Out of the Shadows?

Out of the Shadows?

The Informal Sector in Post-reform India

RAJESH RAJ S.N.

KUNAL SEN

OXFORD
UNIVERSITY PRESS

OXFORD
UNIVERSITY PRESS

Oxford University Press is a department of the University of Oxford.
It furthers the University's objective of excellence in research, scholarship, and
education by publishing worldwide. Oxford is a registered trademark of
Oxford University Press in the UK and in certain other countries

Published in India by
Oxford University Press
YMCA Library Building, 1 Jai Singh Road, New Delhi 110001, India

ISBN-13: 978-0-19-946084-7
ISBN-10: 0-19-946084-1

Typeset in Berling LT Std 9.5/13
by Tranistics Data Technologies, New Delhi 110044
Printed in India by Rakmo Press, New Delhi 110020

To my parents
(Rajesh Raj S.N.)

In memory of my mother
(Kunal Sen)

CONTENTS

TABLES, FIGURES, AND BOX

Tables

Figures

Box

PREFACE

Our interest in the informal sector has been a long-standing one. In the case of Rajesh Raj, this interest goes all the way back to the PhD submitted to the Indian Institute of Technology Madras, Chennai in 2006. We started our collaborative work on the informal sector in 2007 and have maintained this collaboration through a series of journal papers and several research grants from funding sources as diverse as the British Academy, International Growth Centre, Department for International Development (DFID) of the UK government, and the Economic and Social Research Council (ESRC). We were also benefited in our work by the availability of detailed unit-record data with a rich set of information on the informal manufacturing sector brought out by the National Sample Survey Office (NSSO). We are indebted to the NSSO for doing so, as we believe that the availability of such data has been a 'game changer' in our understanding of the informal sector in India.

For some time, we felt that there was a need to put together what we knew about the informal manufacturing sector in India as part of a research monograph, as there has been little systematic research on the Indian informal sector, in spite of its importance. This book is the outcome of our many years of research in this area. In this book, we aim to understand the economic behaviour of the myriad firms that comprise the informal manufacturing sector in India—what characterizes them, what drives them, and how they respond to the rapid economic change that is occurring around them, with the fast pace of economic reforms since 1991. We hope that the readers of this book will find the informal sector in India as fascinating as we did when we started our research and that they agree with us at the end that the informal sector has not received the attention it deserves in our understanding of contemporary economic change in India. We have drawn on our earlier work, including papers published in *Journal of Comparative Economics* and European *Journal of Development Research*. Some of the analysis in Chapter 5 is drawn from Kathuria et. al (2013). Chapter 7 of this book is a substantially updated version of the analysis in Raj and Sen (2012). The authors also would like to thank the following for the copyrighted materials used in this volume: (a) World Bank (2013) for Figures I.1 and I.2; (b) American Economic Association for Figure I.3, as taken from La Porta and Shleifer (2014); and (c) Oxford University Press for Figure I.4, as taken from Hsieh and Klenow (2014).

Over the years, we were fortunate to have many collaborators in our work, the most important of them being Suresh Babu, Sanjay Banerji, Vinish Kathuria, Dibyendu Maiti, and Subash Sasidharan. We learnt a lot from them and are grateful to them for their collaboration with us. We also benefited a great deal in our discussions with Ira Gang, Barbara Harriss-White, Gopal Kadekodi, Ravi Kanbur, K.L. Krishna, Dipak Mazumdar, and Arvind Panagariya. The research that has resulted in this book has been partly funded by a small research grant from the British Academy (SG121855), for which we are grateful. We would also like to thank our host institutions, Centre for Multi-Disciplinary Development Research (CMDR), Dharwad, Karnataka (where Raj was based for most of the period when this book was written), the Department of Economics, Sikkim University (where Raj is presently based), and the Institute for Development Policy and Management (IDPM), the University of Manchester, for providing us with a congenial intellectual environment for the duration of this study. We would like to thank the participants of the workshop we organized in September 2014 at Sikkim University for their helpful comments, and especially the comments received from Amaresh Dubey, Praveen Jha, Nilachal Ray, and Gopalan Sajeevan. We are also grateful to the two anonymous reviewers consulted by Oxford University Press (OUP) for suggestions that have greatly improved the contents of the book. We are indebted to OUP and its editorial team for their constant support. Finally, we would like to thank our respective families, who put up with the long hours that we have spent in writing this book, for their patience, understanding, and good humour.

ABBREVIATIONS

AICTE	All India Council of Technical Education
ASI	Annual Survey of Industries
ATS	Apprenticeship Training Scheme
CLR	Capital–Labour Ratio
CPI	Consumer Price Index
CSO	Central Statistical Office (previously Organization)
CTS	Craftsmen Training Scheme
DGE&T	Directorate General for Employment & Training
DME	Directory Manufacturing Enterprise
EC	Economic Census
EDP	Entrepreneurship Development Programme
EPFMP Act	Employment Provident Fund and Miscellaneous Provisions Act
EUS	Employment and Unemployment Survey
FSU	First Stage Unit
GDP	Gross Domestic Product
GMM	Generalized Method of Moments
GSDP	Gross State Domestic Product
GVA	Gross Value Added
IDA	Industrial Disputes Act
ILO	International Labour Office (a part of the International Labour Organization)
IMF	International Monetary Fund
ISIC	International Standard Industrial Classification
JSS	Jan Shikshan Sansthan

LSI	Large-scale Industry
MHRD	Ministry of Human Resource Development
MoLE	Ministry of Labour and Employment
MP	Madhya Pradesh
MSME	Ministry of Micro, Small, and Medium Enterprises
NCEUS	National Commission for Enterprises in the Unorganized Sector
NDME	Non-directory Manufacturing Enterprise
NIC	National Industrial Classification
NIOS	National Institute of Open Schooling
NSIC	National Small Industries Corporation
NSSO	National Sample Survey Office (previously Organization)
OAME	Own Account Manufacturing Enterprise
OBC	Other Backward Classes
OECD	Organisation for Economic Co-operation and Development
OLS	Ordinary Least Squares
PSL	Priority Sector Lending
QR	Quantitative Restriction
R&D	Research and Development
SC	Scheduled Caste
SDI	Skill Development Initiative
SFA	Stochastic Frontier Analysis
SIDBI	Small Industries Development Bank of India
SIDO	Small Industries Development Organization
SITC	Standard International Trade Classification
SNA	System of National Accounts
SSE	Small-scale Enterprise
SSI	Small-scale Industry
ST	Scheduled Tribe
TE	Technical Efficiency
TFP	Total Factor Productivity
TFPG	Total Factor Productivity Growth
TN	Tamil Nadu
UFS	Urban Frame Survey
UN	United Nations
UNIDO	United Nations Industrial Development Organization

UP	Uttar Pradesh
USU	Ultimate Stage Unit
UT	Union Territory
VSI	Village and Small Industries
WB	West Bengal
WLS	Weighted Least Squares
WPI	Wholesale Price Index
WTO	World Trade Organization

TAKING A 'PRODUCTION LENS' TO INFORMALITY IN INDIA
An Introduction

In classical accounts of economic development, economic growth is seen to be accompanied by a rise in the share of production in modern manufacturing enterprises that are large in size and a corresponding decline in self-employment and informal small manufacturing enterprises (Gollin 2008). Yet in most developing countries, the informal manufacturing sector remains a persistent phenomenon, in spite of rapid economic growth in recent decades. In India, the majority of manufacturing firms and workers are based in the informal sector, which has shown no signs of contracting, in spite of the high rates of economic growth that the country has witnessed since the early 1990s. This is all the more surprising, given the comprehensive economic reforms that the country has undergone since 1991—a time when several barriers to the growth of the formal manufacturing sector were removed. This should have led to a declining importance in the informal manufacturing sector, as more firms are moving to the formal sector. Yet the conundrum is that informal firms remain dominant in terms of numbers in the manufacturing landscape in India.

Why is the presence of a large informal manufacturing sector in a developing country a matter of concern? The coexistence of a large informal sector along with a more modern, formal manufacturing sector is often referred to as 'manufacturing dualism' (Gollin 2014; Lewis 1954). Dualism is a pervasive feature of the manufacturing sectors of most developing economies. Typically, the manufacturing sectors in these economies have a large, less-productive informal sector, where most firms reside along a relatively small, more-productive formal sector, comprising fewer firms (Bourguignon and Morrisson 1998; Little et al. 1987; Temple 2005; World Bank 2005).[1] The persistence in the size of the informal sector, along with large differences in productivity and earnings between the informal and formal sectors, has been a matter of policy concern at the global level (International Labour Office [ILO] 2002; World Trade Organization [WTO] 2009).

Persistence of manufacturing dualism has strong negative implications for both efficiency and equity in the economy. The lack of significant structural change that reallocates workers and firms from the low-productive informal sector to the high-productive formal sector constrains the growth of aggregate productivity in the economy.[2] At the same time, sharp differences in earnings between workers in the informal and formal sectors and the existence of a large pool of workers in the informal sector lead to a high level of income and asset inequality, which may worsen further if the process of economic growth is biased towards the growth of the formal sector (in terms of productivity and capital accumulation) rather than the informal sector (WTO 2009).

While the determinants of the persistence of manufacturing dualism is not well understood, it is commonly believed that an important factor behind the prevalence of dualism is the policy regime, and that trade and industrial policies that inhibit competition and technological change may exacerbate dualism, especially if they are protective of the formal sector or constrain the growth of the informal sector (Gang 1992; Little 1987; Tybout 2000). Economic reforms that allow for a level playing field between the informal and formal sectors may therefore act as a significant positive force in reducing dualism (World Bank 2005). However, it is not clear if this will indeed be the case if economic reforms provide a more favourable environment for the more well-resourced larger firms in the formal sector to expand and reap economies of scale, to obtain best-practice technology, and to seek market opportunities overseas as

---

[1] Duality in manufacturing can be defined in two ways: first, in terms of the size of the two segments—formal and informal sector; and second, in terms of heterogeneity in efficiency of the firms in the two segments (World Bank 2005).

[2] Temple (2005) finds that the lack of structural change that leads to the reallocation of labour from the less-productive 'backward' sector to the more-productive 'modern' sector is an important reason for international differences in aggregate productivity growth.

compared to less well-resourced smaller firms in the informal sector. Therefore, whether economic reforms help reduce manufacturing dualism or exacerbate it is an empirical question.

India has had a long history of manufacturing dualism (Little et al. 1987), with about 80 per cent of manufacturing employment and 17 per cent of manufacturing output being in the informal sector (National Commission for Enterprises in the Unorganized Sector [NCEUS] 2007). It is commonly believed that the dualism evident in the manufacturing sector was a legacy of a set of economic policies that provided protection to the larger manufacturing firms from external competition via an import-substituting industrialization policy regime and also made it difficult for new firms, whether domestic or foreign, to enter existing industries through a strict licensing policy (Panagariya 2008). The Indian government has enacted a far-reaching set of economic reforms since 1991. Yet, two and a half decades after the initiation of economic reforms, we know surprisingly little about the evolution of the informal manufacturing sector in the post-reform phase. Given the importance of the informal sector in India's economy, there has been relatively little scholarship on informal firms. What has been the regional variation of the informal sector, and their growth performance in different industries in the 1990s and the 2000s? Is the performance and characteristics of rural informal firms different from those of urban informal firms? What have been the effects of economic reforms on the informal sector? How has India's deepening integration with the global economy affected this sector? What are the constraints to the growth of informal firms, and what are the roles of access to finance and infrastructure, availability of skilled workers, and assistance from the government in explaining the transition of enterprises from being very small family concerns to larger enterprises employing wage labour? These questions are addressed in this book using a rich set of secondary data sets on informal firms that are representative of the informal manufacturing sector in India. These data sets have been collected by the National Sample Survey Office (NSSO) and go all the way back to 1984–5, with the most recent data set that has been utilized here being from 2010 to 2011.

There is a large existing scholarship on the informal sector in India (Agarwala 2013; Banerjee 1984; Basile 2013; Breman 1996, 2010, 2013; Coelho and Maringanti 2012; Coelho et al. 2012; NCEUS 2007; Shaw and Pandit 2001). Much of this literature approaches the study of informality from a 'labour' or 'consumption' lens, trying to understand how informal workers experience poverty and the nature of the lives they lead. The literature on informality from these perspectives has provided valuable insights into the conditions of work for informal workers and the links of informality to poverty. However, it remains to be understood what the constraints to the growth of informal firms are, and why we see informality persisting.[3] By taking a production 'lens' to informality in this book, the determinants of enterprise performance are made the centre stage of the analysis of informality.

Why is it important to study informality from a production point of view? For the vast majority of the poor, especially in urban areas, the jobs they hold or the enterprises they manage are in the informal sector. Typically, a household enterprise is owned and managed by the same individual who works in the enterprise, whether the enterprise is a roadside stall or a garment firm. These individuals are typically categorized as self-employed and the enterprises they own or manage are called 'own account enterprises'. Of course, not all of the urban poor are owners/managers—there is significant proportion of casual wage workers. However, these wage workers work mostly in enterprises located in the informal sector—the enterprises they work in are those which are no longer own account enterprises and have grown large enough to hire outside workers, but not large or profitable enough to make the transition to the formal sector.

Therefore, whether for the self-employed or for the casual wage workers who compose the urban poor, the route out of poverty is through the enterprises they work in or own/manage, which must become more productive over time and eventually become larger in scale. Poverty here is a consequence of the characteristics of—these usually less-productive enterprises, with very little capital or technology, paying wages far below the wages of those employed in the formal sector. Taking a production lens to informality allows us to study the nature of these enterprises, their characteristics, and their relation to the productivity of the enterprises, and the determinants of firm transition in the informal sector from own account microenterprises to larger firms in the informal sector, who hire casual wage workers.

As we have noted, since the early 1990s, the Indian economy has been one of the world's fastest growing economies, with growth in gross domestic product (GDP) per capita exceeding 7 per cent for

---

[3] A few authors have studied production conditions in the informal sector in India, such as Harriss-White (2003) and Sanyal (2007).

most years since 1991, when radical economic reforms were enacted that dismantled the command-and-control regime of the past. Yet, the available evidence suggests that the growth process has not been inclusive, and, given the high growth rates, the decline in poverty incidence has been much less than what may have been expected (Sen 2014). Looking at informality from a production point of view allows us to clearly relate informality to productivity characteristics of informal firms, and understand what the constraints are to their growth. By doing so, we can better understand how economic growth can be made more inclusive of the informal sector and of the working poor.

Our attempt in this book to study informality in India from a production lens is aided considerably by the availability of unit-level data on informal firms, from the quinquennial surveys of informal manufacturing enterprises undertaken by the NSSO.[4] The unit-level data covers informal firms from family firms or self-employed with one or two workers to larger enterprises employing over ten workers. The surveys ask detailed questions to informal firms, which provide a wealth of information on firm characteristics and behaviour, as well as their performance. We use five rounds of these quinquennial surveys from 1989–90 to 2010–11. Such a rich data set of informal firms that spans over 21 years is rare in the context of a developing country. The availability of this data set for the period encompassing the period of reforms provides us with a unique opportunity to study the effects of the rapid economic changes since 1991 on the Indian informal manufacturing sector (a detailed description of the data has been provided in Appendix A1). Data from the unit-level record are used here in two ways. First, we will conduct a descriptive analysis of patterns of firm growth and stagnation based on the size classes of firms, industry, region, and categories of firms, as well as comparing firm growth in the informal manufacturing sector with that of firms in cognate size classes in the Indian formal manufacturing sector. Second, we will undertake econometric analysis, using repeated cross-sections of the firm-level data wherever appropriate, asking different questions of the data to expand on our knowledge of the determinants of firm growth in the informal sector.

---

[4] For years 1978–89 and 1984–5, we do not have the unit-level data. For these years, we have the industry-level aggregate data, which we use when we examine industry-level patterns of growth and structural change and the effects of international trade on employment.

In the remainder of this introductory chapter, we first discuss some definitional issues relating to the informal sector and spell out clearly what we understand by the informal sector in India. We then set out what we know of the Indian informal sector within the broader context of the informal economy across the developing world. We also discuss the relationship between informality and urban poverty in India. We then discuss the prevailing views in Indian policy circles on what to do with informality. Finally, we present the organization of the book.

Defining the Informal Sector in India

As Godfrey (2011: 233) notes, 'the informal sector represents a problematic construct that defies easy definition'. A bewildering range of definitions are available in the literature on the informal sector. In this book, we choose a legalistic definition, where we define the informal manufacturing sector as a set of firms which have not registered with the official authorities under the Factories Act, 1948. Firms have to register with the Indian government under the Factories Act if they employ 10 or more workers and use electricity in their operations, or if they employ 20 or more workers without the use of electricity in their operations. However, in practice, many do not register under the Factories Act, even when they employ more than 20 workers (Pais 2008). The Factories Act regulates the conditions of work in the formal manufacturing sector, including minimum safety, sanitary, health, and welfare standards, as well as stipulating regulations on hours of work, leaves with wages, and holiday provisions for workers which employers in the formal sector need to follow or face stiff penalties (NCEUS 2009). In addition, firms registered under the Factories Act are required to supply data on the firm's operations on a regular basis to the official statistical agency of India, the Central Statistical Office (CSO) (Kulshreshtha 2011). The informal manufacturing sector, by default, comprises firms which fall outside the scope of the Factories Act; they generally do not pay taxes and are outside the purview of government regulations (Kanbur 2011). Therefore, we take the informal manufacturing sector in India as being identical to what is often termed as the 'unorganized manufacturing sector' in Indian terminology.

The informal sector is the largest employment provider in the manufacturing sector in India, with over 80 per cent of India's workers being employed in the informal sector. The NSSO employs a further classification of informal firms in India as follows: (a) Own Account

Manufacturing Enterprises (OAMEs), which are family-owned firms that only employ workers from within their families; (b) Non-directory Manufacturing Enterprises (NDMEs), which are firms that employ less than six workers, with at least one hired worker; and (c) Directory Manufacturing Enterprises (DMEs) that employ six or more persons, with at least one hired worker. The NSSO classification is very useful for us as it makes clear the distinction between pure household enterprises (OAMEs) which are very small in size, slightly larger enterprises which use both family and non-family labour (NDMEs), and even larger enterprises which employ at least one non-family worker (DMEs). For the rest of the book, we will use the NSSO classification in drawing a distinction between OAMEs, NDMEs, and DMEs in the analysis of informal firms in later chapters.

Indian Informal Sector in the Global Context

What can we say about the Indian informal sector vis-à-vis similar sectors in other countries? As can be seen in Figure I.1, India has

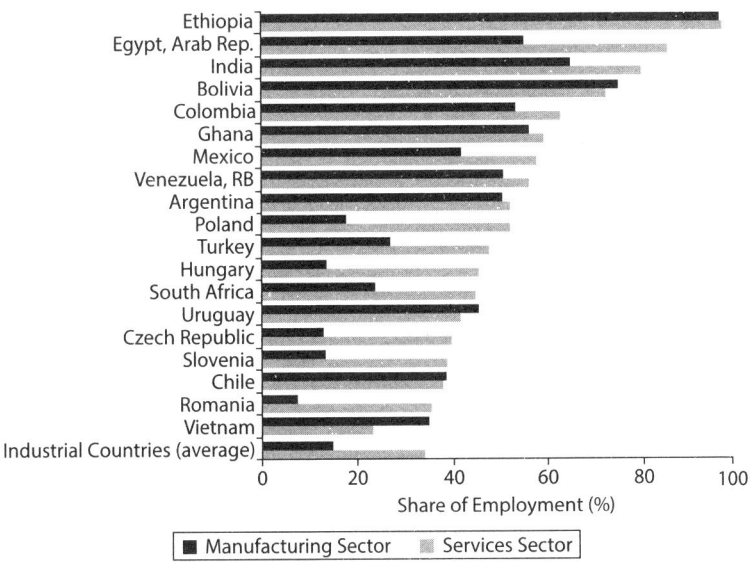

Figure I.1   Share of the Informal Sector in Total Employment: Select Countries
Source: World Bank (2013).

the highest proportion of manufacturing workers employed in the informal sector, after Ethiopia and Egypt. Thus, while the informal sector is important in providing employment in the lowest and low to middle income countries, it is particularly important in India, both in relative and absolute terms. (Given India's population, the number of workers employed in the informal manufacturing sector in India is far higher than in other countries.) 'Manufacturing dualism' is a particularly acute problem in India—the productivity differential between the 90th percentile and 10th percentile of the total factor productivity (TFP) distribution is highest in India after Mexico (Figure I.2). On a more positive note, the ratio of value added by informal firms to value added by formal firms in India is above the median for developing countries at 0.18, though just about barely higher (when the median is 0.15) (Figure I.3). Finally, it can be observed that much of the employment creation in India occurs in the smallest firm-size class, which is mostly populated by firms in the informal sector (Figure I.4). In contrast, in an advanced

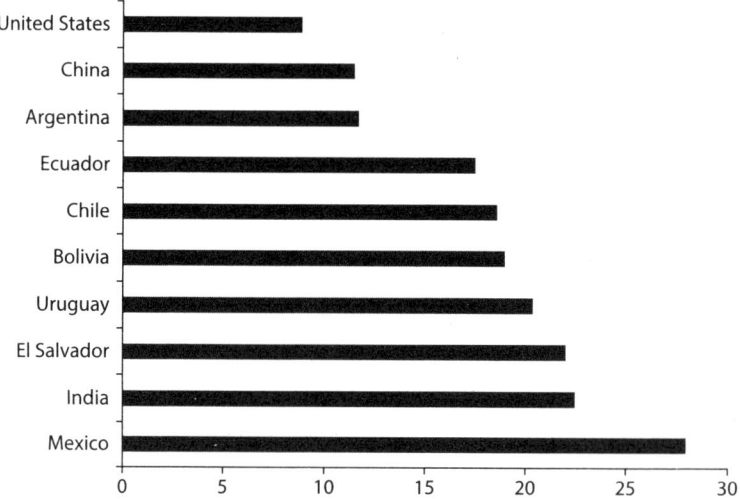

Figure I.2 Productivity Differentials between the Most and Least Productive Firms: Select Countries
Source: World Bank (2013).

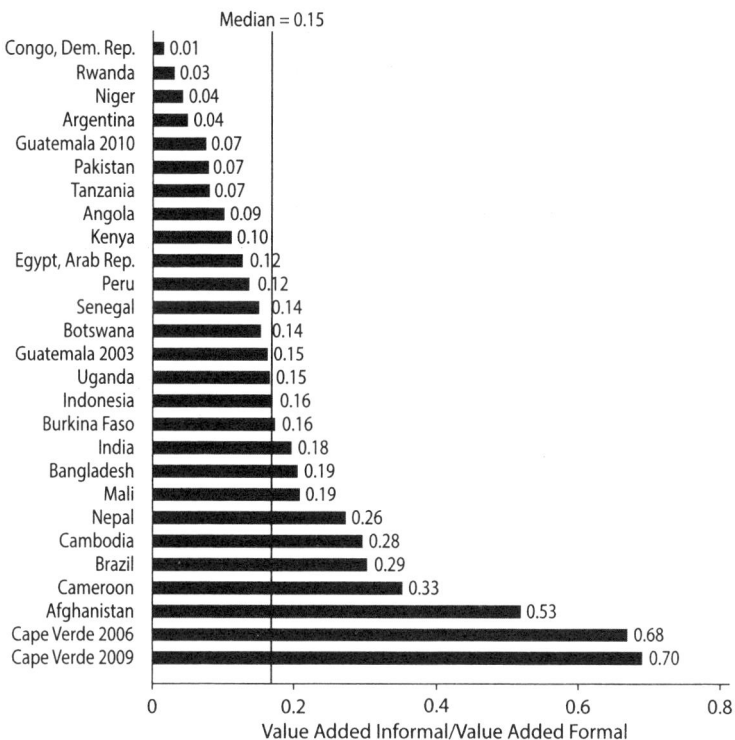

Figure I.3 Ratio of Value Added by Informal Firms to Value Added by Formal Firms: Select Countries
Source: La Porta and Shliefer (2014).

economy such as the US, employment creation occurs mostly in large firms, which are both the source of productivity and employment growth in advanced market economies. In summary, what we find from these selected vignettes of the informal sector and manufacturing firms across the world is that India has a very large incidence of informality among manufacturing firms, and a more severe problem of manufacturing dualism than most other developing countries. This suggests that the persistence of informality and manufacturing dualism in India is a matter that should be of enormous concern both in the scholarly and in the policy communities.

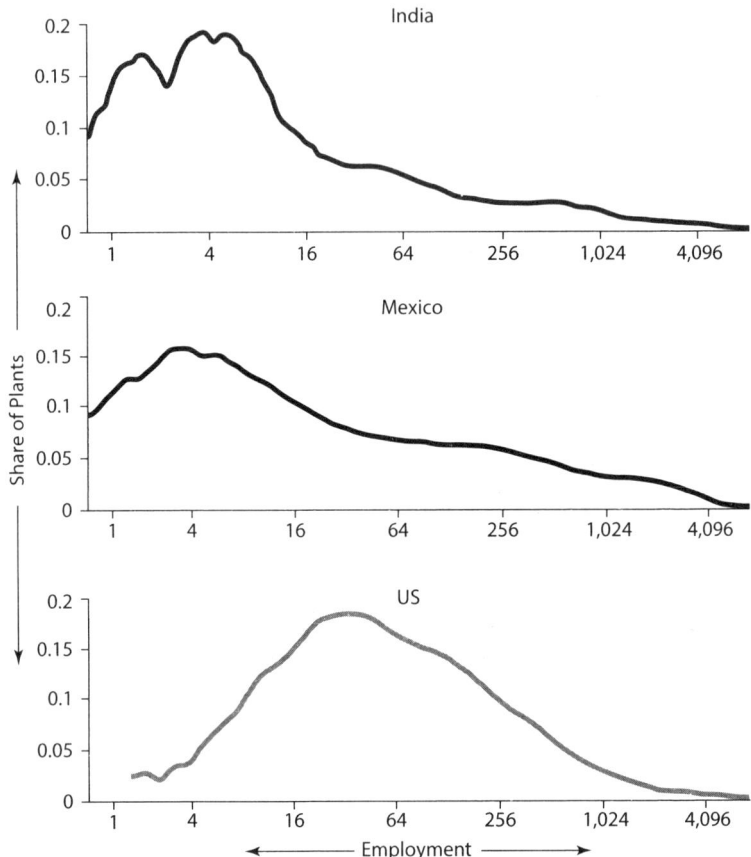

Figure I.4 Distribution of Enterprises by Employment: India, Mexico, and the United States
Sources: 2010–11 ASI-NSS (India), 1998 Economic Census (Mexico), and 1997 Manufacturing Census (United States). Also see Hsieh and Klenow (2014).
Note: Plants are weighted by the per-plant value-added share of each four-digit industry.

The Relationship between Informality and Urban Poverty in India

The surveys on informal sector enterprises undertaken by the NSSO do not collect data on poverty (household consumption data) that could be used to assess the poverty status of these enterprises. The NSSO does a separate survey of individuals (whether working or unemployed) called the Employment and Unemployment Survey (EUS), which collects data on consumption at the household level that can be used to examine the poverty status of workers in different occupational groups. Unfortunately, the NSSO does not match the data on employees and own account workers available in the EUS with the data on the firms that they work in or manage, which are available in the enterprise surveys. Here, we provide a crude estimate of the poverty status of informal wage workers and own account workers using the 66th Round (2009–10) of the EUS, and classifying urban households as poor if their monthly per capita expenditure was below the official state-level urban poverty line. We use three broad classifications—whether the head of the household is self-employed, a salaried worker, or a casual worker (we do not provide similar estimates for rural households, as we cannot make the distinction easily between agriculturalists and non-agricultural enterprises for rural self-employed households). Further, the EUS does not differentiate between self-employed in the formal sector and self-employed in the informal sector (which is mostly household enterprises or family firms), and so the poverty rate reported here for the self-employed includes the self-employed in the formal sector (for example, doctors, lawyers, and other professionals). With this important caveat, we see that the poverty rate for urban casual workers in 2009–10 is over 50 per cent (Figure I.5).

Figure I.5   Poverty Rate by Status Employed (proportion of households below the poverty line)
Source: NSSO, *Employment and Unemployment Survey*, 66th Round, unit-level data, our calculations.

The poverty rate among self-employed is around 28 per cent. In contrast, the poverty rate among salaried workers is around 16 per cent. Thus, there is a close correlation between informality and poverty in urban areas.

In Figure I.6, we plot the urban poverty rate among the self-employed based on the location of their enterprise. We find that the urban poverty rate among enterprises having no fixed location is as high as 40 per cent. In contrast, the poverty rate among self-employed, whose enterprises are fixed in location, but where the production unit is not in their own dwellings, is as low as 16 per cent. These are most likely to be non-family firms, some in the informal sector and some in the formal sector. The poverty rate for the self-employed whose enterprises are located in their own dwellings is around 25 per cent. These are most likely to be family firms.

Next, we try and see whether urban poverty and firm performance have a clear relationship. We present two graphs to examine this issue—first, a scatter plot of labour productivity of family firms versus

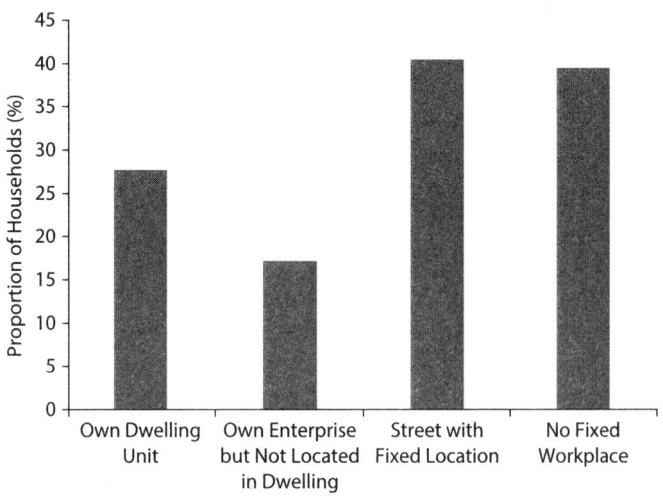

Figure I.6 Poverty Rate by Location of Unit and Self-employment (proportion of households below the poverty line)
Source: NSSO, *Employment and Unemployment Survey*, 66th Round, unit-level data, our calculations.

urban head count ratio by states (29 states for which we have data); second, we also present a scatter plot of labour productivity of non-family firms versus urban head count ratio by states. We present these scatters in Figures I.7 and I.8. We find that while there is a negative relationship between labour productivity of family firms and urban poverty, it is not as pronounced as the negative relationship between labour productivity of non-family firms and urban poverty. This is a remarkable finding (though based on simple bivariate scatters) as it suggests that there is a clear negative relationship between firm performance and urban poverty across states in India. States where non-family firms are more likely to be productive are more likely to observe low urban poverty. This finding provides some support for the argument that the route out of urban poverty seems to be the growth of firms in the informal sector—and for them to make the transition from household enterprises and to become more productive over time.

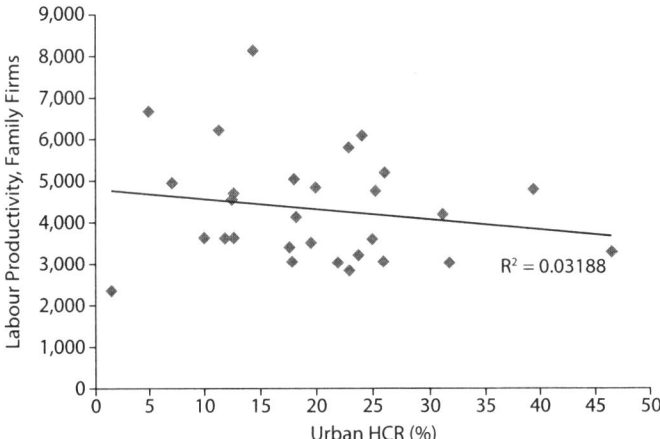

Figure I.7   Scatter Plot of Labour Productivity, Family Firms (OAMEs) vs Urban Head Count Ratio, by States in India
Source: NSSO, 66th Round, 2009–10, *Survey of Unincorporated Non-agricultural Enterprises*, our calculations.
Notes: (a) Labour productivity is the total real value added of the firm divided by the total number of workers, including family workers, in rupees. (b) HCR: Head Count Ratio.

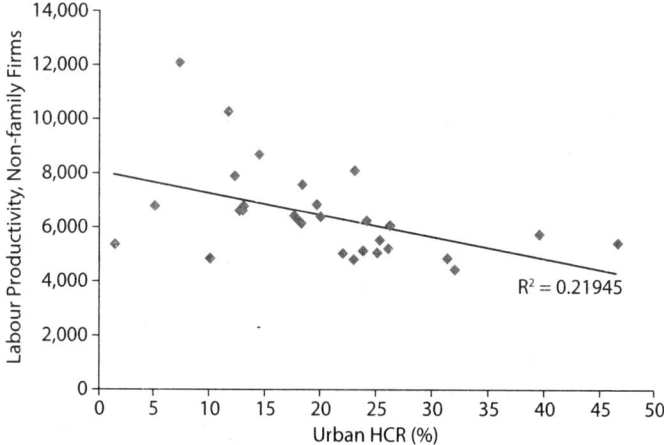

Figure I.8 Scatter Plot of Labour Productivity, Non-family Firms (NDMEs and DMEs) vs Urban Head Count Ratio, by States in India
Source: NSSO, 66th Round, 2009–10, *Survey of Unincorporated Non-agricultural Enterprises*, our calculations.
Notes: (a) Labour Productivity is the total real value added of the firm divided by the total number of workers, including family workers, in rupees. (b) HCR: Head Count Ratio.

What to Do with Informality in India? Two Views

A conundrum that policymakers in India have faced in addressing the large presence of the informal sector is whether the objective of the policy should be to reduce the size of informality in the economy and relocate as many workers as possible to the formal sector, or whether the objective should be to promote the well-being of the informal sector and take steps to enhance its vitality and inherent dynamism. Underpinning this conundrum are two diametrically opposed views of the informal sector. One view takes the informal sector to be a means of exploitation—a site for primitive capital accumulation to take place, unfettered by the regulations and social norms of fairness governing pay and work conditions that are more at play in the formal sector. In such a view, workers in the informal sector are underpaid, they do not have mechanisms for voicing their concerns to their employers, and they work in abysmal conditions. In this perspective, the informal sector is inherently exploitative and the goal of the policy should be to bring in similar regulations and organizations for workers in the informal sector as are found to be present in the formal sector. Here, the key policy concern is not to bring poor people into formalized economies, but the other way around—*to bring formalization to the poor in the informal sector,* by introducing social security legislation, minimum wage legislation, and collective bargaining for informal workers, and to bring the informal sector within the ambit of the state. This view is most clearly reflected in the various reports of the NCEUS, a national body commissioned by the Indian government in 2004 to address the issues faced by enterprises in the informal sector.

Another view takes the informal sector to be the venue for economic dynamism and creativity where households and entrepreneurs make the long but necessary transition from the very small enterprises observed in the early stages of capitalism to the very large corporations that are omnipresent in late capitalism. In this view, any regulations or laws introduced by the state or an attempt to recreate the informal sector as a mirror reflection of the formal sector is merely going to weaken the creative energies of the informal sector and bring the growth of informal enterprises to a grinding halt. In such a view, the most important role that the state can play in encouraging the transition of firms from the informal to the formal sector is to leave the informal sector alone. In this view, the policy emphasis should be on easing the laws and regulations that make the transition to the formal sector cumbersome and fraught with uncertainty, and to provide incentives to informal firms to formalize their enterprises. In essence, this view suggests that *de facto informalization of formal rules* (via diluting laws and regulations that seek to restrict economic activity in the formal sector) should be the key policy thrust to bring the poor into formalized economies. This view is most clearly reflected in the scholarly writings of economists such as Jagdish Bhagwati and Arvind Panagariya.

The view that takes the informal sector as 'a means of accumulation' and the one that takes the informal sector 'as a means of exploitation' differ substantially in the way they would approach the question of how to bring the poor into formalized economies. Put starkly, the former view would bring the poor into formalized economies by *informalizing the formal* sector while the latter view would bring the poor into formalized economies by *formalizing the informal* sector.

In this book, we assess which view is correct by examining the empirical evidence on informal manufacturing firms in India, which may support one view over another. Based on our own findings, we recommend some clear policy directions for the government with respect to the informal sector in India.

Organization of the Book

The book is organized as follows: In Chapter 1, we provide an overview of the theoretical literature on the informal sector, highlighting the differences of perspectives in the literature, and their implications for our understanding of the Indian informal manufacturing sector. In Chapter 2, we provide a brief overview of the evolution of India's economic policies that may have had a direct or indirect effect on the informal manufacturing sector. We also review important studies that have examined the effects of these policies on the Indian informal sector. In Chapter 3, we examine the overall patterns and trends in number of enterprises, employment, and gross value added (GVA) for the informal manufacturing sector, both aggregated and disaggregated by sector, industry, and region (Indian states), for the period 1984–5 to 2010–11. In Chapter 4, we present some stylized facts about firms in the Indian informal manufacturing sector, using unit-level data from the NSSO surveys of unorganized enterprises from 2000–1 to 2010–11. In the next three chapters, we address three analytical issues that are important to our understanding of the informal manufacturing sector in India. In Chapter 5, we assess whether economic reforms in India has exacerbated or reduced manufacturing dualism in India—that is, the efficiency differentials between informal and formal manufacturing firms. In Chapter 6, we examine the determinants of transition of firms in the informal sector, from the very small OAMEs to mid-sized NDMEs to the larger DMEs. In Chapter 7, we ask whether India's increasing integration with the world economy has had an effect on employment in the informal sector, vis-à-vis the formal sector. The concluding chapter (Chapter 8) summarizes the key findings of the analysis in the book and examines their policy implications.

I

THEORETICAL PERSPECTIVES ON
THE INFORMAL ECONOMY

This chapter briefly reviews the main theoretical perspectives on the informal sector.[1] It begins with the dual economy model, which is the dominant conceptual framework for understanding the informal economy. Then, it reviews other approaches to the informal economy—namely, the neo-Marxian, legalist, and the institutionalist perspectives.[2]

The Dual Economy Approach

In the dual economy model, proposed by Harriss and Todaro (1970) and Lewis (1954), there are two sectors operating in the economy: the formal and the informal sector. The formal sector features wage labour, capital-intensive firms, and high marginal productivities that create incentives for capitalists to invest in workers and equipment. The informal sector is characterized by low wages and labour-intensive firms/actors. The informal sector persists primarily because the efficiencies

---

[1] In this chapter, we review the generic theoretical frameworks of the informal sector. Later, we review the literature on determinants of performance of informal firms; the transition of Own Account Manufacturing Enterprises (OAMEs) to Non-directory Manufacturing Enterprises (NDMEs) and Directory Manufacturing Enterprises (DMEs); and the effect of trade on informal sector employment creation in Chapters 5, 6, and 7, respectively.

[2] This chapter draws from Maiti and Sen (2010a and 2010b).

of formal production have yet to displace the more traditional mode of production (Godfrey 2011). The crucial assumption behind the dual economy model is that labour in the informal sector produces with zero marginal productivity primarily because surplus labour exists. As Lewis (1954: 402) noted: 'An unlimited supply of labour may be said to exist in those countries where population is large relative to the capital and natural resources, so that there are large sectors of the economy where the marginal productivity of labour is negligible, zero or even negative.' If surplus labour is not paid its marginal productivity, subsistence wages prove to be much below the marginal productivity of labour in the formal sector, thereby creating an unlimited supply of labour that is willing to move out from the informal sector. In the dual economy model, growth consists in its simplest form of expanding the capitalist formal sector and contracting the informal sector. The expansion of the formal sector requires an increase in savings which can only come from the capitalist sector or from external sources (Gollin 2014). As capital flows into the economy, it can be used to create jobs in the formal sector, which can always be filled by workers moving from the informal sector. As these workers move, the savings rate of the economy increases and this, in turn, leads to a virtuous circle that steadily raises the level of per capita income in the economy.[3] Therefore, an important prediction of the dual economy approach is that the informal sector will shrink as the economy expands and as the formal sector grows. In the Lewisian view, informality is simply a reflection of underdevelopment and should wither away with growth and structural transformation. There is strong evidence in support of this proposition, where richer countries have smaller informal sectors. As La Porta and Shleifer (2014: 119) conclude in their review of the stylized

---

[3] In the original formulation of the dual economy model by Lewis (1954), there are only two sectors—the modern sector, corresponding in large part to the urban sector, and the traditional sector, corresponding in large part to the rural sector. However, a more realistic formulation is provided by Ranis and Stewart (1999), where there are three sectors—a formal urban sector, an informal urban sector, and a subsistence rural sector. This is what we typically observe in most developing countries. In the Ranis-Stewart formulation, the urban informal sector can actually expand with economic growth for some time—again, a feature of the informal sector that can be observed with economic development.

facts of informality across the world, a clear finding of the relationship between informality and economic development is that 'as the economy develops, informality shrinks'.

Other Theoretical Perspectives

The dual economy model is not the only theoretical framework available to understand the existence and functioning of the informal sector. Three other perspectives have also been influential in the literature. These are: (a) the neo-Marxian approach; (b) the legalist view, and (c) the institutionalist approach. Each of these is discussed here in turn.

Neo-Marxian Approach

The neo-Marxian approach does not recognize the informal sector as a separate entity in the process of economic development, and the sector is often seen to be a part of the larger pre-capitalist sector (which also includes feudalism and semi-feudalism). In the classical Marxian tradition, capital and labour are seen as separate entities, and there is no space for economic entities which cannot be seen as either capital or labour. However, as Sanyal (2007) and Sanyal and Bhattacharya (2009) argue, such a view is not consistent with the reality in many developing societies. In the neo-Marxian approach, in contrast to the classical Marxian approach, the informal sector provides an 'economic space in which workers engage in economic activities in ways that are very different from the capitalist organisation of production. In particular, the prevalent form of labour in the informal sector is self-employment, which is different from the usual wage-based employment resting on the alienation of labour from capital' (Sanyal and Bhattacharya 2009: 35). Thus, with the process of globalization and marketization, 'the informal economy, that is, the economy of the surplus labour force, is a product of the process by which the capitalist economy secures its resources minus the people who traditionally survived on it' (Sanyal and Bhattacharya 2009: 37), a process which Sanyal (2007) refers to as 'exclusion' (see also Breman [1985 and 2010] for similar arguments). The pressures of competition and globalization lead to the integration of informal units with global or domestic capital via a process of subcontracting, though these units inhabit a non-capitalist production space (Castells and Portes 1989). Thus, in such a view of the informal economy, the relation of the informal sector to the formal sector is through the coercion or compulsion of the market. A similar view is provided by Adams and Harriss-White (2007: 18) who note that 'informal accumulation and the emergence of extensive informal labour markets co-exist with large economic spaces carved out and apparently well-preserved for right-less work and petty production, trade and services from which it is not possible to accumulate'.[4] As argued by Harriss-White (2010: 170), the informal sector 'may be better thought of as intrinsic to the state-regulated economy and incorporated by it'. In this view, globalization and economic growth may themselves be a cause of informalization, as 'formal registered entities are restructured through process specialization, subcontracting, and job-working, in the effort to reduce costs in economic sectors under competitive pressure' (Harriss-White 2010: 176).[5] Therefore, in contrast to the dual economy approach, the neo-Marxian approach sees the informal sector as a feature of late capitalism, especially in the developing world, and argues that the informal sector will persist in developing countries, in spite of economic growth (Hart 1973). In support of the neo-Marxian approach, the analysis of cross-national data suggests that the decline in informality with rising per capita income across countries has been far slower than may be predicted by the dual economy approach (Gollin 2014).

Legalist Approach

This approach argues that the rigid rules and regulations and the terms and conditions for operating a unit in the formal sector are such that it creates an additional burden for the unit owners, and hence force them to bypass formal rules and regulations by operating in the informal sector. De Soto (1989) argues that the informal sector thrives in order to avoid the cost of formality in terms of stringent rules and regulation, taxes, time, and effort required for complying with formal procedures. According to this approach, the issue of informality is no longer an exclusive problem of development,

---

[4] See also Harriss-White (2002).
[5] See also International Labour Office (ILO) (2009) on the evidence between globalization and informality.

because the cost relating to regulation and enforcement is a relevant issue for any country, whether developed or developing. Therefore, in this approach, 'informal work arrangements are a rational response by micro-entrepreneurs to over-regulation by government bureaucracies' (Becker 2004: 10).

The way out of the informal economy lies in creating institutions and incentives and removing relevant barriers that discourage formality (Godfrey 2011). Firms prefer the informal economy because formal laws (such as property rights protection) and institutional procedures (for example, business registration requirements) make it either impossible or impractical to move to the formal economy. De Soto (2000), in particular, focuses on the lack of property rights for informal firms. Typically, informal firms and entrepreneurs lack title to their land, which prevents them from collateralizing their property to obtain bank loans which can fuel their growth. Similarly, onerous bureaucratic procedures, strict government regulations, and cumbersome bureaucratic approvals can have a significant negative effect on the transition of informal firms to the formal sector. As De Soto (2000: 83) argues, 'if there are costs to becoming legal, there are also bound to be costs to remaining outside the law'. He found that operating a business by extralegal means includes paying 10 to 15 per cent of its annual income in bribes and commissions to authorities. Add to such payments the costs of avoiding penalties, making transfers outside legal channels, and operating from dispersed locations and without credit; the life of the extralegal entrepreneur turns out to far more costly and full of daily hassles than that of the legal businessman. Therefore, exclusion from the formal sector raises the costs of doing business, creating a double penalty for entrepreneurs and households trying to compete informally (Godfrey 2011).

In the legalist view, informal firms are an untapped reservoir of entrepreneurial energy, held back by government regulations (La Porta and Shliefer 2014). In this view, unleashing this energy by reducing entry regulations or improving property rights would fuel growth and development. La Porta and Shleifer (2014), however, point out that the World Bank Enterprise Surveys, which ask informal entrepreneurs to rank their most important constraints to growth, do not show that informal firms see government regulations as their most binding constraint—in fact, less than 10 per cent of either formal and informal firms worry about business licensing and permits and the legal system. Moreover, when informal firms are asked what benefits they may enjoy if they formalize, they mention access to credit and access to raw materials as being the incentives to formalize, rather than more access to government programmes, the legal system, and infrastructure. Finally, La Porta and Shleifer find from their own work that very few informal firms formalize, largely due to the fact that they are much less productive than formal firms.

However, the evidence that La Porta and Shleifer (2014) provide against the legalist view is not wholly convincing. It could be argued that informal firms are less productive than formal firms because of their small size and their lack of access to technology and specialized inputs, which itself may be a function of their desire not to formalize, given the impediments they face to do so. Furthermore, the fact that informal firms do not report bureaucratic procedures as being an important constraint on their growth is not surprising—one of the benefits of being in the informal sector is that firms do not have to deal with government regulations that much. It should also be noted that the legalist view does not advocate for the formalization of informal firms per se. Instead, the legalist view argues for the relaxation of the institutional constraints to firm growth in the informal sector, with appropriate reforms such as the provision of titles to land for informal entrepreneurs.

A further weakness of the La Porta and Shleifer's critique of the legalist view is that they tend to see the informal sector in a homogenous manner, not differentiating between the different types of informal firms. While it could be argued that the presence of too many household enterprises in the informal economy is not desirable, given the low productivity of these enterprises, there are also larger non-household enterprises, particularly in the manufacturing sector that can be sources of growth for the economy. Given the large presence of unskilled and semi-skilled workers in the informal sector, many of whom are employed in the larger non-household enterprises, and who have very little opportunities to move to the formal sector, it would make sense for policymakers in developing countries to simultaneously try and increase the size of the formal sector and, *at the same time,* follow policies that encourage the growth of the more dynamic set of firms in the informal manufacturing sector.

Institutionalist Approach

According to this approach, any type of economic transaction involves discovering efficient terms and conditions. But the parties engaged in economic transactions face hold-up problems in distributing ex post benefits from joint actions because of incompleteness of contracts and opportunistic behaviour of individuals engaged in contracts (Williamson 1985). The participation of third parties or legal institutions to enforce the terms and conditions is either costly or ineffective. Therefore, informal institutions, such as norms and trusts, exist as a mechanism of governance and as a means of enforcement (North 1990; Ostrom 1990). Informality may, therefore, exist in any society, but is more likely to exist in a society where formal rules and regulations are not in place or are not well enforced. This view recognizes that informal institutions are crucial in underpinning economic transactions in the early stages of economic development and act as substitutes for missing or ineffective formal institutions in many developing countries. Informality is seen here as a relation between economic agents (households or firms) and not as a characteristic of the agent—that is, an agent is considered to be in informal sector *not* because of what it does in terms of its activities, but in terms of the relationships it engages in. In this sense, the institutionalist approach has strong similarities with the neo-Marxian approach which takes informality as a relation between capitalist firms and the pre-capitalist entities.

✽   ✽   ✽

In this chapter, we reviewed the main theoretical perspectives on the informal economy. While these various approaches have different starting points and theoretical building blocks, they broadly correspond to the two mutually exclusive and diagonally opposite views discussed earlier—informality as exploitation and informality as accumulation. The underlying vision of the approaches of neo-Marxism and dualism is that informality, whether understood as a relation or as a characteristic of the firm, the sector, or the economy, is inherently exploitative. On the other hand, legalist and institutionalist schools see the informal sector as a means of accumulation and as being inherently dynamic. The informal sector is a place where market activities can flourish unfettered by rules and regulations and can remain outside the reach of the state (as in the legalist school), or where informal relations develop both between different types of informal units as well as between informal and formal units as mechanisms of governance to handle increasingly complex economic exchange and production, and where these relations are ultimately efficiency enhancing (as in the institutionalist school).

This volume looks at the empirical evidence for India to see which of these approaches find the most support in the Indian context. Are they characterized by low-productivity growth and weak economic performance, as suggested by dualism theories? Are informal firms in India in inherent exploitative relationships with formal firms, as argued by the neo-Marxian approach? How dynamic are these firms and have they prospered under the deregulated environment offered to them by economic reforms, as proposed by the legalist approach? We return to these issues in the concluding chapter after we assess the empirical evidence on the performance of informal firms in the post-reform period.

2

THE POLICY CONTEXT

The contribution of small firms towards employment and earnings has been a significant concern for the policymakers of developing countries. The failure of large-scale, modern industrialization strategies to solve the problems of underemployment and poverty had further heightened this apprehension (Liedholm and Mead 1987). As a result, enhancing the growth of small-scale industries (SSIs) has been viewed as an effective way to realize the growth and equity objectives of developing countries. This led to governments of many developing countries to make considerable efforts in improving the productivity and earnings of these firms, which has thus spawned a plethora of policies and programmes to support small firms (Romjin 2001). Many policy instruments have been employed to promote the growth of small firms in developing countries. These instruments include credit support; subsidies for the use of certain inputs; advice on technology, production, and marketing; reservation of certain products for exclusive production by small firms; and exemption from excise and sales taxes (Katrak 1999).

India too has supported its small-scale sector historically. It emerged from the belief that employment generation is critical in a labour-surplus economy, and SSIs, being the most labour-intensive manufacturing enterprises, would be able to absorb the surplus labour (Mohan 2002). It was also expected that, as the small firms are located in rural areas, supporting these firms would help in the geographic decentralization and dispersal of industrial activity.[1] The grounds on which the case of SSI is advocated are that, among others, they are the seedbed from which larger enterprises grow and they help restrict the market power of larger enterprises. Thus, promotion of SSI sector had gained significant importance as an element of industrial policy in India since Independence (Subrahmanya 1995). For instance, during the tenure of the First Five Year Plan, various boards were constituted to promote different segments of SSIs. Majority of these boards were assigned the task of promoting the traditional segments of the sector. On the other hand, planning for the growth of the modern SSIs took two routes: administrative mechanism encompassing institutions that are meant to provide various services and support in the form of technology, marketing, training, finance, and entrepreneurship for small firms and policy instruments covering incentive schemes and the reservation system (Subrahmanya 1995).

As noted by Little et al. (1987), initial measures to help develop small firms include the development of infrastructure, regional development centres, and technical and financial assistance.[2] Later, with the rising concern that the survival and growth of small firms were being adversely affected by competition from larger enterprises in the subsequent years, the government rolled out a reservation policy that made production of some items the exclusive domain of small firms. These policies would have had varied effects on development of small firms, and thus on overall economic welfare. Some of these policies, such as advice on technology, may help improve efficiency of firms and help enhance overall economic welfare, while some other policies, especially reservation policy, restricts competition from larger enterprises and also limits the size of small firms, and thus may have mixed welfare effects (Katrak 1999).

---

[1] Industrial planning in the post-Independence period laid much emphasis on the indispensable role of 'decentralised industrial sector' (synonymous with the then SSI) for employment generation in the economic development of the country (Subrahmanya 1995).

[2] The latter two have been administered by various agencies, including the Small Industries Development Organization (SIDO), the Small Industries Services Institute (SISI), and the Industrial Development Bank of India (IDBI).

These support policies and programmes have spawned considerable amount of literature which have documented them and have debated on the real effect of these policies, especially the protective measures on small firms. The objective of this chapter is to present a thematic review of studies that have examined the role of these support measures on the subsequent performance of SSIs.[3] Alongside, this chapter also reviews studies that have examined the effect of various reform measures initiated in the 1990s on small firms. Industrial delicensing, trade reforms, and dereservation were the key reforms of the product market enacted by the Indian government with respect to the manufacturing sector (Kathuria et al. 2013). The possible role of labour laws acting as a barrier to firm transition forms another source of debate, and a number of studies have also addressed this issue in the context of small firms in the Indian manufacturing sector. Based on the focus of this study, the literature review is classified into the following themes: (a) small-scale industry reservation, (b) regulatory framework, (c) financial sector, (d) trade policy, and (e) other government assistance.

Small-scale Industry Reservation Policy

The origin of the reservation policy for SSIs can be traced to the committee for Village and Small Industries (VSIs) headed by D.G. Karve (Subrahmanya 1995). The committee was constituted to prepare a scheme for the utilization of resources for the development of VSIs, and suggested, among others, reservation of product lines exclusively for manufacturing in small-scale sector. Based on the recommendation of the committee, the reservation policy was initiated in 1967.[4] The objectives of the policy were to (a) ensure the bulk of increased production of consumer goods in the SSI sector, and (b) to increase employment opportunities by setting up SSIs. The main intention, however, was to protect small firms engaged in the

---

[3] In this chapter, we do not make a distinction between informal and formal firms, as the policy framework that the Government of India (GoI) adopted for small firms did not largely differentiate between informal and formal firms.

[4] Despite its introduction in 1967, the policy got a legal backing only in 1984 under Section 29B of the Industries (Development and Regulation) (IDR) Act, 1951 (Narayana 2003).

manufacturing of reserved items from the competition of medium and large firms.[5]

Initially, under this policy, which applies exclusively to manufacturing, 47 products were reserved for production by SSIs. The non-SSI units that produced items which were subsequently reserved are allowed to carry on with the production of same products, but with a caveat that expansion of capacity will not be allowed, while those that had not previously been producing the reserved items are not permitted to set up production (Katrak 1999; Narayana 2003). However, large-scale industries (LSIs), with a minimum export obligation of 75 per cent of their output, are allowed to enter the production of reserved items (Subrahmanya 1995). As the policy is uniformly applicable all over the country, state governments are not empowered to add or remove any products from the reserved list. As argued by Katrak (1999), any such measure for the protection of small firms from large firms demands that products on the reserved list be carefully selected keeping in mind the long-term potential and the comparative advantage of small firms. A careful scrutiny of available government documents rules out adoption of any criteria for inclusion of products into the list of reserved items (Narayana 2003). The only selection criterion mentioned in official documents was the ability of SSIs to manufacture such (reserved) items (Mohan 2002), and thus the choice of products was 'arbitrary' (Hussain 1997; Mohan 2002).

Trends in Reservation

Since 1967, which is the year of implementation of reservation policy, there have been significant changes in the number of items reserved for

---

[5] As mentioned in the Annual Report for 1988–9 (Ministry of Commerce and Industry 1989) by the development commissioner: 'The reservation policy prevents the creation of new capacities in the large-scale sector in areas which are well within the competence of small-scale sector so that small-scale units are able to cater to the additional demand for the reserved items.' Narayana (2003) argues that the reservation policy protected SSIs from vertical competition in production from the non-SSIs in the domestic economy by erecting an entry barrier, and from foreign competition in production by high tariff and non-tariff barriers on reserved products. But the policy allowed horizontal competition among the SSIs for the same product.

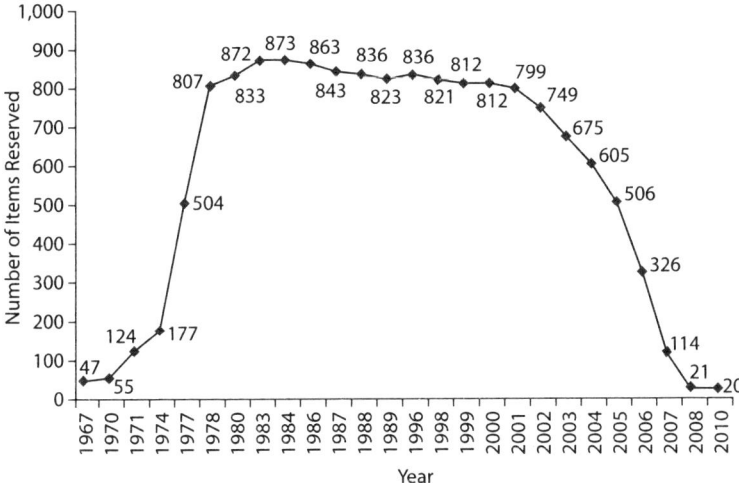

Figure 2.1   Trends in Number of Items Reserved for Exclusive Production under SSI Sector

Sources: Subrahmanya (1995); Martin et al. (2014); various annual reports of Ministry of Small Scale Industries; various budget documents; and different notifications by the Ministry of Commerce and Industry.

production in the small-scale sector. This trend is clearly captured by the inverted, U-shaped curve in Figure 2.1, which depicts the cumulative number of items reserved for exclusive production under the SSI sector in India. Three broad phases can be envisaged as: (a) phase of expansion (Phase I: 1967–86), (b) phase of stagnation (Phase II: 1987–97), and (c) phase of contraction (Phase III: 1998–2010).

Phase I: Phase of Expansion   This phase corresponds to the period 1967–86. The number of items reserved for SSI production consistently increased during this period. By the end of 1970, 55 items were reserved for SSIs. The year 1971 had seen an addition of 73 more items and a deletion of 4 items, thereby resulting in an escalation in the number of items reserved to reach 124 (Subrahmanya 1995). By 1977, the number of items in the reserved list was increased to 504. In effect, the number of reserved items had almost increased 10 times during the 10-year period between 1967 and 1977. The next

10-year period added 359 more items to the reserved list. Thus, by 1986, the number of items reserved for SSI production touched 863 (or 1,045 products).[6]

Phase II: Phase of Stagnation   The period, 1987–97, hardly witnessed any change in the number of items included in the reserved list. In other words, the number of reserved items remained more or less stagnant during this period. The late 1980s and the 1990s also witnessed intense debate on the continuance of this policy which had no parallel anywhere in the world. In the context of economic liberalization measures, the continuance of this policy was considered as an 'aberration' for the economy in general and the industry in particular. Some researchers, thus, argued for a re-examination of this policy as it treated SSIs and LSIs as watertight compartments (Subrahmanya 1995).

Many policy documents and academic studies had emphatically put forth the argument for dereservation during this period. Moreover, they also called for a rapid dereservation within a span of a few years. Many argued that the reservation policy was inconsistent with the other liberalization measures implemented by the Indian government in this period (Desai and Taneja 1993; Sandesara 1993).[7] This period also witnessed a significant rise in studies examining the issue of continuance of reservation policy for small firms and also whether this policy had any influence on the growth of small firms.

Majority of the studies observed that the reservation had virtually not helped small entrepreneurs either to utilize more of the existing capacity or to achieve higher growth in production. Comparing the performance of reserved SSIs with that of unreserved SSIs, Katrak (1999) and Subrahmanya (1995) found that capacity utilization rate was lower in reserved SSIs as compared to the unreserved SSIs, and it was the case in most of the industries. Sandesara (1993) too found that there was considerable under-utilization of capacity in the small-scale sector. His

---

[6] The number of items and number of products changed somewhat because of the adoption of National Industrial Classification (NIC) codes for items to be produced (Rajiv Gandhi Institute for Contemporary Studies 2006).

[7] In fact, as pointed out by Narayana (2003), 563 products out of 1,045 products (or 53.87 per cent) were on the free list of imports.

estimates suggested that capacity utilization for reserved items was 48 per cent, whereas it was 50 per cent in the unreserved SSI sector. In the case of growth performance too, the unreserved SSIs outperformed the reserved SSIs (Katrak 1999; Rajiv Gandhi Institute for Contemporary Studies 2006; Subrahmanya 1995). While the reserved SSIs registered an annual growth rate of 10.3 per cent, the unreserved SSIs grew at an average annual growth rate of 13 per cent over the period 1985–6 to 1987–8 (Subrahmanya 1995). Based on a survey of 1,200 SSI units, Morris et al. (2001) also demonstrated that production of reserved items grew at a retarded rate to that of other producers in the SSIs. Their results clearly showed that the firms that manufactured reserved items ranked poorer in measures of efficiency.[8] Mohan (2002) too argued that policies intended to help small firms have discouraged their growth and slowed down the overall expansion of manufacturing sector. His analysis showed that the growth of employment in manufacturing had slowed down, following a major expansion of the number of products reserved for small firms in 1978. Guhathakurta (1993) has pointed out that the products made by the small firms are of a lower quality than those made by the competing large enterprises. Little et al. (1987) compared protection against advanced domestic factory production to the infant industry argument that was used to seek protection from foreign competition. They argued that reservation created inefficiencies and led to a reduction in overall economic welfare. Panagariya (2008) too argued that the policy of reserving many labour-intensive products for small firms has restricted the growth of Indian exports of these products. In a recent study, García-Santana and Pijoan-Mas (2014) estimated the aggregate productivity costs of small-scale reservation laws in India. Their estimates on the effect of the small-scale reservation laws in the Indian economy gives output per worker losses of 2 per cent for the economy as a whole and 6.8 per cent for manufacturing in particular, and total factor productivity (TFP) losses of 0.75 per cent for the economy and 2 per cent for the manufacturing sector. Thus, the empirical results suggest that reservation has brought little help to production and employment in the small-scale units, or

---

[8] Morris et al. (2001), on the other hand, did not find strong evidence to support the position that inferior capacity utilization and production are the result of reservation.

to the consumers of their products, and therefore destroyed the scale
(as it relates to the size of the firm) and external economies (that arise
mainly from spatial juxtaposing of firms) which could expedite growth
(Katrak 1999; Subrahmanya 1995).

Many studies have also tried to look at the factors that aided the
poor performance of reserved SSI units. Sandesara (1993) attributed
this lacklustre performance of the reserved industries to excessive
entry of small firms into these protected sectors. According to Katrak
(1999), the policy of reservation curbed firm's size, which affected the
overall growth and productivity of small firms. Citing the same reason, Subrahmanya (1995) argued that reservation policy has inhibited
transition of firms in the Indian manufacturing sector. He contended
that measures such as reservation, coupled with various concessions
and benefits, had encouraged SSI units to remain small rather than
transform themselves into larger sized units over a period of time. In
essence, the aim of promotional agencies, of encouraging the growth
of small-scale units, became ineffective as the growth of firms beyond
the threshold guided by the reservation policy would practically make
these firms ineligible for these benefits (Subrahmanya 1995). In turn,
many enterprises that wished to grow beyond the official ceiling for
small firms had split their operations into two or more units.[9] In other
words, small-scale reservation policy had always provided an incentive for entrepreneurs to expand horizontally with more small units,
rather than vertically into larger, middle-sized units (Mazumdar and
Sarkar 2009). According to Mohan (2002), the inability of small firms
to invest in capital stock beyond a limit restricted the growth of small
firms. He maintained that the firms making reserved products were
not allowed to upgrade their technology as they would have had to
stop making such products if their investment grew above the allowed
limits for the SSI. This has affected the overall efficiency of these firms
and, as pointed out by Holmström (1993), they became inefficient over
time. Inclusion of a diverse set of products under the reserved category
without any comparative costs–benefits of the small firms is also often
cited as a reason for the lethargic performance of reserved SSI units

---

[9] It needs to be mentioned that the official ceiling of defining a small-
scale enterprise (SSE) pertained to a production unit (factory) rather than to
an enterprise.

(Ghosh 1988; Guhathakurta 1993; Little et al. 1987).[10] According to a number of scholars, the Indian industrial policy of 'reservation for the small scale' is an important factor behind the absence of medium-sized firms in India (Martin et al. 2014), and thus explain the presence of the missing middle[11] or the dualism in the Indian manufacturing sector (Kumar and Gupta 2008; Mazumdar 2010).

Whatever be the reasons highlighted for the poor performance of small firms in the reservation sector, the arguments for dereservation are clear from these studies. As is evident from the studies reviewed, arguments in favour of abolition of reservation policy (or dereservation) emerged from the intrinsic weaknesses of the policy—namely, inadequate capacity for production, restriction on capacity expansion, absence of economies of scale in production, lack of exposure to vertical competition, and, above all, prevention of entry decisions by firms based on economic considerations (for example, profits and export earnings) (Narayana 2003). Mohan (2002) argued for complete elimination of the reservation policy on the ground that small firms will be free and will be able to grow in terms of investment, expansion, and upgrade. It was also mentioned that the reservation policy is incompatible with the measures of trade policy in regard to removal of the quantitative restrictions (Mohan 2002; Narayana 2003). Supporting the need for dereservation, Morris et al. (2001) observed that the impact of dereservation would be largely non-volatile for most firms. In their opinion, only a handful of products among the reserved ones would shift completely into the larger sector following the dereservation, and the effect would be higher in the consumption of lifestyle goods. Based on case studies of four industries, Shridharan (2002) too argued that dereservation would have only limited impact on majority of products reserved for small firms.

A number of committees appointed by the Government of India (GoI) on various occasions had also suggested dereservation of items reserved for the small-scale sector. The advisory group on consumer goods industry constituted by the Planning Commission had recommended

---

[10] Interestingly, the reserved list included some traditional products such as textiles, modern consumer goods such as electronics, and also capital goods such as machine tools (Katrak 1999).

[11] The missing middle problem of the Indian industry refers to the fact that there are fewer mid-sized firms as compared to small-sized and large-sized firms.

in its report submitted in 1989 (Planning Commission 1989) that the policy of reservation should be progressively abandoned over the next two years. The report submitted by the Vijayaraghavan Committee appointed by the Advisory Committee on Reservation constituted by the Ministry of Commerce and Industry, GoI, in 1996 recommended selective dereservation of items. The committee had suggested dereservation of only 95 products out of 1,045 products.[12] On the contrary, the Planning Commission's study group constituted by the GoI in 2001 had recommended for the continuance of the reservation policy as the committee observed that the SSI sector was making significant contribution to employment, output, and export (GoI 2001). Taking an opposite view, the Abid Hussain Committee, constituted by the GoI in 1997 to review the policy on the SSIs, had recommended total abolition of the reservation policy (GoI 1997). However, the committee was of the opinion that some transitional arrangements need to be made for small firms affected by dereservation.

Not surprisingly, one of the results of these debates has been the consensus among researchers and policymakers that the SSI sector has to embrace the changes occurring in the economy. This resulted in the appointment of a special committee by the Advisory Committee on Reservation in 1996 to review the reservation policy and to reconsider the list of items in the reserved list. It culminated in the policy of dereservation announced in 1997, where the government had decided to gradually dereserve the products originally reserved for small firms (Katrak 1999; Rajiv Gandhi Institute for Contemporary Studies 2006).

Phase III: Phase of Contraction   The period, 1998–2010, witnessed significant reduction in a number of items (or products) reserved for production by small firms. Based on the recommendations from the special committee appointed by the Advisory Committee on Reservation, over 800 items out of 821 items were dereserved between 1998 and 2010. While there were a few items removed from the list in earlier years, large-scale dereservation started in 1997 (with the dereservation of 15 items), and gained momentum in 2001

---

[12] The technical unfeasibility of manufacturing new and quality products within the then investment limit for the SSIs was the main criterion suggested by the Vijayaraghavan Committee for dereservation (Narayana 2003).

(with 50 items being dereserved). From 2002 to 2005, approximately 100 to 200 items were dereserved each year, with only 326 items remaining reserved by the end of 2005 (Figure 2.1). The largest dereservation of items occurred between 2005 and 2006, when 212 items were removed from the list. In the subsequent year, 93 items were taken out from the list and by the end of 2010, 20 items needed to be removed from the list of items reserved for small firms.

In this context, a question of great importance to the policy is whether dereservation has benefited the SSI sector in general and industrial sector in particular. The study by the Rajiv Gandhi Institute for Contemporary Studies (2006) noticed that dereservation has not been followed by any significant fall in SSI output in most dereserved product segments. Out of the 12 products analysed, only one product recorded decline in output during the dereservation period. The study also found some indications to support technology improvements following the dereservation. It also showed that there was a fall in the growth of imports of dereserved items following the dereservation. Martin et al. (2014) examined whether dereservation made any positive impact on the growth of employment, output, investment, and wages for workers. To explore the impact of dereservation on performance, the study classified the factories into incumbents (those already producing reserved products) and entrants (those that moved into the space of the products after the product was dereserved). We found that the dismantling of small-scale reservation policies has contributed to an increase in employment of nearly 3 per cent across India. According to the study, the average incumbent stagnated while the average entrant grew following dereservation. The study also noticed that entrants into a previously reserved product space experienced significant increase in employment, output, investment, and wages. Employment and output increased on an average by 8 per cent and capital investment by 10 per cent. Average real wages increased by approximately 7 per cent. Interestingly, they further noticed that factories that were protected by the reservation policy cut down the number of workers, reduced their output, and reduced their capital stock in the dereservation period. Their district-level results suggest that between 2000 and 2007, a district facing the average amount of dereservation would have experienced a 3 to 6 per cent increase in overall employment. On the other hand, Panagariya (2008) argued that 'it is a mistake to expect that dereservation by itself will lead to the emergence of large-scale manufacturing'. Responding to the criticism that low growth of manufacturing sector is due to the slow process of trimming the SSI reservation list, he claimed that many items belonging to unskilled-labour-intensive manufacturing, such as toys, footwear, and several apparel products, were out of the reservation list for several years, but they did extremely poor on the export front.

Regulatory Framework

In India, small firms which intend to make the transition to the formal sector face different regulatory costs of formality at different employment size levels (Ramaswamy 2013). Some of the important legislations are listed in Table 2.1.[13]

Table 2.1   Important Labour Regulations

S. No.	Name of the Act	Responsibility
1	Factories Act, 1948	Enacted by the central government and enforced by the state governments
2	Employment Provident Fund and Miscellaneous Provisions (EPFMP) Act, 1952	Enacted by the central government, which has the sole responsibility for enforcement
3	Employees State Insurance Act, 1948	Enacted by the central government, which has the sole responsibility for enforcement
4	Industrial Disputes Act (IDA), 1947	Enacted by the central government and enforced by both the central and state governments
5	Minimum Wages Act, 1948	Enacted by the central government and enforced both by the central and state governments

Source: Planning Commission (2006).

[13] Though there are 45 different national- and state-level labour legislations in existence, according to Zagha (1998), it is the IDA of 1947 that has the most detrimental effect on the entry of large firms into unskilled-labour-intensive industries. Dougherty (2009), on the other hand, argued that it is not the IDA alone that is harming labour market outcomes—it is the wider range of labour legislations.

These labour regulations are commonly believed to enhance the estimated cost of employment adjustment for manufacturing firms in response to changes in the product market (Ramaswamy 2013). To Panagariya (2008), these complex sets of labour laws emerged as the key barrier to the emergence of large-scale, unskilled-labour-intensive firms. It was argued that, to escape these regulations, firms would try to stay below the threshold size defined by these regulations. Ramaswamy (2013) argued that firms could employ non-permanent workers to stay below the threshold size as the size thresholds are determined by the number of permanent workers employed in a given factory. Textile firms had been practicing this for a long time in India (Mazumdar and Sarkar 2013).

Implications of the Labour Law Regime

Despite the fact that most of these labour regulations are meant to control the activities pertaining to registered (or formal) firms (Besley and Burgess 2004), an excessively restrictive regulatory regime with respect to employment of labour is also said to be responsible for the increase in employment share of the informal or unorganized sector. Besley and Burgess (2004) showed that states which amended the IDA in a pro-worker direction experienced reduction in manufacturing activities in the formal sector, but led to increased activities in the informal sector. They have further noticed that labour regulation discouraged registration in the formal sector, thereby encouraging firms to remain in the informal sector. The labour law regime in India has also resulted in wages in the organized sector that are substantially higher than those in the unorganized sector (Glinskaya and Lokshin 2005; Panagariya 2008). Besides high wages, the absence of an alternative to exit at a reasonable cost discouraged the entry of large-scale firms into unskilled-labour-intensive sectors (Panagariya 2008).

Some scholars have even argued that the limited applicability of important laws for the firms in informal sector are in a way responsible for the emergence of a dual labour market in India with the associated outcome of the considerably larger sections of informal sector labour being deprived of protection from laws in many spheres (National Commission for Enterprises in the Unorganized Sector [NCEUS] 2009). Hence, due to the presence of these labour regulations, average firm size remained much smaller in India (Krueger 2013). Supporting this evidence, Mazumdar and Sarkar (2009) and Ramaswamy (2013) have observed that size-dependent labour regulations and fiscal incentives work against Indian firms in their vertical growth, thereby giving rise to the phenomenon of the missing middle in the size distribution of manufacturing firms. Another study that investigated regulations that become applicable at the 10-worker threshold is Chatterjee and Kanbur (2013). They focus on the Factories Act and consider it as one of the possible reasons for the presence of missing middle among the manufacturing firms in India. The study differentiates between and quantifies two sides of the missing middle: (a) enterprises who adjust out of the regulation (avoiders) and (b) enterprises who evade the regulation (evaders). The study estimates that the evaders and the avoiders together comprise 1.9 per cent of firms and 11.1 per cent of employment. The authors therefore argue that the focus on (de)regulation as a route to employment and productivity growth has to be balanced with a focus on improving the productivity of those enterprises which would not be affected greatly by the regulation in question.

Financial Sector

In the 1950s and 1960s, the Indian financial sector operated in a fairly liberal environment. A main feature of the Indian banking sector during this period was that a large proportion of bank credit went to the industrial sector and, within it, to the large borrowers, with the agricultural sector getting a little over 2 per cent of bank credit (Sen and Vaidya 1997). It was thus felt among Indian policymakers that there was a need for extensive social control of the Indian banking system in line with the prevailing socialistic mood in the country. The idea gaining currency was that banks should be allocating more credit to social sectors of the economy. Following the nationalization of the banking sector in July 1969, banks were increasingly pressurized to lend to the 'priority sector', comprising agriculture and allied activities, SSIs, retail trade, transport operators, professionals, and craftsmen. While this meant that more credit was available to small-scale firms, medium and large firms may have received a lower share of bank credit in the process.

The gradual set of reforms initiated in the mid-1980s left untouched the policies relating to the provision of credit to firms in the industrial sector. More radical reforms had to wait till 1991 when, as part of the structural adjustment programme, the statutory liquidity ratio was substantially reduced. The interest rates on short-term loans (provided predominantly by the commercial banks) have also been deregulated in a phased manner since 1992 and, by 1994, commercial banks were completely free to set their own lending rates. On balance, the financial liberalization measures implemented since 1991 have led to a relatively easier access to capital markets for firms and may have eased borrowing constraints on their investment decisions under the new policy regime. Despite these significant developments in the financial sector, the long-standing system of direct credit remains largely unchanged. Formally, banks are required to direct 40 per cent of their credit to the priority sectors, notably agriculture and SSIs.

Rao (2014) argued that despite the rightful inclusion and stress on lending to the micro, small, and medium enterprise (MSME) sector, the same has not benefited from adequate credit from the banking sector. It has been argued that medium-sized MSME units benefited the most from the priority sector lending (PSL) regime. This has been also highlighted by a committee appointed under the chairmanship of M.V. Nair to review the PSL regime, which suggested not to encourage bank lending to medium-sized MSME units, and advocated for making the micro segment the specific target under the PSL. However, it needs to be mentioned that this kind of regulation seems to 'incentivize' small-scale units to remain as they are and not to grow and attain scale and competitiveness since bank funding would be denied to them as they grow larger. As argued by Rao (2014), successful entrepreneurs tend to create multiple small units rather than consolidate operations. He maintained that the best possible alternative would be to lend to those small units who put in the right governance structures to become bigger and more competitive.

Studies examining the impact of PSL on small-scale firms are scanty. One such study by Chari (2004) showed how state credit played an important role in establishing the knitwear industrial cluster in Tiruppur, which accounted for 85 per cent of the cotton knitwear production in India in 1997. He argued that the State Bank of India's liberal credit policy was an instrumental factor in the remarkable transformation of peasant workers into small-scale entrepreneurs in Tiruppur.

Trade Policy

Until the early 1990s, India had a highly restrictive trade regime. Average import-weighed tariffs surpassed 80 per cent, over 90 per cent of tradable goods were protected by quantitative restrictions on imports, consumer goods were in the negative list, and foreign investment was subject to strict limitations (Chadha et al. 2003).[14] In 1991, as part of the comprehensive economic reform programme initiated that year, the country has embarked on a series of major trade reforms leading to significant liberalization of the trade regime with respect to capital and intermediate goods. The period also witnessed significant reduction in tariff and non-tariff barriers, phasing out of quantitative restrictions, and easing of the limitations on the entry of foreign investment (Alessandrini et al. 2011). Import licensing was virtually abolished with respect to the imports of most machinery and equipment and of manufactured intermediate goods (Ahluwalia 1999). The peak tariff rate reduced from 77 per cent in 1989–90 to 56 per cent in 1994–5, and then to 31.8 per cent in 2000–1 (Figure 2.2). By the end of 2005–6, the tariff rate remained at 29 per cent, and the rate was the highest in the food products industry and the lowest in the publishing industry (Figure 2.3). There was, however, little change in trade policy with respect to consumer goods which remained in the negative (banned) list (Balasubramanyam 2003).[15]

Giving a view contrary to classical trade theories, studies since the late 1990s have highlighted that trade liberalization does not necessarily lead to rising welfare of unskilled labour (Sinha 2011). In contrast, these studies observed that increasing openness due to trade may lead to rising informalization of work and increased wage

---

[14] The unweighted average of tariffs on manufactured goods was quite high at 147 per cent, with most tariff lines for manufacturing clustered around a range of 140 to 160 per cent (Sen 2008). Unweighted average tariff is the unweighted average of effectively applied rates or most favoured nation rates for all products subject to tariffs calculated for all traded goods. Weighted average tariff is the average of effectively applied rates or most favoured nation rates weighted by the product import shares corresponding to each partner country (World Bank 2010).

[15] The negative list included list of items on which no tariff concessions or any other form of barrier reduction was offered.

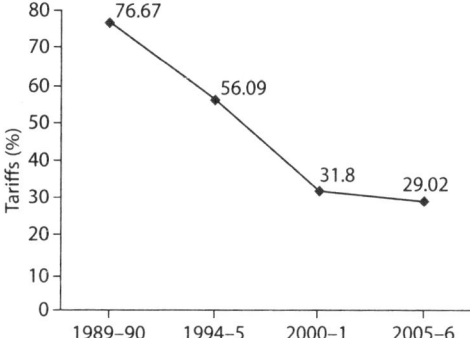

Figure 2.2 Trend in Trade Reforms (tariffs in per cent)
Source: Trade and industrial output data of the World Bank Trade Database.
For more details, see Nicita and Olarreaga (2006).
Note: Tariffs represent percentage of import duties levied on an industry.

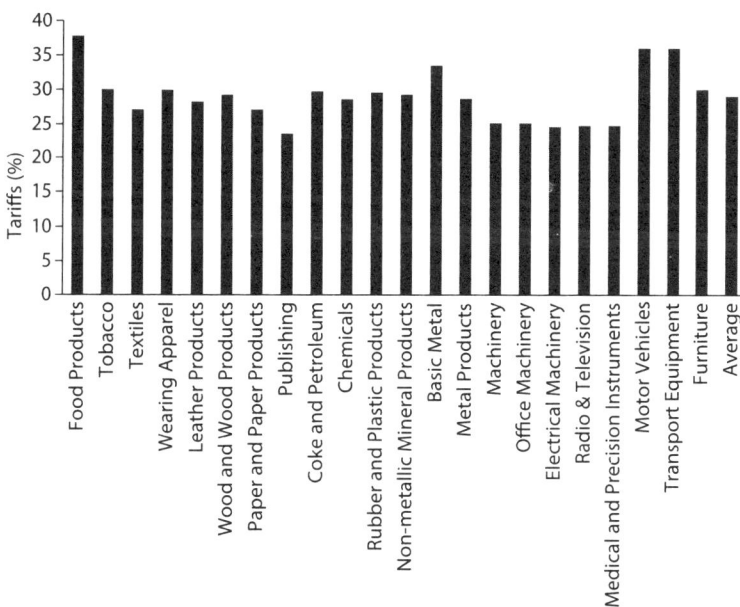

Figure 2.3 Industry-wise Status of Trade Reforms: 2005–6 (tariffs in per cent)
Source: Trade and industrial output data of the World Bank Trade Database.
Note: Tariffs represent percentage of import duties levied on an industry.

differentials across formal and informal manufacturing sector, rather than a greater degree of economic integration. For instance, studies by Carr and Chen (2002), Harriss-White (2003), Sinha et al. (2007), and Stallings and Peres (2000) contradicted the assumptions of neoclassical economic theories of international trade and found that there has been a surge in informal activities following openness due to trade. What has been the effect of the trade policy changes on openness, on Indian manufacturing in general, and on small-scale sector in particular? It has been argued that changes in import duties at the national level might have influenced the import competitiveness of small firms (Narayana 2003). Similarly, removal of quantitative restrictions (QRs) was expected to increase imports into domestic markets and, thereby, expose the domestic producers to international competition. Tybout (2000) was of the opinion that trade reforms in the form of reduced tariffs would have had a pro-competitive effect only on those firms that are in direct competition with imports, and majority of these firms are in the formal sector. Since informal firms cater primarily to the local market and do not compete directly with imports, the efficiency enhancing effects of trade reforms would be less for these firms. On the other hand, informal firms would be better able to adjust their use of labour and capital in response to trade reforms as compared to formal firms who face various policy-induced impediments to the adjustment of factors of production. Besides, there can also be an indirect impact on informal firms if they are working as subcontractors for formal firms.

While analysing the import performance of the sensitive items for the SSIs, Narayana (2003) observed that the impact of removal of the QRs on small firms appeared to be negligible at the all-India level. Nataraj (2011) examined the impact of trade liberalization on firm productivity and found that unilateral reduction in the tariffs of final goods increased the average productivity of small, informal firms in Indian manufacturing sector, and that the lower tariffs of final goods are associated with the exit of the least productive firms in the informal sector. Marjit and Kar (2007) found that trade liberalization has led to a rise in real wage and real fixed assets in the informal manufacturing sector of India. Ahsan and Mitra (2014) too showed that trade liberalization led to an increase in the share of wages in total revenue for small firms.

Other Government Assistance

While there are no comprehensive and specific programmes for supporting the technology, marketing, and training needs of firms in the informal sector, informal firms would have benefited from a number of initiatives devised to support SSIs. Indian government has implemented many of these initiatives through two principal organizations—the Small Industries Development Organization (SIDO) and the National Small Industries Corporation (NSIC) Limited. These institutions assisted small enterprises through a set of specially tailored schemes which facilitate marketing support, credit support, technology support, training and upgrade of skills, and other support services. Some of the schemes implemented under the aegis of SIDO include Credit Linked Capital Subsidy Scheme for Technology Upgradation, ISO 9000/ISO 14001 Certification Reimbursement Scheme, and Assistance to Entrepreneurship Development Institutes. The NSIC, for example, offers various technology support schemes to small units through its 'Technical Services Centres' and 'Extension Centres'. These services range from guidance on the use of new techniques, provision of material-testing facilities through accredited laboratories to classroom and practical training for upgrading the skills.

Training for Skill Upgrade

Vocational training programmes aimed at skill development are rolled out by various ministries/departments, commissions, councils, autonomous bodies and institutions, as well as by public–private partnership bodies (NCEUS 2009). The Ministry of Human Resource Development (MHRD) and the Ministry of Labour and Employment (MoLE) are the two major ministries responsible for skill development. There have also been initiatives from other ministries/institutions, but they are mostly sectoral in nature and target-group oriented. All of these formal vocational training programmes under the aegis of the MHRD and MoLE, such as the diploma-level courses offered by polytechnics; the Craftsmen Training Scheme (CTS) and the Apprenticeship Training Scheme (ATS) of Directorate General for Employment & Training (DGE&T); and the diploma programmes in engineering and architecture, hotel management and catering technology, and pharmacy offered by the All India Council of Technical Education (AICTE), insist on a minimum level of educational qualification. Additionally, these pro-grammes have not been explicitly geared towards the informal sector, or at least not towards the most vulnerable informal workers (NCEUS 2009). This is clearly evident from the case studies carried out by the NCEUS which showed that those who receive formal training either start their own enterprises or go for wage employment in the informal sector (NCEUS 2009). Therefore, the need of the hour is to devise programmes that take into account the structural characteristics of the informal sector and target those at lower ends.

Of course, there exist some schemes that are explicitly based on the needs of the informal sector under the aegis of different ministries of the government. Community polytechnics, Jan Shikshan Sansthan (JSS), National Institute of Open Schooling (NIOS) initiated by the MHRD, Skill Development Initiative (SDI) launched in 2007 by the MoLE to train one million people in five years, and entrepreneurship develop-ment programmes (EDPs) organized by the Ministry of Micro, Small, and Medium Enterprises (MSME ministry) to impart training to the new entrants to the workforce so as to develop skills, entrepreneurship, and managerial capabilities are some examples.[16] Though there exist several formal and informal schemes to promote skill development for workers in the informal sector, it is clearly evident that governmental system for skill development and training is dispersed, characterized by overlaps and multiplicity of schemes and, above all, woefully inad-equate, especially for workers in the informal sector (NCEUS 2009).

✻   ✻   ✻

The overall discussion in this chapter clearly suggests that there have been considerable changes in the policies and programmes supporting the small firms in the Indian manufacturing sector, especially since the economic reforms of 1991. The rest of the book examines the implica-tions of the reform process for growth and performance of informal manufacturing firms.

---

[16] These programmes are explained in detail in NCEUS (2009).

3

CHANGE AND CONTINUITY IN THE INDIAN INFORMAL MANUFACTURING SECTOR

In this chapter, we set out the stylized facts of the Indian informal manufacturing sector with respect to its evolution over time. We examine the overall patterns and trends in number of enterprises, employment, and gross value added (GVA) for the entire informal manufacturing sector over the period 1984–5 to 2010–11 in the next section.[1] We do the same for broad industrial groups and by location (rural/urban) with a view to identifying whether the informal sector in some industries have exhibited stronger growth than in other industries, and whether patterns and trends in the key indicators of informal sector performance have differed across rural and urban areas. The third section looks at regional patterns in output, employment, and enterprise growth across 15 major Indian states,[2] to see whether there are spatial variations in

---

[1] Appendix 3A, given at the end of this chapter, presents a discussion on the construction of variables.

[2] It is important to note here that the state of Andhra Pradesh was bifurcated into two states—Telangana and Andhra Pradesh—in 2014. As the period for this study ends in 2010–11, we use the data for combined Andhra Pradesh. Similarly, in 2000, Bihar, Madhya Pradesh, and Uttar Pradesh were bifurcated and three new states—Uttarakhand, Chhattisgarh, and Jharkhand—were formed. We merged data for these three states with their parent states so as to have consistent data for the entire study period.

enterprise, employment, and output growth in the informal manufacturing sector in India. The fourth section looks at patterns and trends in the number of enterprises, employment, and GVA by enterprise type— Own Account Manufacturing Enterprises (OAMEs), Non-directory Manufacturing Enterprises (NDMEs), and Directory Manufacturing Enterprises (DMEs)—to see whether the variation in output, enterprise, and employment growth across the industry and across the state is particularly evident in one type of informal firms relative to other types. The last section presents the key findings of the analysis.

Growth of the Informal Manufacturing Sector: Aggregate Trends

We first compare the growth performance of the informal manufacturing sector with that of the formal manufacturing sector. The rate of growth of real output has fluctuated considerably in both the formal and informal manufacturing sectors during 1978–2011 (Table 3.1). Output growth accelerated in the formal manufacturing sector in the mid-1980s, then slowed down in the 1990s, and again accelerated in the 2000s. Real output grew the fastest during the 2000s, especially during the early 2000s, at an annual growth rate of over 11 per cent. Considerable volatility is visible in output growth in the informal sector too. Output grew at a rate of 12.17 per cent in the early 1980s and then slowed down to 5.77 per cent in the second half of the 1980s.

Table 3.1   Real Output Growth in the Formal, Informal, and Total Manufacturing Sectors (in per cent)

Year	Output Growth			Employment Growth		
	Formal	Informal	Total	Formal	Informal	Total
1978–84	4.80	12.17	6.34	2.25	12.74	10.44
1984–90	9.38	5.77	8.53	1.07	−0.93	−0.59
1990–5	7.20	−3.46	5.21	2.58	−2.03	−1.14
1995–2001	6.45	11.48	7.24	0.09	3.69	2.96
2001–6	11.41	10.66	11.28	2.67	−0.34	0.22
2006–11	10.26	−7.15	7.94	6.86	−0.85	0.89

Source: Authors' calculations based on ASI and NSSO data sets.
Note: Growth rates are annual average compound growth rates. Output growth rates are reported for real output, computed at 1993–4 prices.

The first half of the 1990s witnessed negative output growth, but this got reversed during 1994–2001. The late 1990s and the early 2000s witnessed faster output growth of 11.5 per cent and 10.7 per cent, respectively, but the sector again witnessed a reversal in output growth in the late 2000s.

As of 2011, the informal sector employs about three-quarters of the manufacturing workforce (about 35 million people) in the country (see Table 3.2). The share remained the same for most part of the period under study except for a marginal decline observed between 2005–6 and 2010–11. The latter period witnessed the share of manufacturing workers employed by the informal sector declining by 7 per cent, from 80 per cent in 2005–6 to 73 per cent in 2010–11. Both the sectors witnessed considerable expansion in employment over the period 1978–2011. Our estimates suggest that employment in the formal manufacturing sector and informal manufacturing sector increased at an annual rate of 2.4 per cent and 2.3 per cent, respectively, in this period. In absolute terms, the addition to employment in the formal sector was 0.1 million per annum, while the number of workers has more than doubled in the informal sector during this period.

Similar to real output, the volatility in growth was clearly evident for employment in both sectors (Table 3.1). Though the number of workers has consistently increased in the formal sector, its rate of increase has considerably fluctuated over time. Employment growth slowed down in the mid-1980s, then accelerated in the first half of the 1990s, and

Table 3.2 Employment Trends in the Formal and Informal Manufacturing Sectors (in '0000s): 1978–9 to 2010–11

Year	Formal Sector	Informal Sector	Total Manufacturing Sector	Share of Informal Sector in Total Employment (%)
1978–9	595	1,669	2,264	73.7
1984–5	680	3,428	4,108	83.4
1989–90	717	3,272	3,989	82.0
1994–5	814	2,953	3,767	78.4
2000–1	819	3,704	4,503	81.8
2005–6	911	3,641	4,553	80.0
2010–11	1,269	3,489	4,758	73.3

Source: Authors' calculations based on ASI and NSSO data sets.

again decelerated in the late 1990s. The sector witnessed faster expansion in employment in the 2000s, especially during the second half of the 2000s. A different growth trend is observed for employment in the informal sector. After a period of increase in the first half of the 1980s, there is a decline in employment for the period 1984–5 to 1994–5. This was reversed in the second half of the 1990s with an annual growth rate of 3.69 per cent. However, the last two sub-periods of 2000s witnessed a steady decline in employment in the informal sector.

Industry-wise Patterns

Table 3.3 reports the industry-wise share in number of enterprises, employment, and GVA for the informal manufacturing sector over the period 1984–5 to 2010–11.[3] It can be seen that the bulk of the activities in the informal manufacturing sector are concentrated in five industry groups producing food products, beverages, cotton products, textiles, and wood products.[4] In 2010–11, these five industry groups together accounted for 81 per cent of total enterprises, 71 per cent of total employment, and 60 per cent of total value added (TVA) in the sector. Our analysis also reveals that their contribution is significantly higher in the rural sector than in the urban sector. However, their contribution to both rural as well as urban areas has declined over time.

We now discuss the growth performance of the sector in terms of growth in enterprises, employment, and GVA at the industry level. We present growth rates for the entire period of 1984–5 to 2010–11 and for its two sub-periods, 1984–5 to 1994–5 and 1994–5 to 2010–11 in Table 3.4.[5] This latter decomposition would help in capturing the impact of reforms on the growth performance of the sector. As discussed earlier, the sector has witnessed significant growth for the period 1984–5 to 2010–11. There was a decline in number of enterprises, but employment and GVA grew substantially during this period. The acceleration in informal sector activities for the overall period is evidently due

---

[3] We use real GVA and its construction is presented in Appendix 3A at the end of this chapter.

[4] These industry groups are explained in detail in Table A1.3 of Appendix A1.

[5] We do not have disaggregated data for 1978–9, so our disaggregated analysis from this section onwards starts from 1984–5.

Table 3.3 Share in Enterprises, Employment, and GVA by Industry Group: 1984–5 to 2010–11 (in per cent)

Industry	Number of Enterprises						Employment						Gross Value Added					
	1984–5	1989–90	1994–5	2000–1	2005–6	2010–11	1984–5	1989–90	1994–5	2000–1	2005–6	2010–11	1984–5	1989–90	1994–5	2000–1	2005–6	2010–11
Food Products	18.5	17.8	19.5	16.4	13.6	12.0	19.2	17.5	19.1	17.2	15.8	12.9	18.2	18.7	18.1	15.7	15.3	13.8
Beverages	7.7	14.3	11.6	13.7	18.2	14.5	7.2	10.9	9.1	10.5	13.1	10.1	4.6	5.2	4.7	4.1	4.1	3.5
Cotton Products	15.7	12.9	10.2	7.3	6.4	15.6	21.3	14.1	12.4	9.4	8.9	17.1	12.4	12.1	11.0	8.8	9.4	14.9
Textiles	20.8	8.4	8.9	23.3	27.4	25.6	16.3	8.7	10.3	19.5	22.0	19.1	13.3	6.9	8.6	19.4	18.4	16.6
Wood Products	17.5	24.5	23.3	18.7	15.0	13.0	14.4	20.0	18.3	16.1	13.6	11.8	17.4	21.0	15.0	9.8	12.1	11.6
Paper Products	0.8	1.3	1.4	1.4	1.7	0.7	1.2	1.9	1.9	2.0	2.1	1.0	2.5	4.3	3.5	3.3	3.4	1.3
Leather Products	3.0	2.2	1.7	1.1	0.9	0.7	2.2	1.7	1.7	1.1	1.4	0.9	3.5	1.6	2.5	1.7	1.9	1.0
Chemicals	0.4	1.4	1.2	1.3	2.5	1.3	0.6	1.7	1.2	1.5	2.4	1.5	1.3	2.5	1.3	1.6	1.9	1.5
Rubber Products	0.7	0.5	0.7	0.6	0.5	1.1	1.1	0.8	1.1	1.0	0.8	1.6	1.3	2.3	3.0	1.9	1.1	2.4
Non-metallic Minerals	5.9	6.6	6.9	4.8	3.8	3.5	7.6	8.7	8.8	8.2	6.4	8.3	4.4	5.9	6.7	8.9	5.7	8.1
Basic Metals	0.3	0.2	0.3	0.3	0.2	0.3	0.4	1.9	0.4	0.4	0.3	0.4	1.2	1.3	1.2	1.1	1.1	0.7
Metal Products	4.1	3.9	4.7	5.2	5.3	3.7	4.2	5.1	5.8	6.4	7.0	5.3	12.3	9.4	12.4	13.5	14.2	9.4
Transport Equipment and Parts	0.3	0.2	0.2	0.2	0.2	0.2	0.3	0.4	0.4	0.5	0.6	0.4	4.4	1.3	1.2	1.3	1.3	1.0
Other Manufacturing Products	4.3	5.7	9.4	5.7	4.3	7.9	4.0	6.5	9.5	6.2	5.6	9.7	3.2	7.5	10.8	8.8	10.0	14.1
Total	100.0	100.0	100.0	100.0	100.0	100.0	100.0	100.0	100.0	100.0	100.0	100.0	100.0	100.0	100.0	100.0	100.0	100.0

Source: Authors' calculations based on NSSO data.

Table 3.4 Growth of Number of Enterprises, Employment, and GVA by Industry Group (in per cent)

Industry	Number of Enterprises			Employment			Gross Value Added		
	1984–95	1995–2011	1984–2011	1984–95	1995–2011	1984–2011	1984–95	1995–2011	1984–2011
Food Products	–3.08	–1.03	–1.82	–1.53	–1.52	–1.52	–0.43	4.43	2.53
Beverages	0.42	3.46	2.28	0.91	1.58	1.32	–0.16	9.05	5.41
Cotton Products	–7.67	4.77	–0.20	–6.71	3.01	–0.84	–1.05	7.31	4.02
Textiles	–11.41	8.97	0.63	–5.89	4.88	0.60	–5.03	10.42	4.20
Wood Products	–0.74	–1.68	–1.32	0.87	–1.79	–0.78	–1.80	6.22	3.06
Paper Products	2.53	–2.36	–0.51	3.44	–3.00	–0.57	3.44	1.89	2.48
Leather Products	–8.79	–3.67	–5.67	–4.02	–2.71	–3.22	–3.49	–5.16	–4.52
Chemicals	7.67	2.58	4.51	6.26	2.28	3.79	0.01	21.92	12.97
Rubber Products	–3.87	4.79	1.37	–1.08	3.39	1.65	8.45	15.83	12.93
Non-metallic Minerals	–2.05	–2.24	–2.17	–0.06	0.58	0.33	4.08	8.44	6.74
Basic Metals	–3.79	3.26	0.49	–1.49	0.27	–0.41	–0.97	16.57	9.48
Metal Products	–2.44	0.51	–0.63	1.79	0.37	0.92	0.61	6.82	4.39
Transport Equipment and Parts	–4.54	–0.03	–1.79	1.23	0.47	0.76	–12.59	15.28	3.64
Other Manufacturing Products	4.25	0.87	2.16	7.38	1.09	3.46	12.98	16.27	14.99
Total	–3.57	2.01	–0.18	–1.48	0.94	0.00	–0.17	10.55	6.30

Source: Authors' calculations based on NSSO data.

Note: Growth rates are annual average compound growth rates. Gross value added growth rates are reported for real gross value added, computed at 1993–4 prices.

to the better performance of the sector during the post-reform period (1994–5 to 2010–11). The latter period witnessed significant expansion of activities in the informal sector leading to considerable increase in the number of enterprises, employment, and GVA. Growth of GVA was the fastest (at 10.6 per cent per annum), followed by number of enterprises (at 2 per cent per annum) and employment (at 1 per cent per annum).[6] This significant growth performance in the post-reform period has more than compensated for the slump in growth recorded by the sector in the preceding period 1984–5 to 1994–5, which has seen considerable decline in enterprises, employment, and GVA.

It can be observed that growth rates differ significantly across two-digit industries.[7] Majority of industries have recorded significant gains in the post-reform period. Manufacturers of cotton products, textiles, rubber products, basic metals, and transport equipment and parts are the principal gainers. These industries have substantially increased their size in the sector in terms of enterprises, employment, and real output, leaving behind their poor performance in the pre-reform period. Manufacture of leather products is the only industry group that witnessed deterioration in performance in terms of all these variables in the post-reform period. This industry recorded significant deceleration in enterprises, employment, and GVA in both the periods.

The estimated growth rates of GVA show that in the first sub-period, growth rates varied from a high 12.98 per cent in the manufacture of other industrial goods to a low –12.59 per cent in the transport industry.

[6] However, it can be noted from Table 3.1 that there has been considerable volatility in the growth of the informal sector from 1995 to 2011.

[7] The National Industrial Classification (NIC) uses letters and digits to represent the hierarchy (levels of production) and relations among categories of economic activity. In other words, all the production activities are grouped into several 'activity groups' or 'tabulation categories' in a hierarchical manner. These activities are first grouped into 'section', which is alphabetically coded from A through U. Every section is then divided into 'division', with two digit numeric code. Every division is further divided into a 'group' with three digit numeric code. Each group gets divided into 'class' with a four digit numeric code and every four digit class is divided into a five digit 'sub-class' (Central Statistical Organization [CSO] 2008). In this chapter, we use the 'two-digit' classification of industrial activities in the manufacturing sector.

A marginal increase can be observed in the inter-industry variation in growth rates in the second period. There is a significant increase in value addition in the post-reform period in industries producing chemicals, rubber products, basic metals, and transport equipment and parts. As shown in Table 3.4, these four industries recorded a very high growth rate of 22 per cent, 15.8 per cent, 16.6 per cent, and 15.3 per cent, respectively, in this period. The manufacture of leather products is the only industry group that has registered a negative growth in value added in the period following reforms. The leather industry experienced a decline in the GVA by 5.16 per cent in this period.

Figure 3.1 shows the rate of growth of value added in the two-digit industries, with the rate of growth in the period 1994–5 to 2010–11 plotted on the x-axis and the rate of growth in the period 1984–5 to 1994–5 on the y-axis. The origin of the scatter plot corresponds to the growth rates for the sector as a whole: –0.2 per cent and 10.6 per cent for the first and second sub-periods, respectively. The first quadrant represents those industries whose growth rates are above the average for the sector as a whole in both periods, and the second quadrant includes those industries with growth rates above the average in the post-reform period but below the average in the period prior to reforms. The third quadrant encompasses industries with growth rates below the average for the sector in both the periods, while the fourth quadrant includes industries with growth rates higher than the average in the pre-reform period but lower than the average in the post-reform period.

Rubber products, chemicals, and a miscellaneous category called 'other manufacturing products' have registered growth rates above the average for the informal manufacturing sector in both the first (pre-reform) and the second (post-reform) sub-periods (see Figure 3.1, quadrant I). In contrast, five industries—leather, cotton, wood, food, and beverages (see Figure 3.1, quadrant III)—have witnessed output growth below the average for the sector in both periods.

Manufacturing of basic metals, textiles, and transport equipment and parts experienced a turnaround in the growth performance—from a negative growth trend in the pre-reform period to a positive growth performance in the post-reform period (see Figure 3.1, quadrant IV). It appears that these industries have benefited the most from the reforms initiated in the 1990s. On the other hand, non-metallic minerals, metal products, and paper products (see Figure 3.1, quadrant II) seem to have lost ground in the post-reform period. These industries have registered growth rates

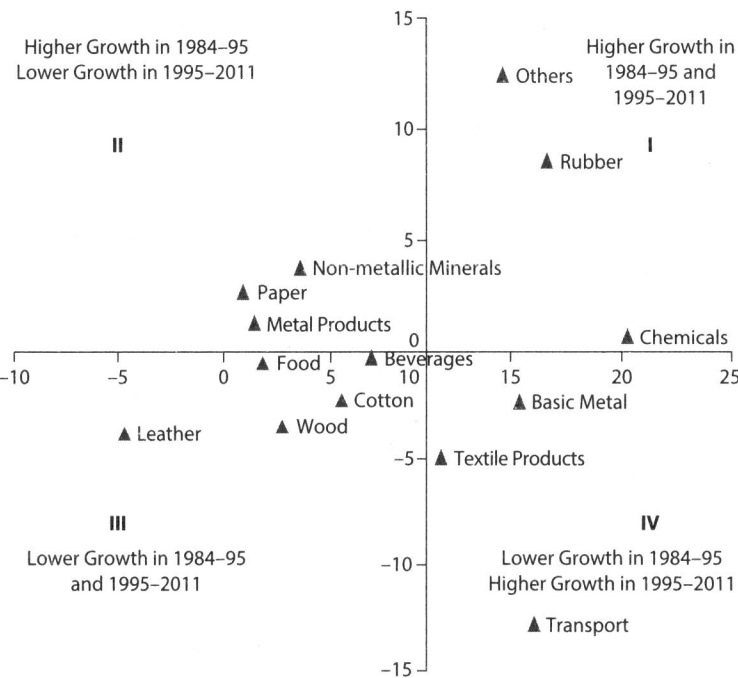

Figure 3.1   Growth of Gross Value Added in Two-digit Industries
Source: Authors' calculation from NSSO data.
Notes: (a) The origin represents the average growth for the informal manufacturing
sector in India.
  (b) Growth rates are annual average compound growth rates. Gross value added
  growth rates are reported for real gross value added, computed at 1993–4 prices.

that are lower than those in the preceding sub-period. We find that the
manufacture of paper products recorded lower growth rate in this period,
after an impressive performance in the sub-period 1984–5 to 1994–5.

Given that the major chunk of the manufacturing work force is
employed in the informal sector, it would be pertinent to also consider
growth of employment along with output growth as a performance criterion. Thus, Figure 3.2 presents the growth performance of two-digit
industries for the period 1984–2011, with the rate of growth of value
added on the x-axis and the rate of growth of employment on the y-axis.
The origin of the scatter plot corresponds to the growth rates for the
informal manufacturing sector as a whole: 6.3 per cent and –0.98 per
cent, respectively, of GVA and employment. It is found that only

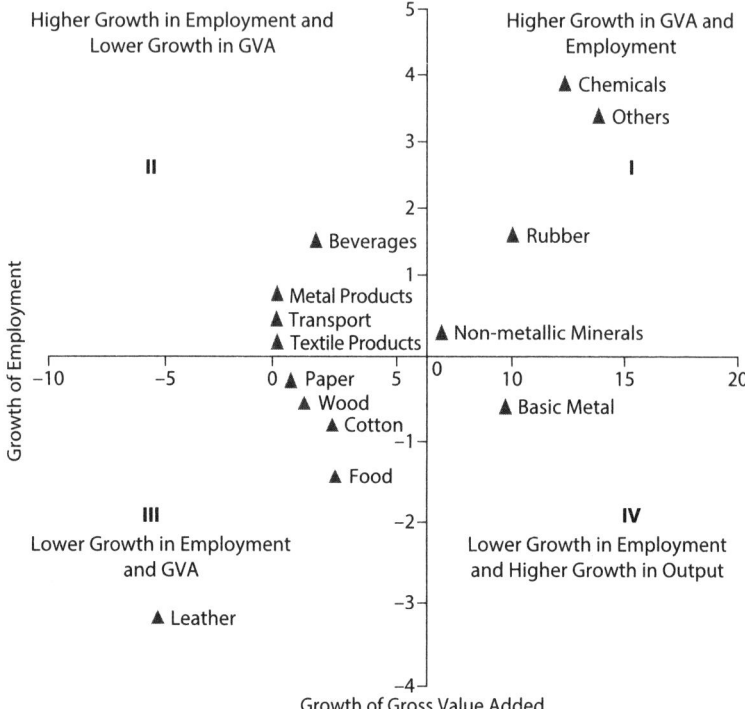

Figure 3.2 Growth of Employment and Gross Value Added: 1984–5 to 2010–11
Source: Authors' calculation from NSSO data.
Notes: (a) The origin represents the average growth for the informal manufacturing
sector in India.

(b) Growth rates are annual average compound growth rates. Gross value added
growth rates are reported for real gross value added, computed at 1993-4 prices.

four industries—chemicals, rubber, non-metallic minerals, and other
manufacturing products—have recorded output and employment
growth rates higher than the average for the sector as a whole (Figure
3.2, quadrant I). Five industries have registered growth rates below the
average for the sector in both the variables (Figure 3.2, quadrant III).
In industries such as basic metals, output grew faster than the average
for the sector, but employment grew slower (Figure 3.2, quadrant II).
On the other side, beverages, metal products, transport equipment and
parts, and textiles witnessed growth performance that is higher than

the average growth in employment, but lower than average growth in output (Figure 3.2, quadrant IV).

Growth Trends by Location: Rural and Urban Sector

We now look at the trends in growth of the informal manufacturing for rural and urban areas separately, as we would expect that the patterns of growth could differ significantly, depending on the location of the enterprise. Trends similar to the one observed at the aggregate level is noticed for the rural sector too. After a period of decline in the first sub-period, that is 1984–5 to 1994–5, the rural segment of the sector regained the growth momentum by registering positive growth rates during 1994–5 to 2010–11 (see Table 3.5). Growth of GVA increased at a rapid rate in the post-reform period, with a growth rate of over 9 per cent per annum. The number of enterprises too overcame their abysmal growth phase in the first sub-period by registering significant gains in the second sub-period; the number of rural enterprises grew at a rate of 0.4 per cent per annum in the second sub-period. On the other hand, employment continued to decline in the second sub-period as well. However, the rate of decline slowed down in this period.

Majority of the industries posted impressive growth performance in value added in the period that witnessed significant reforms in the Indian industrial sector. Chemicals, rubber products, basic metals, transport equipment and parts, and other manufacturing products are the industries that witnessed most significant expansion in the second sub-period in the rural segment of the informal manufacturing sector. The leather industry is the only industry that has reported consistent decline in enterprises, employment, and GVA in both sub-periods. The largest increase in enterprises and workers in the post-reform period occurred in the textile and basic metals industries. The value addition to output was the highest in chemicals, transport, and basic metals industries.

The post-reform period has witnessed significant expansion of informal sector in urban areas too. The number of enterprises and employment reported a turnaround in growth performance from a negative growth in the first sub-period to a positive growth in the second sub-period. During this period, enterprises, employment, and GVA grew at the rates of 5.5 per cent, 3.7 per cent, and 11.2 per cent per annum, respectively (Table 3.6). This is a remarkable improvement considering

Table 3.5 Growth of Number of Enterprises, Employment, and GVA in the Rural Informal Manufacturing Sector by Industry (in per cent)

Industry	Number of Enterprises			Employment			Gross Value Added		
	1984–95	1995–2011	1984–2011	1984–95	1995–2011	1984–2011	1984–95	1995–2011	1984–2011
Food Products	-2.9	-2.2	-2.5	-1.6	-2.9	-2.4	1.3	2.8	2.2
Beverages	0.8	3.5	2.5	1.4	1.6	1.5	0.2	9.5	5.8
Cotton Products	-8.3	2.5	-1.8	-8.0	0.6	-2.8	-1.8	4.0	1.7
Textiles	-10.5	6.2	-0.6	-5.5	2.0	-1.0	-6.9	9.2	2.7
Wood Products	-0.7	-2.5	-1.8	0.8	-2.8	-1.4	-3.6	5.9	2.1
Paper Products	8.8	-2.8	1.5	7.8	-2.9	1.1	6.0	5.4	5.7
Leather Products	-11.4	-8.7	-9.8	-8.9	-6.0	-7.2	-10.1	-6.5	-7.9
Chemicals	12.5	1.7	5.7	11.0	0.5	4.4	10.7	20.3	16.5
Rubber Products	-5.0	-2.6	-3.5	-5.0	0.6	-1.6	3.0	16.5	11.1
Non-metallic Minerals	-2.0	-3.0	-2.6	-0.1	0.2	0.1	4.9	8.1	6.9
Basic Metals	-8.7	6.0	0.1	-4.2	4.4	1.0	-0.5	19.8	11.5
Metal Products	-4.9	-0.1	-2.0	-2.6	-0.4	-1.3	-1.6	7.8	4.1
Transport Equipment and Parts	-11.1	-2.1	-5.7	-6.6	1.3	-1.8	-6.1	21.0	9.8
Other Manufacturing Products	5.3	-2.7	0.3	9.1	-2.7	1.7	9.3	15.3	13.0
Total	-3.6	0.4	-1.1	-1.9	-0.7	-1.2	-1.0	9.5	5.4

Source: Authors' calculations based on NSSO data.

Note: Growth rates are annual average compound growth rates. Gross value added growth rates are reported for real gross value added, computed at 1993–4 prices.

Table 3.6 Growth of Number of Enterprises, Employment, and GVA in the Urban Informal Manufacturing Sector by Industry (in per cent)

Industry	Number of Enterprises			Employment			Gross Value Added		
	1984–95	1995–2011	1984–2011	1984–95	1995–2011	1984–2011	1984–95	1995–2011	1984–2011
Food Products	−3.9	2.6	0.1	−1.4	2.1	0.7	−2.6	6.4	2.9
Beverages	−1.1	3.4	1.6	−0.7	1.6	0.7	−0.9	7.9	4.4
Cotton Products	−5.6	8.8	3.0	−3.2	6.1	2.4	−0.4	9.4	5.5
Textiles	−14.1	14.5	2.5	−6.6	8.7	2.6	−3.5	11.1	5.2
Wood Products	−0.7	1.7	0.8	1.3	1.2	1.3	1.1	6.6	4.4
Paper Products	0.8	−2.2	−1.0	2.4	−3.0	−1.0	3.2	1.3	2.0
Leather Products	−3.1	−0.2	−1.3	1.3	−1.3	−0.3	0.3	−4.8	−2.9
Chemicals	4.7	3.3	3.8	3.6	3.5	3.5	−2.3	22.5	12.3
Rubber Products	−3.4	6.4	2.5	0.0	3.8	2.3	9.4	15.7	13.2
Non-metallic Minerals	−2.2	1.4	0.0	0.4	2.4	1.6	1.2	9.6	6.3
Basic Metals	−1.9	2.3	0.7	−0.9	−0.9	−0.9	−1.0	15.9	9.1
Metal Products	1.7	1.2	1.4	5.7	0.8	2.7	1.1	6.6	4.5
Transport Equipment and Parts	0.4	0.6	0.5	4.5	0.3	1.9	−13.0	14.4	3.0
Other Manufacturing Products	2.8	4.0	3.6	5.5	4.1	4.6	14.1	16.5	15.6
Total	−3.5	5.5	1.9	−0.3	3.7	2.1	0.5	11.2	7.0

Source: Authors' calculations based on NSSO data.
Note: Growth rates are annual average compound growth rates. Gross value added growth rates are reported for real gross value added, computed at 1993–4 prices.

the fact that the number of enterprises and employment had declined at –3.5 per cent per annum and –0.3 per cent per annum, respectively, in the pre-reform period. In this period, GVA too grew at a very low annual rate of 0.5 per cent.

Similar to the rural sector, the rates of growth, however, showed marked variation across the two-digit industries. The inter-industry variation in growth rates declined for the number of enterprises and employment and increased for GVA in the post-reform period. Manufacture of chemicals, textiles, transport equipment and parts, and other manufacturing products witnessed significant expansion in the number of enterprises, employment, and GVA in the urban informal manufacturing sector. Among these industries, manufacture of textiles is the largest industry group accounting for significant share in the selected indicators. This industry registered significant gains in all the variables by switching over from a negative growth performance in the first sub-period to a positive growth perfor-mance in the second sub-period. We notice that only two industry groups—namely, metal products and other manufacturing prod-ucts—have recorded positive growth rates in both pre-reform and post-reform periods.

Regional Patterns of Growth and Structural Change in Informal Manufacturing

As is evident from the earlier discussion, the informal manufacturing sector in India has registered substantial growth in recent years. This has also resulted in an increase in the size of the sector relative to the other sectors of the economy, especially as employment provider. Our analysis also reveals that the performance of this sector over the years in terms of value addition and employment generation is impres-sive. However, the analysis carried out till now is at the economy-wide level across industries. These aggregate trends could mask considerable regional variations. Given the geographical size of the economy and the heterogeneity of activities, it would be worthwhile to examine the regional dispersion of informal manufacturing. This section sketches a regional profile of informal manufacturing activities in India and its growth trends. This, in our view, would unravel the inter-state varia-tions in activities and growth trends.

State-wise Distribution of Informal Manufacturing

This section presents an analysis of informal manufacturing activity across states. Three indicators are considered to sketch the geographical spread. They are: the number of enterprises, employment, and GVA. Six time periods, starting from 1984–5 till 2010–11, are compared to understand the extent of changes over time. Table 3.7 shows that Uttar Pradesh (UP) and West Bengal (WB) had the maximum number of enterprises in 1984–5; UP had close to 30 per cent of the total number of enterprises in the country. Over the time, by 2010–11 the share of UP had fallen by half to 14.8 per cent. There is a remarkable constancy in the shares of most states in the distribution of enterprises, employment, and output, with only Andhra Pradesh (AP) being able to increase its share. There is a regional concentration in informal sector activities in the country, with the top three states (Tamil Nadu [TN], WB, and UP) accounting for more than 40 per cent of the total number of enterprises in the country. However, a decline is also noticed in concentration over the years as the combined share of the top three states declined and share of bottom three states (Assam, Haryana, and Punjab) increased during the period under consideration (that is 1984–5 to 2010–11). With regard to employment too, a similar trend can be observed for UP and WB, the states with the highest share. While UP witnessed a declining employment share over time, WB improved its share in employment. As observed in the case of number of enterprises and employment, the combined share of top three states in GVA (TN, UP, and WB) has also witnessed significant decline over the years. Maharashtra and Gujarat registered impressive increase in their share in GVA since 1984–5 while UP registered a significant decline over time.

State-wise Distribution of Informal Manufacturing in Rural and Urban Areas

This section looks at the state-wise evolution of the informal sector, separately for rural and urban areas. The scenario at the rural level is presented in Table 3.8. It can be noted that the share of UP in total number of enterprises declined to half over the time, while WB and AP increased their shares over time. In the case of employment too, a similar trend is noticed. UP witnessed a decline in its share while WB experienced an increase in its share in employment. States like TN have

Table 3.7 Share of Major States in Number of Enterprises, Employment, and GVA in Informal Manufacturing Sector in India: 1984–5 to 2010–11 (in per cent)

State	Number of Enterprises						Employment						Gross Value Added					
	1984–5	1989–90	1994–5	2000–1	2005–6	2010–11	1984–5	1989–90	1994–5	2000–1	2005–6	2010–11	1984–5	1989–90	1994–5	2000–1	2005–6	2010–11
Andhra Pradesh	8.3	10.3	9.3	9.9	9.3	9.8	8.1	9.4	8.0	9.4	8.4	9.3	6.3	4.9	5.5	7.1	5.4	8.4
Assam	1.3	1.0	2.2	1.7	2.2	1.3	1.2	0.9	2.0	1.4	1.8	1.3	1.2	1.1	1.3	1.4	1.8	1.5
Bihar	7.5	7.8	9.3	7.7	8.2	4.7	7.1	6.8	7.7	6.9	6.8	4.1	4.0	3.6	5.2	5.5	4.3	3.2
Gujarat	2.4	3.5	4.6	3.3	4.0	8.6	1.7	5.0	5.9	4.2	5.3	9.6	5.8	12.1	11.5	7.9	8.0	13.0
Haryana	1.1	1.3	0.7	1.2	1.4	1.1	1.3	1.2	0.9	1.2	1.5	1.4	2.5	1.9	2.3	2.1	3.5	2.4
Karnataka	4.3	5.5	6.2	6.3	5.8	5.2	4.4	5.4	5.9	5.8	5.6	4.5	6.9	5.9	4.7	5.3	6.5	5.2
Kerala	3.3	3.9	2.2	3.1	4.0	3.0	3.8	4.0	2.2	3.0	4.0	2.9	5.4	3.4	2.2	3.7	4.4	4.5
Madhya Pradesh	6.1	4.5	4.2	6.1	6.4	6.4	4.0	3.9	3.8	5.5	6.3	5.7	4.6	3.4	4.7	3.7	4.8	3.4
Maharashtra	7.2	6.7	5.6	7.6	6.8	8.4	6.1	7.5	7.4	8.4	8.3	9.7	9.6	15.3	15.4	14.4	17.3	14.2
Odisha	4.2	6.5	11.0	6.0	5.8	3.7	4.8	7.1	10.4	6.3	5.8	3.8	1.6	1.9	2.8	2.1	2.4	1.9
Punjab	1.5	1.9	1.3	2.1	1.8	2.3	1.5	1.8	1.4	2.1	1.7	2.3	2.3	2.0	3.0	4.2	2.9	3.1
Rajasthan	3.7	4.1	3.1	3.8	3.9	3.8	3.4	3.8	2.5	3.3	3.7	3.7	4.9	6.3	3.3	4.4	4.6	4.8
Tamil Nadu	9.4	9.1	8.8	9.4	9.0	10.0	11.3	9.9	9.4	9.8	9.6	10.5	15.8	12.7	11.8	11.3	10.6	13.5
Uttar Pradesh	28.5	15.4	16.7	14.8	14.7	14.8	28.5	15.3	18.0	16.0	15.5	16.2	19.4	12.8	15.8	13.7	12.6	11.2
West Bengal	11.2	18.4	14.7	17.0	16.7	16.7	12.9	18.0	14.6	16.7	15.7	15.0	9.9	12.5	10.5	13.2	10.8	9.7

Source: Authors' calculations based on NSSO data.

Table 3.8 Share of Major States in Number of Enterprises, Employment, and GVA in Rural Informal Manufacturing Sector in India: 1984–5 to 2010–11 (in per cent)

State	Number of Enterprises						Employment						Gross Value Added					
	1984–5	1989–90	1994–5	2000–1	2005–6	2010–11	1984–5	1989–90	1994–5	2000–1	2005–6	2010–11	1984–5	1989–90	1994–5	2000–1	2005–6	2010–11
Andhra Pradesh	7.9	10.9	9.9	10.4	9.2	10.2	7.5	10.4	8.7	10.2	8.9	10.3	6.2	7.0	7.6	8.7	7.0	9.6
Assam	1.5	1.2	2.7	2.1	2.8	1.9	1.4	1.1	2.5	1.8	2.4	1.9	1.9	1.5	2.1	2.2	3.0	2.9
Bihar	8.8	9.1	11.0	9.4	10.2	6.9	8.7	8.5	9.6	8.9	9.0	6.3	6.8	6.1	8.8	9.2	7.5	6.2
Gujarat	1.5	2.3	2.3	2.1	2.6	2.8	0.9	2.7	2.6	2.4	2.9	3.6	3.2	5.9	5.6	3.9	4.1	5.4
Haryana	1.0	0.9	0.6	0.9	1.0	0.8	1.0	0.9	0.7	0.8	1.0	1.2	1.4	1.0	1.8	1.4	2.5	2.1
Karnataka	3.5	5.2	6.2	5.9	5.7	5.5	3.6	5.0	6.2	5.5	5.7	4.6	5.7	5.6	5.4	5.1	7.2	5.2
Kerala	2.9	4.2	2.4	3.6	4.2	3.4	3.3	4.4	2.5	3.6	4.4	3.4	4.3	4.6	3.7	5.5	7.1	6.8
Madhya Pradesh	5.7	4.6	4.2	6.2	6.3	6.8	3.2	4.0	3.8	5.7	6.5	6.6	4.8	3.7	3.7	4.0	6.0	4.7
Maharashtra	6.0	5.7	3.9	5.8	4.7	6.4	5.1	5.6	4.2	5.3	4.4	6.2	6.6	9.7	5.4	7.4	6.3	7.4
Odisha	5.2	8.0	14.0	7.9	7.4	5.6	6.2	9.3	14.3	8.9	8.0	6.3	3.0	3.1	5.6	3.7	3.9	3.9
Punjab	1.3	1.3	0.8	1.6	1.3	1.7	1.1	1.1	0.7	1.4	1.0	1.3	1.2	1.2	1.6	2.8	1.7	1.9
Rajasthan	3.5	3.6	2.8	3.4	3.4	3.2	3.2	3.4	2.3	2.8	3.2	2.9	5.3	6.9	4.1	4.6	4.8	5.0
Tamil Nadu	6.6	6.6	6.6	7.3	7.2	7.0	7.7	7.2	7.0	7.2	7.9	7.1	10.9	11.4	10.8	8.0	11.1	10.3
Uttar Pradesh	33.4	15.2	16.5	15.0	14.9	15.6	34.2	15.3	18.3	16.5	16.2	17.7	28.2	13.7	19.5	16.0	13.9	14.2
West Bengal	11.2	21.0	16.2	18.4	18.9	22.1	12.8	21.4	16.5	19.0	18.4	20.5	10.6	18.7	14.5	17.5	13.9	14.5

Source: Authors' calculations based on NSSO data.

been able to maintain a steady share during this period. When looking at the share in GVA, states like WB, AP, and Maharashtra recorded an increase in their share, while UP witnessed a decline. Again, TN has been able to maintain a steady share throughout the study period. It can thus be concluded that, over time, the share of UP declined in the employment, enterprises, and GVA in the rural informal manufacturing sector, while states like WB have significantly gained.

Unlike the rural sector, we do not find any significant improvement in any state's share in enterprises in the urban sector during the period 1984–5 to 2010–11 (Table 3.9). The share pattern across Indian states remained more or less the same over the period. It is also evident that, unlike in the rural sector, there is no drastic decline for UP in the urban sector. But TN registers a steady decline in its share in enterprises. Karnataka, Maharashtra, and AP were able to maintain a steady share for this 26-year period. Similar trend is seen with regard to employment in the urban informal manufacturing sector. While considering GVA, it can be found that three states—Gujarat, Maharashtra, and TN—accounted for over 50 per cent of the total contribution to GVA of the firms in the urban sector. It is found that concentration is higher in GVA, with Maharashtra alone accounting for close to 26 per cent of GVA originating from the urban segment. It should also be noted that the share of Maharashtra has increased drastically along with that of Gujarat over the period 1984–5 to 2010–11. Over the time, states like WB and Karnataka were able to maintain a steady share, while UP witnessed a decline.

Next, the state-wise rural and urban break-up of total enterprises and employment of the informal sector from 1984–5 to 2010–11 is examined. In 1984–5, informal manufacturing was predominantly rural in orientation in terms of number of enterprises and employment (Table 3.10). This is evident from the fact that in states like Odisha, UP, Bihar, and Assam, more than 85 per cent of the enterprises and employment were in the rural sector. However, by 2010–11, there is an increase in urban orientation, especially in states like Haryana, Maharashtra, Punjab, Gujarat, and TN, with more than 50 per cent of the enterprises and employment originating from the urban segment. Kerala and WB presented an alternate scenario with decline in urban share of enterprises and employment despite rapid urbanization in these states. Despite the rural dominance in enterprises and employment, GVA

Table 3.9 Share of Major States in Number of Enterprises, Employment, and GVA in Urban Informal Manufacturing Sector in India: 1984–5 to 2010–11 (in per cent)

State	Number of Enterprises						Employment						Gross Value Added					
	1984–5	1989–90	1994–5	2000–1	2005–6	2010–11	1984–5	1989–90	1994–5	2000–1	2005–6	2010–11	1984–5	1989–90	1994–5	2000–1	2005–6	2010–11
Andhra Pradesh	9.5	8.5	7.4	8.5	9.4	9.2	9.4	7.1	6.3	7.7	7.4	8.1	6.3	3.2	3.9	5.8	4.2	7.6
Assam	0.7	0.6	0.6	0.8	0.8	0.4	0.7	0.6	0.6	0.7	0.8	0.5	0.7	0.8	0.6	0.8	0.9	0.7
Bihar	3.7	3.7	4.1	3.6	3.3	1.6	3.3	3.1	3.3	3.0	2.9	1.5	1.9	1.7	2.4	2.3	2.0	1.5
Gujarat	4.9	7.2	12.2	6.3	7.4	17.0	3.8	10.3	13.9	7.8	9.6	16.6	7.7	17.2	16.2	11.3	11.0	17.6
Haryana	1.5	2.3	1.2	1.9	2.3	1.6	1.8	2.0	1.3	2.0	2.6	1.6	3.3	2.6	2.7	2.8	4.2	2.5
Karnataka	6.6	6.3	6.1	7.4	6.3	4.8	6.3	6.2	5.0	6.4	5.5	4.4	7.7	6.1	4.2	5.5	6.1	5.3
Kerala	4.5	2.9	1.7	1.9	3.5	2.5	5.1	3.1	1.5	1.9	3.1	2.4	6.2	2.5	1.1	2.2	2.4	3.1
Madhya Pradesh	7.2	4.4	4.2	5.7	6.8	5.7	5.8	3.8	4.0	5.1	5.8	4.6	4.5	3.1	5.4	3.5	3.9	2.6
Maharashtra	10.9	9.9	11.1	12.0	12.0	11.2	8.4	12.0	15.0	14.5	15.4	13.7	11.8	19.8	23.3	20.3	25.5	18.2
Odisha	1.2	1.8	1.4	1.3	1.8	1.0	1.4	1.8	1.1	1.2	1.6	0.9	0.5	0.9	0.6	0.7	1.2	0.7
Punjab	2.2	3.4	2.7	3.2	3.0	3.3	2.5	3.5	2.9	3.4	3.0	3.5	3.1	2.8	4.2	5.4	3.9	3.8
Rajasthan	4.2	5.8	3.9	4.9	4.9	4.6	4.0	4.8	2.9	4.1	4.6	4.5	4.5	5.9	2.6	4.2	4.5	4.7
Tamil Nadu	17.5	16.8	15.9	14.4	13.3	14.4	20.2	16.3	15.1	14.9	12.9	14.5	19.4	13.7	12.6	14.1	10.3	15.5
Uttar Pradesh	14.2	16.0	17.4	14.4	14.1	13.6	14.5	15.3	17.2	14.9	14.3	14.5	13.0	12.1	12.9	11.7	11.6	9.4
West Bengal	11.0	10.2	10.1	13.7	11.1	8.9	12.9	10.1	10.0	12.2	10.7	8.6	9.3	7.6	7.4	9.6	8.5	6.8

Source: Authors' calculations based on NSSO data.

Table 3.10 Rural–Urban Share in Number of Enterprises, Employment, and GVA by Major States: 1984–5 to 2010–11 (in per cent)

State	Number of Enterprises				Employment				Gross Value Added			
	1984-5		2010-11		1984-5		2010-11		1984-5		2010-11	
	Rural	Urban	Rural	Urban	Rural	Urban	Rural	Urban	Rural	Urban	Rural	Urban
Andhra Pradesh	70.4	29.6	61.6	38.4	66.4	33.6	59.8	40.2	41.7	58.3	42.9	57.1
Assam	86.6	13.4	86.9	13.1	83.8	16.2	81.5	18.5	66.8	33.2	72.3	27.7
Bihar	87.2	12.8	85.8	14.2	86.6	13.4	83.1	16.9	71.7	28.3	71.7	28.3
Gujarat	47.1	52.9	19.0	81.0	37.7	62.3	20.4	79.6	23.6	76.4	15.5	84.5
Haryana	67.2	32.8	42.6	57.4	58.4	41.6	46.0	54.0	23.3	76.7	33.6	66.4
Karnataka	60.2	39.8	62.4	37.6	58.4	41.6	55.1	44.9	35.0	65.0	37.2	62.8
Kerala	64.6	35.4	66.6	33.4	61.6	38.4	62.3	37.7	33.8	66.2	56.9	43.1
Madhya Pradesh	69.4	30.6	63.2	36.8	57.9	42.1	62.4	37.6	43.5	56.5	51.7	48.3
Maharashtra	61.3	38.7	45.4	54.6	59.8	40.2	34.6	65.4	29.0	71.0	19.6	80.4
Odisha	92.4	7.6	89.1	10.9	91.9	8.1	88.7	11.3	80.7	19.3	75.7	24.3
Punjab	62.9	37.1	41.7	58.3	52.4	47.6	31.1	68.9	22.3	77.7	23.0	77.0
Rajasthan	70.6	29.4	50.2	49.8	66.4	33.6	43.0	57.0	46.3	53.7	38.7	61.3
Tamil Nadu	52.0	48.0	41.2	58.8	48.4	51.6	36.3	63.7	29.2	70.8	28.6	71.4
Uttar Pradesh	87.1	12.9	62.3	37.7	85.3	14.7	58.7	41.3	61.5	38.5	47.6	52.4
West Bengal	74.6	25.4	78.2	21.8	71.0	29.0	73.5	26.5	45.4	54.6	56.2	43.8
Total	74.2	25.8	59.1	40.9	71.1	28.9	53.8	46.2	42.3	57.7	37.5	62.5

Source: Authors' calculations based on NSSO data.

Note: Rural implies share of rural sector in total and urban implies share of urban sector in total.

from the urban sector was substantial during the period 1984–5 to 2010–11. In the case of Maharashtra and Gujarat, it can be found that the urban sector's contribution to GVA has registered a steep increase. However, it is also found that the number of states with more than 50 per cent urban share in GVA has declined from 11 in 1984–5 to 9 in 2010–11. In Assam, Bihar, and Odisha, the distribution of enterprises, employment, and GVA tilted deeply towards the rural sector, while in Gujarat and Maharashtra, the distribution of enterprises, employment, and GVA was heavily skewed towards the urban sector.

Although informal manufacturing continues to be largely rural, over time, there was erosion in the dominance of rural segment in the informal sector. It can be found that, especially in recent years, there is a gradual change in the rural–urban distribution of enterprises, workers, and GVA. The swing in all cases was in favour of urban centres. In the case of employment, a steadily declining share of rural sector is noticed. Rural areas accounted for 71 per cent of employment in the informal manufacturing sector in 1984–5 and only 54 per cent in 2010–11. But in the case of GVA, the decline started only in the 1990s and continued unabated in the period after the 1990s too. More than 5 per cent drop can be noticed in the rural share in GVA between 1984–85 and 2010–11. In the case of enterprises too, a drop in rural share was noticed during the period under study. In fact, the sector witnessed significant decline in number of enterprises in rural areas between 1984–5 and 2010–11 (a drop by 15 per cent).

Regional Growth Trends

Although the previous discussion on the changes in the share reveals interesting trends in regional and rural–urban orientation, it fails to capture trends in growth which leads to structural changes within the informal sector. This section presents trends in growth across states in the three key indicators of growth and structural change: number of enterprises, employment, and GVA. Growth rates across states at the rural and urban segments are also examined here.

It may be noticed that during the period 1984–95, referred to as the 'pre-reform era', the informal manufacturing sector registered slow growth in all the three indicators considered (see Table 3.11). The growth rates of enterprises and employment were better only in states

Table 3.11 Growth of Number of Enterprises, Employment, and GVA in the Informal Manufacturing Sector by Major States: 1984–5 to 2010–11 (in per cent)

State	Number of Enterprises			Employment			Gross Value Added		
	1984–95	1995–2011	1984–2011	1984–95	1995–2011	1984–2011	1984–95	1995–2011	1984–2011
Andhra Pradesh	-3.6	2.4	0.1	-2.8	2.0	0.1	-3.4	9.4	4.2
Assam	0.9	-1.2	-0.4	2.5	-1.7	-0.1	-1.5	4.2	1.9
Bihar	-2.6	-2.1	-2.3	-1.9	-2.9	-2.5	0.5	-2.5	-1.4
Gujarat	1.8	6.1	4.4	10.0	4.1	6.4	4.7	10.2	8.0
Haryana	-8.8	4.9	-0.6	-6.2	4.1	0.0	-2.8	4.3	1.5
Karnataka	-1.1	1.0	0.2	0.2	-0.6	-0.3	-5.8	9.3	3.2
Kerala	-8.4	4.1	-0.9	-7.9	2.8	-1.4	-10.4	8.1	0.6
Madhya Pradesh	-8.2	4.8	-0.4	-3.0	3.5	1.0	-2.1	6.0	2.8
Maharashtra	-7.2	4.7	0.0	-0.7	2.7	1.4	2.5	4.8	3.9
Odisha	4.9	-4.6	-1.1	5.1	-5.1	-1.3	3.7	0.4	1.7
Punjab	-6.4	6.1	1.1	-3.4	4.3	1.3	0.4	2.9	1.9
Rajasthan	-6.5	3.4	-0.5	-5.5	3.4	-0.1	-6.1	7.0	1.8
Tamil Nadu	-5.4	2.9	-0.4	-4.5	1.8	-0.7	-5.0	7.3	2.4
Uttar Pradesh	-9.7	1.3	-3.1	-7.1	0.4	-2.6	-4.2	9.0	3.7
West Bengal	-2.1	2.9	1.0	-1.4	1.2	0.2	-1.6	8.0	4.2
Total	-4.7	2.1	-0.6	-2.7	1.0	-0.4	-2.2	5.0	2.2

Source: Authors' calculations based on NSSO data.

Note: Growth rates are annual average compound growth rates. Gross value added growth rates are reported for real gross value added, computed at 1993–4 prices.

Table 3.12 Growth of Number of Enterprises, Employment, and GVA in the Rural Informal Manufacturing Sector by Major States: 1984–5 to 2010–11 (in per cent)

State	Number of Enterprises			Employment			Gross Value Added		
	1984–95	1995–2011	1984–2011	1984–95	1995–2011	1984–2011	1984–95	1995–2011	1984–2011
Andhra Pradesh	-2.3	0.7	-0.5	-1.3	0.4	-0.3	0.3	7.0	4.4
Assam	1.7	-1.7	-0.4	3.3	-2.4	-0.2	-0.4	3.9	2.2
Bihar	-2.3	-2.4	-2.4	-1.8	-3.2	-2.7	0.8	-2.7	-1.4
Gujarat	-0.5	1.7	0.8	7.8	1.5	3.9	3.7	8.0	6.3
Haryana	-9.6	2.5	-2.3	-6.7	2.9	-0.9	1.2	4.1	3.0
Karnataka	1.3	-0.3	0.3	2.7	-2.5	-0.5	-2.3	7.3	3.5
Kerala	-6.2	2.8	-0.8	-5.5	1.2	-1.4	-3.1	6.4	2.6
Madhya Pradesh	-7.3	3.6	-0.8	-1.2	2.9	1.3	-4.3	8.6	3.5
Maharashtra	-8.5	3.7	-1.2	-4.7	1.8	-0.7	-3.7	6.4	2.4
Odisha	5.4	-5.1	-1.2	5.6	-5.6	-1.5	4.6	-0.5	1.4
Punjab	-8.7	5.0	-0.5	-6.6	3.1	-0.7	0.9	2.8	2.1
Rajasthan	-6.5	1.2	-1.8	-5.7	0.8	-1.8	-4.4	4.6	1.1
Tamil Nadu	-4.5	0.8	-1.2	-3.7	-0.5	-1.8	-1.9	5.0	2.3
Uttar Pradesh	-11.0	0.1	-4.3	-8.7	-0.9	-3.9	-5.3	8.0	2.7
West Bengal	-0.9	2.5	1.1	-0.3	0.7	0.3	1.4	7.4	5.1
Total	-4.5	0.5	-1.5	-2.8	-0.6	-1.5	-1.8	3.9	1.7

Source: Authors' calculations based on NSSO data.

Note: Growth rates are annual average compound growth rates. Gross value added growth rates are reported for real gross value added, computed at 1993–4 prices.

Table 3.13 Growth of Number of Enterprises, Employment, and GVA in the Urban Informal Manufacturing Sector by Major States: 1984–5 to 2010–11 (in per cent)

State	Number of Enterprises			Employment			Gross Value Added		
	1984–95	1995–2011	1984–2011	1984–95	1995–2011	1984–2011	1984–95	1995–2011	1984–2011
Andhra Pradesh	−7.9	7.1	1.1	−6.3	5.6	0.8	−7.1	11.9	4.2
Assam	−6.0	3.1	−0.5	−3.5	2.9	0.4	−4.2	4.8	1.2
Bihar	−4.6	−0.2	−1.9	−2.5	−1.1	−1.6	−0.6	−1.9	−1.4
Gujarat	3.5	7.8	6.2	11.1	5.1	7.4	5.0	10.6	8.5
Haryana	−7.2	7.5	1.6	−5.5	5.3	1.0	−4.4	4.4	0.9
Karnataka	−6.2	4.0	0.0	−4.8	3.1	0.0	−8.3	11.0	3.1
Kerala	−14.1	8.0	−1.1	−13.8	7.0	−1.5	−18.2	11.4	−1.1
Madhya Pradesh	−10.5	7.7	0.3	−5.9	4.8	0.5	−0.8	4.1	2.2
Maharashtra	−5.3	5.7	1.3	3.4	3.3	3.3	4.3	4.5	4.4
Odisha	−4.5	3.5	0.3	−4.7	3.0	−0.1	−1.0	4.9	2.6
Punjab	−3.3	6.9	2.9	−0.8	5.0	2.7	0.3	2.9	1.9
Rajasthan	−6.4	6.8	1.5	−5.3	6.7	1.9	−7.8	9.1	2.3
Tamil Nadu	−6.4	5.0	0.4	−5.3	3.7	0.1	−6.7	8.5	2.4
Uttar Pradesh	−3.6	4.0	1.0	−0.8	2.8	1.4	−2.6	9.9	4.9
West Bengal	−6.4	4.8	0.4	−4.9	2.9	−0.2	−4.8	8.7	3.3
Total	−5.5	5.6	1.2	−2.4	3.9	1.4	−2.5	5.8	2.5

Source: Authors' calculations based on NSSO data.

Note: Growth rates are annual average compound growth rates. Gross value added growth rates are reported for real gross value added, computed at 1993–4 prices.

like Gujarat, Odisha, and Assam, while GVA grew in Bihar, Gujarat, Maharashtra, Odisha, and Punjab. However, for the period 1995–2011, referred to as the 'post-reform era', the informal sector can be found registering strong growth rates in all the three variables considered. The highest growth rate of enterprises and employment in this era was registered in Gujarat, Punjab, and Haryana. Based on the average for the 15 states, it can be seen that GVA grew at a rate of 5 per cent per annum in the post-reform period. It is even interesting to note that GVA increased at a faster rate in all the states except Bihar and Odisha, and it grew the fastest in Gujarat, AP, and Karnataka.

Viewed from a rural–urban perspective, we find that the pre-reform growth was significantly lower than the growth of informal sector in the post-reform period in both rural and urban areas (see Tables 3.12 and 3.13). In the post-reform period, we find that only Odisha and Bihar recorded negative growth rates in employment, enterprises, and GVA in the rural segment. The rural sector expanded much faster in the post-reform period in Madhya Pradesh (MP), Gujarat, and Maharashtra. In the urban sector, a similar trend can be discerned. The growth rates were significantly lower for Bihar in the post-reform period. This state witnessed massive reduction in enterprises, employment, and GVA in the urban sector during this period. The major beneficiaries were Kerala, Gujarat, and AP. These three states recorded the fastest growth in enterprises, employment, and GVA in the urban sector during the post-reform period. It can also be noticed that 8 out of 15 states registered more than 6 per cent growth in GVA during this period.

Patterns and Trends in the Informal Manufacturing Sector: By Enterprise Type

As mentioned in the Introduction, the informal manufacturing sector in India comprises three types of enterprises: Own Account Manufacturing Enterprises (OAMEs) employing only family labour; Non-directory Manufacturing Enterprises (NDMEs) employing both hired and family labour, but less than six workers; and Directory Manufacturing Enterprises (DMEs), also employing both hired and family labour, but six or more workers. This section looks at these very different types of enterprises more closely, replicating the analysis of the patterns and trends in growth and structural change that was presented for the overall informal manufacturing sector in the previous two sections, separately for OAMEs, NDMEs, and DMEs. We first report the share of these enterprise types on the basis of number of enterprises, employment, and GVA for the total, rural, and urban sectors, respectively, in Figures 3.3, 3.4, and 3.5.[8] In the informal manufacturing sector, the OAME is the typical enterprise type, accounting for the bulk of the enterprises (86 per cent) (Figure 3.3). A substantial share of the workforce is also employed by OAMEs. More than 65 per cent of the informal sector workers are employed in the OAMEs. But their contribution to GVA is significantly lower (32 per cent), thereby reflecting the fact that they are less productive compared to NDMEs and DMEs.

A significant erosion is found in the dominance of OAMEs over time. A steadily increasing share of DMEs in the number of enterprises, employment, and GVA can be observed for the period 1984–5 to 2005–6 (Figure 3.3). The shift in favour of the DME group is more evident in its share in GVA that rose by over 14 per cent between 1984–5 and 2005–6. This considerably increased the share of DMEs in GVA from 29 per cent in 1984–5 to 44 per cent in 2005–6. The obvious casualty was the OAME category which has seen its share declining from 46 per cent in 1984–5 to 32 per cent in 2005–6 (a 14 per cent reduction). In employment too, NDMEs and DMEs have significantly increased their share, while OAMEs witnessed a 9 per cent decline. However, OAMEs still account for a considerable share in informal sector enterprises despite witnessing a significant decline in their share in employment and GVA. Their share remained constant at 85 per cent all through the 1980s, 1990s, and the early 2000s.

The share of OAMEs in number of enterprises, employment, and GVA has declined in both rural and urban areas (Figures 3.4 and 3.5, respectively). The shift towards DMEs is more evident among the rural firms than the urban ones. Despite their waning dominance, OAMEs continued to occupy a larger share in enterprises, employment, and GVA among rural enterprises. DMEs and NDMEs together accounted

---

[8] Data on three indicators for these enterprise types is available only for the period 1984–2006. The latest survey round for the period 2010–11 does not provide information separately for NDMEs and DMEs. In view of this, the discussion here is confined to the period 1984–2006.

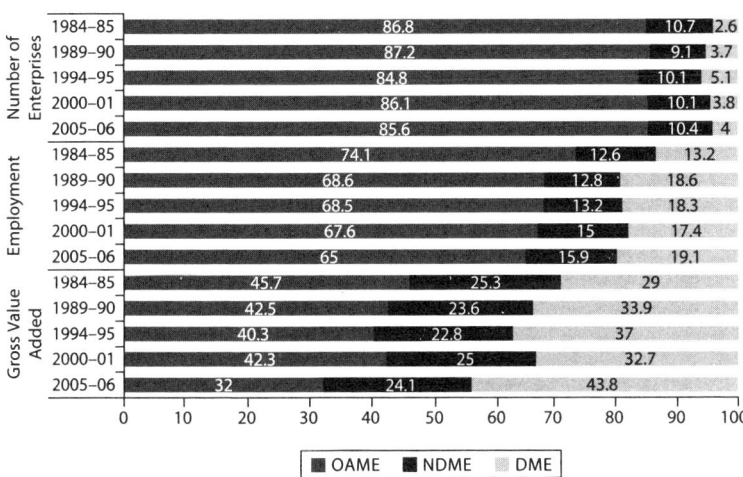

Figure 3.3 Share in Enterprises, Employment, and Gross Value Added by Enterprise Type
Source: Authors' calculation from NSSO data.
Note: Shares reported are percentage shares.

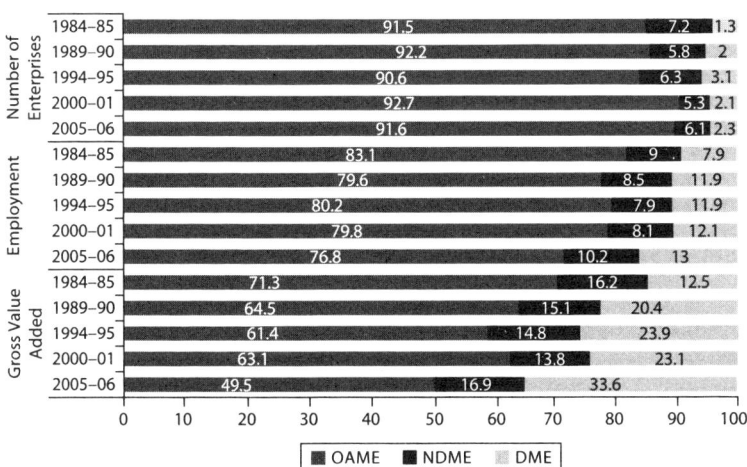

Figure 3.4 Share in Enterprises, Employment, and Gross Value Added in the Rural Informal Manufacturing Sector by Enterprise Type
Source: Authors' calculation from NSSO data.
Note: Shares reported are percentage shares.

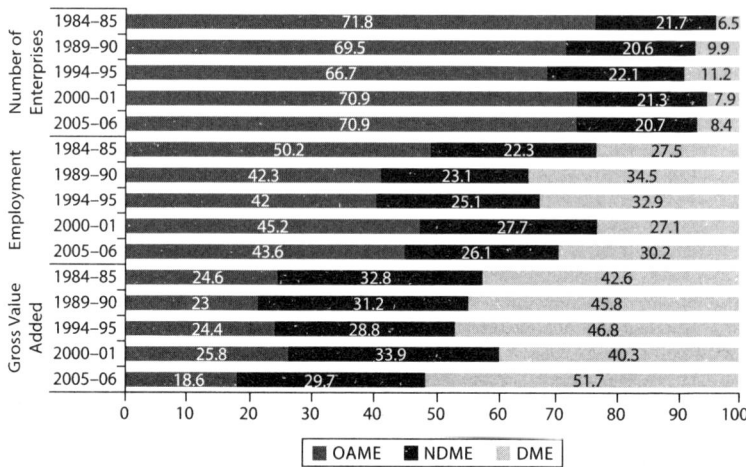

Figure 3.5   Share in Enterprises, Employment, and Gross Value Added in the Urban Informal Manufacturing Sector by Enterprise Type
Source: Authors' calculation from NSSO data.
Note: Shares reported are percentage shares.

for about 80 per cent of GVA and 56 per cent of total employment in the urban sector in 2005–6 (Figure 3.4) as against their combined share of 51 per cent in GVA and 23 per cent in employment in the rural informal manufacturing sector (Figure 3.5).

Key Indicators by the Type of Enterprise and Industry Group

Table 3.14 reports the shares based on the enterprise type for the number of enterprises, employment, and GVA for major industry groups. Textiles, beverages, wood products, and food products were the industry groups with major shares in the OAME category in 2005–6. Among them, beverages industry has significantly improved its relative significance by 2005–6 over 1984–5. Its increasing importance is more evident in its contribution to the number of enterprises and employment. The relative significance of textiles in the OAME category has also improved considerably in this period. The industry's share in GVA has gone up by 10 per cent during this 20-year period.

Table 3.14 Enterprise Type-wise Share in Enterprises, Employment, and GVA by Industry: 1984–5 to 2005–6 (in per cent)

Industry	Number of Enterprises						Employment						Gross Value Added					
	1984–5			2005–6			1984–5			2005–6			1984–5			2005–6		
	OAME	NDME	DME	OAME	NDME	DME	OAME	NDME	DME	OAME	NDME	DME	OAME	NDME	DME	OAME	NDME	DME
Food Products	17.0	31.0	18.4	12.8	18.2	20.3	18.2	28.0	16.5	14.6	18.0	18.2	17.8	25.6	12.4	18.9	15.6	12.0
Beverages	8.4	3.5	3.9	21.0	1.4	0.9	8.0	4.4	5.0	19.6	1.4	1.0	7.2	2.3	2.5	9.8	1.0	1.2
Cotton Products	16.5	9.5	17.3	5.7	8.7	15.0	23.3	11.3	19.3	6.7	10.8	14.5	13.9	8.5	13.3	7.1	8.5	12.1
Textiles	20.6	24.3	12.9	28.6	23.5	13.8	15.6	24.6	12.4	24.7	21.7	13.2	15.1	16.1	7.9	25.9	18.0	12.3
Wood Products	18.8	9.5	6.4	15.6	14.1	4.9	16.7	10.1	6.1	16.6	13.3	3.8	25.1	12.9	8.8	17.6	15.6	5.0
Paper Products	0.4	2.5	4.7	1.4	3.3	3.6	0.5	2.6	3.7	1.4	3.4	3.3	0.5	3.5	4.9	1.6	3.7	4.8
Leather Products	3.1	2.2	2.0	0.7	2.0	2.8	2.3	2.4	1.6	0.7	2.3	2.6	4.8	2.1	2.8	1.4	2.4	2.0
Chemicals	0.2	1.2	2.2	2.6	0.5	3.4	0.2	1.3	1.8	2.4	0.6	3.7	0.2	1.3	3.3	1.1	0.6	3.5
Rubber Products	0.7	0.7	2.8	0.2	1.6	2.5	0.7	0.7	3.5	0.3	1.7	1.9	0.4	1.3	2.8	0.2	1.3	1.7
Non-metallic Minerals	6.2	3.6	8.0	3.6	3.2	8.4	7.5	4.8	11.	5.2	3.6	12.7	5.5	2.1	4.6	3.8	3.4	8.9
Basic Metals	0.2	0.8	1.9	0.1	0.6	1.0	0.1	0.9	1.5	0.1	0.6	0.9	0.3	1.0	3.0	0.2	0.5	2.3
Metal Products	3.6	6.6	12.6	3.8	15.2	12.5	3.1	4.5	10.3	3.8	15.0	11.1	5.5	11.3	24.2	5.6	16.6	20.0
Transport Equipment and Parts	0.2	0.8	1.5	0.1	0.7	2.4	0.1	0.7	1.2	0.1	0.8	2.0	0.3	9.8	6.1	0.1	1.0	2.6
Other Manufacturing Products	4.3	4.0	5.6	3.8	6.8	8.5	3.7	3.7	5.7	3.7	6.7	11.0	3.5	2.3	3.5	6.7	11.8	11.6
Total	100.0	100.0	100.0	100.0	100.0	100.0	100.0	100.0	100.0	100.0	100.0	100.0	100.0	100.0	100.0	100.0	100.0	100.0

Source: Authors' calculations based on NSSO data.

In NDMEs, bulk of the contribution in enterprises, employment, and GVA emanated from industries producing food products, wood products, and metal products. These industries together accounted for about 71 per cent of the total enterprises, 68 per cent of the total workforce, and 66 per cent of the total value addition in the NDME category in 2005–6. Wood products and metal products experienced significant expansion in their relative size over the period 1984–5 to 2005–6, while food products and textiles witnessed a decline in their relative importance.

A substantial contribution in the number of enterprises, employment, and GVA in 2005–6 in the DME group came from food products, cotton products, textiles, and metal products. Manufacture of food products was the largest contributor in the total number of enterprises and workers (Table 3.14). In terms of share in GVA, metal products industry was the biggest contributor, which accounted for one-fifth of the TVA by the DMEs. The industry's contribution in GVA, however, declined between 1984–5 and 2005–6. In 1984–5, about one-fourth of the total value added in the DME group emanated from this industry. Besides textiles, only non-metallic minerals industry improved its relative position in the sector in terms of the share in all the selected indicators.

As mentioned before, the OAME is the typical type of enterprise in the informal manufacturing sector accounting for more than 85 per cent of all enterprises, 65 per cent of total employment, and 35 per cent of GVA in the sector (Table 3.15). It can be found that the share of these very small (mostly family) units is declining over time, and the relative significance of NDMEs and DMEs is rising.

Our analysis shows that manufacture of leather products, transport equipment and parts, cotton products, food products, non-metallic minerals, and basic metals have contributed significantly to the growing share of DMEs (Table 3.15). In 8 out of 14 industries, DMEs contributed more than 50 per cent in GVA, and in 10 industries, their contribution was significantly higher than that of the NDMEs and the OAMEs. Notably, about four-fifths of the value addition in basic metals and transport industries in 2005–6 originated from the DMEs. In essence, the significantly higher contribution of DMEs in GVA in most industries signifies the higher productivity of units in the sector. Transport industry was the only industry group where the contribution

Table 3.15 Enterprise Type-wise Share in Number of Enterprises, Employment, and GVA by Industry: 1984–5 to 2005–6 (in per cent)

Industry	Number of Enterprises						Employment						Gross Value Added					
	1984–5			2005–6			1984–5			2005–6			1984–5			2005–6		
	OAME	NDME	DME	OAME	NDME	DME	OAME	NDME	DME	OAME	NDME	DME	OAME	NDME	DME	OAME	NDME	DME
Food Products	79.6	17.9	2.5	80.1	13.9	6.0	70.2	18.4	11.3	59.9	18.1	22.1	45.3	35.2	19.5	42.5	26.5	31.0
Beverages	93.9	4.8	1.3	99.0	0.8	0.2	83.1	7.7	9.2	96.8	1.7	1.5	72.2	12.3	15.5	82.0	6.3	11.7
Cotton Products	90.7	6.5	2.8	76.4	14.1	9.5	81.0	6.7	12.3	49.3	19.4	31.3	52.0	17.1	30.9	25.8	23.3	50.9
Textiles	85.9	12.5	1.6	89.1	8.9	2.0	70.9	19.0	10.1	72.9	15.6	11.5	52.7	30.3	17.1	48.3	25.3	26.4
Wood Products	93.3	5.8	0.9	88.9	9.8	1.3	85.6	8.8	5.6	79.1	15.5	5.4	67.0	18.5	14.5	50.0	33.6	16.4
Paper Products	50.2	34.1	15.7	70.4	20.8	8.8	29.5	28.3	42.2	43.9	26.0	30.1	8.5	35.3	56.3	15.9	28.2	55.9
Leather Products	90.4	7.9	1.7	63.6	23.8	12.6	76.7	13.7	9.6	35.7	26.9	37.4	62.7	14.8	22.6	24.8	32.7	42.5
Chemicals	53.5	31.9	14.6	92.2	2.1	5.7	27.8	30.4	41.8	66.4	3.9	29.7	6.7	24.2	69.1	20.6	8.2	71.1
Rubber Products	79.5	10.4	10.1	42.7	35.6	21.7	48.3	7.9	43.8	22.1	33.5	44.5	13.0	24.4	62.6	7.8	30.1	62.1
Non-metallic Minerals	90.1	6.4	3.4	82.1	8.9	9.0	72.7	8.0	19.3	53.0	9.0	38.0	57.8	12.1	30.1	22.8	15.3	61.9
Basic Metals	53.0	30.1	16.9	54.1	28.3	17.7	26.6	26.2	47.2	24.8	28.2	46.9	9.8	20.7	69.5	6.4	11.1	82.5
Metal Products	75.3	16.9	7.8	61.0	29.6	9.4	54.0	13.5	32.5	35.6	34.0	30.3	20.7	22.9	56.4	13.7	30.5	55.9
Transport Equipment and Parts	52.7	32.6	14.6	27.4	31.8	40.8	26.3	25.7	48.0	8.3	22.3	69.3	3.5	56.5	40.0	3.5	20.3	76.2
Other Manufacturing Products	86.8	9.8	3.3	75.7	16.4	7.9	69.4	11.8	18.7	43.4	18.9	37.7	50.7	18.0	31.3	23.2	30.8	46.1
Total	86.8	10.7	2.6	85.6	10.4	4.0	74.1	12.6	13.2	65.0	15.9	19.1	46.6	25.2	28.9	34.4	26.0	39.6

Source: Authors' calculations based on NSSO data.

by DMEs in the number of enterprises and employment surpassed the contribution from OAMEs and NDMEs. Essentially, OAMEs constituted bulk of the enterprises and workers in most industries in the sector. Their share in number of enterprises exceeded 80 per cent in six industries in 2005–6. They accounted for more than 50 per cent of the work force in food products, beverages, textiles, wood products, chemicals, and non-metallic minerals. However, their share in GVA exceeded 50 per cent only in beverages and wood products. Nevertheless, in spite of these changes over time, the OAMEs still accounted for a dominant share in most of the traditional industries such as food products, beverages, textiles, and wood products—the largest industry groups in the sector in terms of their share in the informal manufacturing sector. NDMEs witnessed a significant improvement in their relative importance in industries producing cotton products, wood products, leather products, rubber products, non-metallic minerals, and metal products (Table 3.15).

The DMEs, as mentioned earlier, gained in relative importance in both the rural and urban segments of the informal manufacturing sector. In the rural areas, the relative importance of DMEs increased considerably in food, cotton, leather, non-metallic minerals, and transport industries (Table 3.16). Despite their declining importance, OAMEs still accounted for a major share in enterprises and employment in majority of the industries in rural areas. The presence of OAMEs in terms of enterprises and workers was significantly higher than the NDMEs and the DMEs in food products, beverages, cotton products, textiles, leather products, wood products, and metal products. On the contrary, their relative contribution in GVA was found to be considerably low reflecting the low productivity level of OAMEs in rural areas. Our computations show that the OAMEs lost 20 per cent of their share, on an average, in GVA to NDMEs and DMEs over time. The DMEs alone made huge gains in value added as its share in GVA shot up from 11.9 per cent in 1984–5 to 27.7 per cent in 2005–6 (a gain of 16 per cent).

The dominance of OAMEs declined considerably in many industries in the urban segment of the informal sector too (Table 3.17). The relative importance of OAMEs fell considerably in food products, cotton products, wood products, leather products, rubber products, non-metallic minerals, and metal products over the period 1984–5 to

Table 3.16 Enterprise Type-wise Share in Number of Enterprises, Employment, and GVA by Industry, Rural Sector: 1984–5 to 2005–6 (in per cent)

Industry	Number of Enterprises						Employment						Gross Value Added					
	1984–5			2005–6			1984–5			2005–6			1984–5			2005–6		
	OAME	NDME	DME	OAME	NDME	DME	OAME	NDME	DME	OAME	NDME	DME	OAME	NDME	DME	OAME	NDME	DME
Food Products	83.3	14.7	2.1	84.3	9.7	6.0	75.6	15.0	9.5	64.4	12.9	22.7	59.0	29.8	11.2	52.0	16.5	31.5
Beverages	94.2	4.6	1.2	99.3	0.5	0.1	82.7	7.7	9.6	97.5	1.2	1.3	78.8	11.0	10.2	83.2	3.5	13.3
Cotton Products	94.7	3.8	1.4	83.3	12.5	4.1	89.3	4.2	6.6	61.4	21.0	17.6	77.4	7.7	14.9	44.0	27.4	28.6
Textiles	91.0	8.1	0.9	93.6	5.6	0.8	80.7	12.1	7.2	84.4	10.4	5.3	70.9	19.5	9.5	70.2	18.6	11.2
Wood Products	95.8	3.9	0.4	93.2	6.3	0.5	91.9	6.1	2.0	87.6	10.1	2.3	84.3	12.0	3.7	65.3	25.1	9.7
Paper Products	76.7	17.7	5.6	90.2	6.3	3.5	60.2	22.6	17.3	71.5	10.0	18.5	20.4	21.5	58.1	40.3	17.0	42.7
Leather Products	96.0	3.9	0.2	85.7	8.0	6.2	90.7	8.3	1.0	49.2	11.3	39.5	90.4	8.5	1.1	43.2	17.5	39.3
Chemicals	75.6	17.0	7.4	94.1	1.3	4.6	55.3	20.9	23.8	69.1	2.8	28.1	17.2	27.1	55.7	32.7	7.8	59.5
Rubber Products	84.6	9.1	6.3	58.0	29.3	12.7	56.7	9.6	33.7	35.6	29.5	34.9	18.5	16.8	64.6	14.8	29.8	55.4
Non-metallic Minerals	92.1	5.1	2.8	85.6	6.0	8.4	75.9	6.7	17.4	55.3	6.2	38.6	62.2	7.3	30.5	24.3	10.8	64.9
Basic Metals	81.7	13.5	4.8	69.2	20.4	10.4	60.1	17.7	22.2	33.4	26.4	40.2	22.6	19.0	58.4	6.9	7.8	85.3
Metal Products	90.5	8.1	1.4	82.5	15.9	1.6	79.5	13.6	6.9	68.1	25.2	6.7	66.8	17.3	16.0	39.9	35.7	24.4
Transport Equipment and Parts	69.7	28.0	2.3	42.5	19.7	37.7	53.7	34.4	12.0	13.0	11.3	75.7	56.7	29.3	14.0	5.8	11.1	83.2
Other Manufacturing Products	95.2	3.5	1.2	85.2	9.1	5.7	85.0	5.7	9.3	56.0	12.0	32.0	75.5	9.4	15.1	37.8	14.2	48.1
Total	91.5	7.2	1.3	91.6	6.1	2.3	83.1	9.0	7.9	76.8	10.2	13.0	74.1	16.4	11.9	53.7	18.6	27.7

Source: Authors' calculations based on NSSO data.

Table 3.17 Enterprise Type-wise Share in Number of Enterprises, Employment, and GVA by Industry, Urban Sector: 1984–5 to 2005–6 (in per cent)

Industry	Number of Enterprises						Employment						Gross Value Added					
	1984–5			2005–6			1984–5			2005–6			1984–5			2005–6		
	OAME	NDME	DME	OAME	NDME	DME	OAME	NDME	DME	OAME	NDME	DME	OAME	NDME	DME	OAME	NDME	DME
Food Products	65.0	30.5	4.5	64.6	29.3	6.1	49.8	31.7	18.5	44.4	35.7	20.0	31.1	40.8	28.2	27.4	42.4	30.3
Beverages	93.0	5.6	1.4	97.3	2.2	0.5	84.5	7.7	7.8	93.6	3.9	2.6	57.9	15.2	26.9	77.8	16.2	6.1
Cotton Products	75.5	16.4	8.1	65.9	16.5	17.6	53.9	15.1	31.0	38.2	17.9	43.8	26.2	26.7	47.1	16.3	21.2	62.5
Textiles	74.0	22.9	3.1	80.7	15.0	4.4	51.7	32.6	15.6	55.6	23.5	20.9	35.9	40.1	24.0	32.1	30.3	37.6
Wood Products	79.1	16.7	4.2	64.1	30.0	5.9	57.3	21.0	21.7	42.3	39.0	18.7	32.3	31.5	36.2	24.3	48.0	27.8
Paper Products	45.1	37.3	17.6	55.7	31.6	12.7	23.7	29.4	46.9	31.7	33.2	35.2	7.4	36.5	56.1	11.4	30.2	58.3
Leather Products	72.1	21.1	6.8	55.7	29.4	14.9	51.9	23.3	24.8	32.5	30.7	36.8	36.8	20.6	42.6	22.1	34.9	42.9
Chemicals	43.7	38.5	17.7	87.5	4.2	8.3	16.5	34.3	49.2	60.4	6.4	33.1	5.5	23.8	70.7	11.5	8.5	80.0
Rubber Products	77.2	10.9	11.9	33.0	39.6	27.4	45.6	7.3	47.1	14.9	35.6	49.6	11.8	26.1	62.2	5.2	30.2	64.6
Non-metallic Minerals	77.0	15.4	7.6	64.7	23.5	11.8	51.5	16.8	31.7	41.4	23.8	34.8	45.1	26.1	28.8	17.8	30.8	51.4
Basic Metals	37.6	39.0	23.3	45.5	32.8	21.8	17.5	28.5	53.9	21.2	29.0	49.7	8.0	20.9	71.1	6.2	12.5	81.3
Metal Products	41.0	36.8	22.2	35.7	45.7	18.6	21.1	13.3	65.6	16.7	39.2	44.1	8.6	24.4	67.0	7.6	29.2	63.1
Transport Equipment and Parts	30.7	38.6	30.7	20.9	37.0	42.0	7.8	19.8	72.4	6.3	27.2	66.5	1.0	57.7	41.2	2.8	23.1	74.1
Other Manufacturing Products	77.2	17.1	5.7	70.4	20.5	9.1	54.9	17.6	27.6	37.8	22.0	40.2	41.5	21.2	37.3	19.7	34.8	45.6
Total	71.8	21.7	6.5	70.9	20.7	8.4	50.2	22.3	27.5	43.6	26.1	30.2	24.0	32.5	42.9	20.0	31.5	48.5

Source: Authors' calculations based on NSSO data.

2005–6. Though the OAMEs still account for a considerable share in the number of enterprises, its relative importance declined in 9 out of 14 industries during the period 1984–5 to 2005–6. The decline was more dramatic in the manufactures of rubber and leather products. In a number of industries, the share of OAMEs in the number of enterprises also increased. For instance, the share of OAMEs in chemicals has more than doubled in this period, from 43.7 per cent in 1984–5 to 87.5 per cent in 2005–6. Interestingly, the decline in the share of OAMEs in employment and GVA was relatively slower in urban areas as compared to rural areas. In 8 industries, DMEs accounted for a share of more than 50 per cent in GVA in 2005–6, and in 11 industries, its share was higher than the OAMEs and the NDMEs. Manufacture of beverages was the only industry group where the OAMEs contributed a higher share in GVA than the NDMEs and the DMEs. In food products and wood products, a higher share in GVA in 2005–6 came from the NDMEs. In the case of employment, OAMEs still contributed a larger share in food products, beverages, textiles, wood products, chemicals, and non-metallic minerals. In other industry groups, major contribution in employment in 2005–6 originated from the DMEs (Table 3.17).

Growth Trends by the Type of Enterprise

We now examine the growth performance of each type of enterprise in the rural, urban, and the combined informal manufacturing sector for the two sub-periods, 1984–5 to 1994–5 and 1994–5 to 2005–6, and for the overall period, 1984–5 to 2005–6, by broad industry group. There is considerable expansion of activities in the DME category during 1994–5 to 2005–6 (Tables 3.18, 3.19, and 3.20). Both OAMEs and NDMEs witnessed an abysmal growth performance in the first sub-period as enterprises, employment, and GVA have declined in this period. However, they witnessed a turnaround in growth performance in the post-reform period. DMEs, on the other hand, experienced a steady growth in the number of enterprises, employment, and GVA in both the pre-reform and the post-reform period. In DMEs, employment and GVA accelerated their growth performance in the post-reform period, while the number of enterprises reported a slowdown.

The number of OAMEs and NDMEs grew at a rate of over 3 per cent per annum over the period 1994–5 to 2005–6, while the DMEs increased at a rate of 1 per cent per annum. Employment generation

Table 3.18 Industry-wise Growth of Enterprises by Enterprise Type: 1984–5 to 2005–6 (in per cent)

Industry	Number of Enterprises								
	1984–95			1995–2006			1984–2006		
	OAME	NDME	DME	OAME	NDME	DME	OAME	NDME	DME
Food Products	-2.8	-5.8	3.0	-0.5	0.0	2.1	-1.6	-2.8	2.5
Beverages	0.0	2.7	11.8	8.2	-10.8	-17.7	4.2	-4.6	-4.8
Cotton Products	-8.7	-2.7	2.5	-1.8	1.1	0.3	-5.1	-0.7	1.3
Textiles	-11.6	-14.2	2.6	14.7	13.9	2.1	1.3	-0.5	2.4
Wood Products	-0.8	0.0	1.6	-1.4	3.0	-0.1	-1.1	1.6	0.7
Paper Products	3.6	2.3	-1.3	6.7	0.0	2.6	5.2	1.1	0.7
Leather Products	-9.8	-5.2	5.1	-5.1	3.5	2.2	-7.4	-0.7	3.6
Chemicals	12.7	-7.1	1.4	11.1	-1.3	6.9	11.9	-4.1	4.2
Rubber Products	-9.8	7.0	6.3	-0.6	0.8	-2.9	-5.1	3.7	1.4
Non-metallic Minerals	-2.3	-2.8	3.7	-3.2	1.0	1.0	-2.7	-0.8	2.3
Basic Metals	-2.8	-5.5	-4.3	0.4	2.3	2.1	-1.1	-1.5	-1.0
Metal Products	-4.4	2.2	1.5	4.2	5.2	2.4	0.0	3.8	2.0
Transport Equipment and Parts	-7.2	-4.3	1.5	-0.1	2.9	7.3	-3.6	-0.6	4.5
Other Manufacturing Products	4.5	0.4	7.1	-5.4	4.1	1.4	-0.8	2.3	4.1
Total	-3.8	-4.1	3.3	3.1	3.2	0.9	-0.2	-0.3	2.0

Source: Authors' calculations based on NSSO data.
Note: Growth rates are annual average compound growth rates.

Table 3.19 Industry-wise Growth of Employment by Enterprise Type: 1984–5 to 2005–6 (in per cent)

Industry	Employment								
	1984–95			1995–2006			1984–2006		
	OAME	NDME	DME	OAME	NDME	DME	OAME	NDME	DME
Food Products	-1.7	-2.8	1.0	-1.1	1.2	4.0	-1.4	-0.7	2.6
Beverages	1.7	-4.5	-4.4	6.0	-3.4	-6.1	4.0	-3.9	-5.3
Cotton Products	-9.6	0.2	0.9	-2.8	2.1	0.3	-6.1	1.2	0.6
Textiles	-6.8	-10.2	2.6	10.5	11.9	2.2	1.9	0.8	2.4
Wood Products	0.8	2.1	0.0	-1.4	3.3	-0.4	-0.4	2.7	-0.2
Paper Products	5.6	6.2	-1.1	4.6	-0.3	3.9	5.1	2.7	1.5
Leather Products	-6.8	-0.7	5.0	-4.4	2.9	4.1	-5.6	1.2	4.5
Chemicals	13.7	-2.8	3.8	10.5	-2.3	7.5	12.0	-2.6	5.7
Rubber Products	-11.7	12.3	1.5	2.4	0.8	-2.9	-4.6	6.1	-0.9
Non-metallic Minerals	-0.7	-1.8	2.6	-3.2	1.7	2.8	-2.0	0.0	2.7
Basic Metals	2.4	-1.9	-4.2	-3.8	1.4	2.8	-0.9	-0.2	-0.6
Metal Products	-2.0	10.4	1.8	3.3	4.7	2.9	0.7	7.4	2.4
Transport Equipment and Parts	-1.5	2.0	2.1	-3.6	2.4	7.1	-2.6	2.2	4.7
Other Manufacturing Products	7.6	4.5	8.1	-7.1	3.9	3.0	-0.3	4.2	5.4
Total	-2.3	-1.1	1.8	1.4	3.7	2.3	-0.3	1.4	2.1

Source: Authors' calculations based on NSSO data.
Note: Growth rates are annual average compound growth rates.

Table 3.20 Industry-wise Growth of GVA by Enterprise Type: 1984–5 to 2005–6 (in per cent)

Industry	Gross Value Added								
	1984–95			1995–2006			1984–2006		
	OAME	NDME	DME	OAME	NDME	DME	OAME	NDME	DME
Food Products	1.3	-3.2	-0.2	5.7	8.0	12.5	3.6	2.5	6.2
Beverages	0.5	-0.2	-4.1	8.9	1.9	9.6	4.8	0.9	2.8
Cotton Products	-6.0	0.8	3.5	5.9	8.9	8.2	0.0	5.0	5.9
Textiles	-10.0	-11.1	6.5	22.9	23.3	10.6	6.0	5.5	8.6
Wood Products	-3.2	2.1	-1.6	6.1	9.6	8.6	1.6	5.9	3.6
Paper Products	11.1	5.1	0.3	8.1	5.2	12.0	9.5	5.2	6.3
Leather Products	-6.9	0.1	0.9	1.3	11.0	8.6	-2.7	5.6	4.8
Chemicals	12.1	-2.9	-1.3	12.6	5.1	14.5	12.4	1.2	6.7
Rubber Products	-0.4	10.2	9.0	3.1	0.4	-0.6	1.4	4.9	3.8
Non-metallic Minerals	0.9	2.3	8.9	2.0	12.0	10.6	1.5	7.3	9.8
Basic metals	8.5	-1.1	-3.2	-3.3	3.3	13.2	2.1	1.2	5.1
Metal Products	-1.6	4.2	-0.4	9.2	10.4	12.1	3.9	7.4	5.9
Transport Equipment and Parts	-4.1	-17.4	-9.1	1.9	6.2	13.3	-1.0	-5.8	2.0
Other Manufacturing Products	10.8	10.0	17.1	2.9	16.8	8.8	6.6	13.5	12.7
Total	-1.7	-1.0	2.5	8.1	10.8	10.2	3.3	5.0	6.5

Source: Authors' calculations based on NSSO data.

Note: Growth rates are annual average compound growth rates. Gross value added growth rates are reported for real gross value added, computed at 1993–4 prices.

in the post-reform period was the fastest among the NDMEs (3.7 per cent per annum), followed by the DMEs (2.3 per cent per annum) and the OAMEs (1.4 per cent per annum). Despite registering a slow growth in enterprises and employment, GVA grew at a faster rate of over 10 per cent per annum in DMEs. Growth of GVA was highest in NDMEs (at the rate of 11 per cent per annum) and lowest in OAMEs (at the rate of 8 per cent per annum).

Many industries had seen significant expansion of activities in the OAME, NDME, and DME categories in the post-reform period. Textiles industry, which witnessed a contraction of its activities in NDMEs and DMEs in the first sub-period, registered the largest increase in the number of enterprises, employment, and GVA in the post-reform period. In fact, this largest industry in the sector has, in part, helped in pulling up the growth rates of OAMEs and NDMEs in the three variables in the post-reform period. Chemicals and metal products industries appeared to have aided the growth of DMEs in the period 1994–5 to 2005–6. These industries witnessed the highest growth in the number of enterprises, employment, and GVA during this period. It can be also seen that significant decline in the growth of the number of DMEs in the post-reform period was mainly due to the huge decline registered by beverages industry. This industry witnessed substantial reduction in the number of enterprises and employment in the NDME and DME categories, but reported considerable gains in GVA. Barring a few, almost all the industries have registered a positive growth in GVA in the post-reform period among all the types of enterprises. Manufacturing of rubber products in the DME category and basic metals industry in the OAME category were the only exceptions.

Regional Trends in OAMEs, NDMEs, and DMEs

An examination of the state-wise distribution by the type of enterprise reveals that OAMEs account for the largest share in enterprises and employment in majority of the states in 1984–5 (Table 3.21). There was hardly any change in the distribution of enterprises by 2005–6. However, the share of the OAMEs in employment declined in many states during this period. The decline was the fastest in Haryana, Maharashtra, and Rajasthan. On the other hand, the share of family enterprises in employment witnessed a significant increase in another industrialized state—Gujarat. There was a 19 per cent

Table 3.21 Region-wise Share in Number of Enterprises, Employment, and GVA by Enterprise Type: 1984–5 to 2005–6 (in per cent)

State	Number of Enterprises						Employment						Gross Value Added					
	1984–5			2005–6			1984–5			2005–6			1984–5			2005–6		
	OAME	NDME	DME	OAME	NDME	DME	OAME	NDME	DME	OAME	NDME	DME	OAME	NDME	DME	OAME	NDME	DME
Andhra Pradesh	87.6	10.4	2.0	88.9	7.5	3.6	76.1	13.4	10.5	68.1	12.9	19.0	50.5	19.5	30.0	53.8	24.5	21.7
Assam	84.2	14.5	1.3	88.5	10.3	1.2	71.7	20.5	7.8	74.6	18.1	7.3	50.7	33.8	15.5	55.7	33.3	11.0
Bihar	89.8	9.4	0.7	94.5	5.2	0.4	82.8	13.8	3.4	89.6	8.2	2.3	69.7	15.6	14.7	76.6	15.7	7.7
Gujarat	59.0	33.8	7.2	79.9	10.5	9.6	26.6	25.9	47.5	45.7	12.4	42.0	23.3	30.4	46.2	24.2	16.1	59.7
Haryana	82.7	14.5	2.8	70.6	22.8	6.5	69.8	18.6	11.6	43.0	31.8	25.2	20.2	45.1	34.8	22.8	35.5	41.7
Karnataka	84.8	10.5	4.7	84.1	8.4	7.5	58.1	13.9	28.0	56.1	13.3	30.6	42.4	19.4	38.3	24.3	21.7	54.0
Kerala	77.8	18.1	4.0	75.1	20.3	4.6	52.6	25.0	22.3	48.4	30.1	21.4	44.6	37.7	17.6	23.0	43.4	33.6
Madhya Pradesh	90.3	8.2	1.4	93.1	5.2	1.7	79.7	10.2	10.1	82.5	9.1	8.4	61.0	27.0	12.0	48.8	20.9	30.4
Maharashtra	82.6	13.4	4.0	74.7	15.5	9.8	64.0	14.6	21.4	42.6	20.0	37.4	33.3	30.5	36.2	16.7	28.7	54.6
Odisha	91.9	7.4	0.6	95.4	3.9	0.7	88.0	9.0	3.0	90.8	5.3	3.9	73.0	16.3	10.7	66.8	14.6	18.6
Punjab	80.6	16.3	3.0	76.1	19.8	4.0	63.4	23.7	12.9	52.2	31.1	16.7	29.2	24.8	46.1	31.9	41.2	26.8
Rajasthan	89.4	9.3	1.3	86.9	9.7	3.4	79.6	13.7	6.6	61.6	15.7	22.7	61.2	21.3	17.6	42.5	23.8	33.7
Tamil Nadu	80.6	15.6	3.8	80.2	13.9	5.9	60.3	20.6	19.1	52.2	21.1	26.6	37.1	28.5	34.4	27.8	27.8	44.3
Uttar Pradesh	91.6	7.2	1.2	85.8	11.2	2.9	86.4	7.9	5.7	70.3	15.3	14.4	59.9	18.8	21.3	44.9	24.8	30.3
West Bengal	83.9	13.0	3.1	88.4	8.9	2.6	71.4	16.5	12.1	72.4	14.9	12.6	43.9	23.1	33.0	40.5	24.9	34.6
Total	86.6	11.1	2.3	86.0	10.1	3.9	74.3	13.8	11.8	65.8	15.4	18.8	46.3	25.0	28.7	35.3	25.9	38.9

Source: Authors' calculations based on NSSO data.

increase in the share of OAMEs in employment in this state. Bihar, MP, and Odisha were the other states that registered an increase in employment share by OAMEs. The share of DMEs in employment increased substantially in Haryana, Maharashtra, and Rajasthan. Gujarat and Kerala witnessed a decline in the share of DMEs in employment. In terms of GVA, there was a decline in the share of OAMEs and an increase in the share of NDMEs and DMEs over time. In Gujarat, Karnataka, and Maharashtra, DMEs accounted for more than 50 per cent of the GVA in 2005–6, and in Kerala and Punjab, NDMEs accounted for a majority of the GVA. In Odisha, Bihar, Assam, AP, and MP, it was the OAMEs which contributed substantially to the GVA.

Regional Growth Trends: By the Type of Enterprise

The analysis of growth based on the type of enterprise across states reveals interesting patterns (see Tables 3.22 and 3.23). In terms of the number of enterprises, DMEs grew at a slower pace than OAMEs and NDMEs in the post-reform period. DMEs experienced a slowdown in the post-reform era, while OAMEs and NDMEs reported a turnaround (Table 3.22). In Kerala and Haryana, the number of OAMEs, NDMEs, and DMEs grew faster in the post-reform era. The post-reform era also witnessed a decline in the number of OAMEs in Odisha, NDMEs in Haryana, and DMEs in AP, Bihar, Gujarat, Karnataka, Punjab, and UP. Industrialized states such as Gujarat and Maharashtra, which registered a higher growth of enterprises in the pre-reform era, reported significant slowdown in the number of DMEs in the post-reform era. In fact, the number of DMEs declined in Gujarat in the post-reform period.

In employment, NDMEs recorded a higher growth in the post-reform era as compared to OAMEs and DMEs. This substantial increase in the growth of employment in NDMEs can be attributed to the higher growth rate reported in Kerala, Haryana, and Rajasthan. Employment in OAMEs grew the fastest in Kerala, Haryana, and MP, while addition to employment in DMEs was faster in Assam and Rajasthan. In terms of GVA, OAMEs and NDMEs record negative growth rates in the pre-reform period but there was a significant turnaround in the post-reform era (Table 3.23). Even DMEs recorded an improved growth rate in the post-reform era, overcoming the low growth phase in the preceding

Table 3.22 Enterprise Type-wise Growth of Number of Enterprises and Employment in the Informal Manufacturing Sector by Major States: 1984–5 to 2005–6 (in per cent)

State	Number of Enterprises									Employment								
	1984–95			1995–2006			1984–2006			1984–1995			1995–2006			1984–2006		
	OAME	NDME	DME	OAME	NDME	DME	OAME	NDME	DME	OAME	NDME	DME	OAME	NDME	DME	OAME	NDME	DME
Andhra Pradesh	-4.1	-2.8	6.1	3.6	-0.8	-0.2	-0.1	-1.7	2.7	-2.6	-5.0	-1.6	1.2	4.1	6.9	-0.6	-0.3	2.8
Assam	1.2	-0.5	-4.6	3.3	1.2	7.7	2.3	0.4	1.7	3.6	0.6	-7.6	0.6	1.8	10.4	2.0	1.2	1.4
Bihar	-2.2	-8.6	0.2	1.9	2.2	-6.8	0.0	-3.1	-3.5	-1.5	-7.7	4.1	1.2	1.6	-7.8	-0.1	-2.9	-2.3
Gujarat	4.2	-7.7	7.9	2.2	-0.1	-1.1	3.2	-3.8	3.1	15.1	4.1	8.9	1.7	-0.8	0.7	7.9	1.5	4.5
Haryana	-9.6	-6.8	-0.9	8.4	11.4	9.2	-0.6	2.3	4.3	-9.5	-5.3	3.5	6.3	11.8	5.4	-1.6	3.3	4.5
Karnataka	-1.6	-3.3	7.7	2.9	2.6	-1.1	0.7	-0.3	3.0	0.4	-2.2	0.7	1.1	3.5	1.9	0.8	0.7	1.3
Kerala	-8.6	-7.7	-7.2	8.5	9.0	8.6	0.0	0.7	0.8	-8.4	-7.7	-7.1	7.2	9.2	6.3	-0.5	0.8	-0.3
Madhya Pradesh	-8.4	-7.1	-2.5	7.7	1.6	3.2	-0.3	-2.7	0.4	-3.2	-0.6	-3.8	7.2	3.2	5.8	2.1	1.4	1.1
Maharashtra	-9.0	-4.4	5.3	5.8	3.4	1.6	-1.5	-0.3	3.4	-5.0	2.6	5.3	3.4	2.9	2.7	-0.7	2.8	3.9
Odisha	5.5	-7.5	2.4	-3.0	2.8	0.2	1.0	-2.2	1.3	5.9	-7.1	0.7	-3.7	3.0	2.9	0.7	-1.9	1.9
Punjab	-7.5	-4.3	3.6	6.8	6.0	-0.6	-0.3	0.9	1.4	-7.1	-2.7	5.6	5.8	5.8	-1.9	-0.6	1.7	1.6
Rajasthan	-6.4	-7.8	-3.5	4.8	6.9	11.7	-0.7	-0.4	4.2	-5.4	-6.8	-5.1	3.0	8.2	17.6	-1.1	0.8	6.2
Tamil Nadu	-5.5	-7.0	0.6	3.3	3.8	1.6	-1.0	-1.5	1.1	-5.5	-5.6	-0.8	1.9	3.6	1.8	-1.7	-0.9	0.5
Uttar Pradesh	-10.4	-6.2	2.9	1.9	2.5	-1.9	-4.1	-1.7	0.3	-8.9	-2.0	3.0	0.6	1.8	-0.3	-4.1	-0.1	1.3
West Bengal	-1.6	-5.5	-2.4	4.3	4.0	3.1	1.4	-0.6	0.5	-0.8	-4.3	-2.0	2.2	4.5	3.6	0.8	0.2	0.9
Total	-4.9	-5.9	2.8	3.1	3.3	0.9	-0.8	-1.2	1.8	-3.4	-3.4	1.3	1.5	3.7	2.5	-0.8	0.3	2.0

Source: Authors' calculations based on NSSO data.
Note: Growth rates are annual average compound growth rates.

Table 3.23 Enterprise Type-wise Growth of GVA in the Informal Manufacturing Sector by Major States: 1984–5 to 2005–6 (in per cent)

State	Gross Value Added								
	1984–95			1995–2006			1984–2006		
	OAME	NDME	DME	OAME	NDME	DME	OAME	NDME	DME
Andhra Pradesh	−2.6	−1.4	−6.9	9.1	9.6	9.8	3.4	4.2	1.5
Assam	−0.2	−1.4	−8.1	12.7	12.8	16.7	6.4	5.8	4.2
Bihar	1.5	−0.8	−4.7	7.7	9.2	6.7	4.7	4.3	1.1
Gujarat	7.6	−1.8	6.2	3.9	6.2	7.2	5.7	2.3	6.8
Haryana	−0.6	−7.6	0.2	12.6	16.5	12.4	6.1	4.3	6.4
Karnataka	−5.9	−4.8	−6.3	7.5	13.0	17.2	0.9	4.2	5.3
Kerala	−14.0	−10.1	−5.0	14.0	17.8	17.2	−0.3	3.6	6.1
Madhya Pradesh	−5.6	0.8	3.7	11.3	4.6	13.5	2.9	2.7	8.7
Maharashtra	−3.5	0.4	7.4	10.0	12.3	10.3	3.3	6.5	8.9
Odisha	4.7	0.2	1.0	6.1	10.2	16.2	5.4	5.3	8.7
Punjab	0.5	1.8	−0.5	10.1	13.1	5.0	5.5	7.6	2.3
Rajasthan	−5.5	−6.9	−7.1	9.0	15.3	21.3	1.8	4.1	6.8
Tamil Nadu	−6.1	−7.3	−2.5	6.9	10.8	8.6	0.5	1.8	3.1
Uttar Pradesh	−6.4	−3.4	−0.2	6.9	9.3	6.8	0.3	3.1	3.4
West Bengal	0.2	−1.5	−4.5	7.4	10.6	13.6	3.9	4.7	4.5
Total	−3.3	−3.2	0.1	8.0	11.1	10.4	2.5	4.0	5.4

Source: Authors' calculations based on NSSO data.

Note: Growth rates are annual average compound growth rates. Gross value added growth rates are reported for real gross value added, computed at 1993–4 prices.

period. In the post-reform period, OAMEs recorded very high growth rates in Kerala, Haryana, Assam, and MP; NDMEs reported high GVA growth in Kerala, Rajasthan, and Haryana; and DMEs recorded high growth rates in Karnataka, Kerala, Odisha, Rajasthan, and Assam.

✿　　✿　　✿

This chapter provided the stylized facts of the informal manufacturing sector in India from the 1980s to the 2000s. It looks at the overall trends in three key indicators of the informal sector—the number of enterprises, employment, and GVA. We did this by analysing the major industrial groups, by region (that is, by comparing major states), and by location (that is, by looking at whether the informal firm is based in a rural or an urban area). This chapter also looked at the evolution of the key indicators by the type of enterprise in the informal sector—that is, whether the firm is an OAME, DME, or NDME. The analysis showed quite remarkable changes in the informal manufacturing sector in the post-reform period, and evidence of strong growth in output in this sector in the post-1995 period (albeit with high volatility). However, there is less evidence of a corresponding increase in employment in the informal manufacturing sector in the post-1995 period, and the share of the informal sector in the total manufacturing workforce is remarkably constant. Among industrial groups, informal firms are mostly concentrated in food products, beverages, cotton products, textiles, and wood products. Most industries witnessed strong growth in the post-reform period (with the exception of leather). The success-ful industries as far as output and employment growth are concerned, both in the pre-reform and post-reform periods, are chemicals, rubber, non-metallic minerals, and miscellaneous products, while basic metals, textiles, and transport equipment and parts witnessed a turnaround in the growth of output in the post-reform period (and in the case of basic metals, in the growth of employment as well).

The growth patterns of the number of enterprises, output, and employment differ, as expected, between the rural and urban sectors. The urban informal manufacturing sector grew at a faster rate than the rural informal manufacturing sector, and within the urban sector, strong growth in output was observed in chemicals, textiles, transport, and other manufacturing products. With respect to regional patterns, there was surprisingly little change in the distribution in the share of enterprises across Indian states, and in their employment and output shares as well, contrary to what one may expect in a period of significant change in the Indian economy. There was a steady decline of rural informal enterprises in total informal enterprises across most Indian states, suggesting a clear urban bias in the growth of informal manufacturing firms in India.

Disaggregating informal enterprises by the type of enterprise— OAME, NDME, and DME—we saw a clear fall in the relative share of OAMEs in total enterprises, and a relative increase in the share of DMEs over time. This is evident for both rural and urban areas. While OAMEs are very different in their characteristics than NDMEs and DMEs, we found little evidence of segmentation in industrial location across these three types of enterprises, with all the three categories being present in industries such as food and beverages, cotton goods, and textiles. However, there is a strong presence of NDMEs and DMEs in more capital-intensive sectors such as chemicals and basic metals. The decline in the share of OAMEs in total enterprises is also evident from most states, though there are important exceptions such as Gujarat.

The analysis of this chapter suggests that the informal manufacturing sector has witnessed significant change, especially in its overall output and employment performance post-reform, as well as increased growth in some industries, and not in others. A typical informal firm is more likely to be based in urban region now than 20 years back, and family firms have gradually diminished in importance over time. At the same time, there is little change in the distribution of informal enterprises across states in India, and we do not see significant regional variation in the growth of the informal sector over time. Thus, both change and continuity were present in equal measure in the informal manufacturing sector in the post-reform period.

Appendix 3A: Construction of Variables

Real Gross Value Added

Gross value added figures have been used to represent output. Use of GVA at constant prices to represent output is a common practice in the Indian empirical literature (Ahluwalia 1991; Balakrishnan and Pushpangadan 1994, 1998; Goldar 1986). Studies on the unorganized manufacturing sector in India have, by and large, used the single deflation method to deflate the GVA (Rani and Unni 2004; Unni et al. 2001). The implicit deflators of domestic product of the unregistered manufacturing available at the two-digit industry group level have been used to deflate GVA at the industry level. The advantage of using this deflator is that it not only takes care of the general changes in the price level in the economy, but also the changes in the prices of those goods and services that constitute the GVA, namely, the output and inputs. In this sense, this deflator has the advantage of the double deflation method. At the state level, the gross state domestic product (GSDP) figures pertaining to the unregistered manufacturing sector have been used to deflate the nominal values of GVA. The GVA figures are expressed in 1993–4 prices.

Employment

Total number of persons engaged is taken as the measure of labour input. It includes workers, working proprietors, and supervisory/managerial staff members, where workers include full-time, part-time, hired, and other workers.

Number of Enterprises

The unorganized manufacturing sector comprises three types of enterprises—OAMEs, NDMEs, and DMEs. Data for each type of enterprise (OAMEs, NDMEs, and DMEs) and by location (rural and urban) have been summed up to arrive at the number of enterprises in the sector.

4

FIRMS IN THE INDIAN INFORMAL MANUFACTURING SECTOR
Characteristics and Evolution over Time

There is extensive literature available on firms in developed countries—on their characteristics, the structure of the markets they operate in, and their performance (Carlton and Perloff 2004; Scherer and Ross 1990). In the Indian context, there is a well-developed literature that has studied the characteristics and the behaviour of firms in the formal manufacturing sector (Gokarn et al. 2004; Mookherjee 1995). However, very little is known about the nature of firms in the Indian informal manufacturing sector. This is surprising, given that the majority of manufacturing firms in India are located in this sector. Like firms in the formal sector, enterprises in the informal manufacturing sector combine labour and capital to produce output, and some firms do it better than others. This depends on the inherent abilities of managers and owners, and specific characteristics of firms such as a firm's size and age. In contrast to firms in the formal sector, which often operate in monopolistic or oligopolistic market structures (that have implications for their behaviour and performance), firms in the informal sector operate in market structures which are close to perfect competition or are characterized by monopolistic competition. This is one important difference between the industrial organization prevalent in the formal sector and the organization that is prevalent in the informal sector. Another important difference between firms in the formal and informal sectors is that social norms which can act as barriers to entry for some firms are likely to play a more important role in informal markets than in formal markets (Fafchamps 2004; Iversen et al. 2009).

This chapter presents some stylized facts about firms in the Indian informal manufacturing sector using unit-level data from the surveys of unorganized enterprises from 2000–1 to 2010–11, conducted by the National Sample Survey Office (NSSO). We begin by analysing the evolution of firm size across the three different categories of firms in the Indian informal manufacturing sector—Own Account Manufacturing Enterprises (OAMEs), Non-directory Manufacturing Enterprises (NDMEs), and Directory Manufacturing Enterprises (DMEs)—first in the aggregate, and then by state and industry. We also look at firm size and productivity based on different sets of firm's characteristics (location of the firm, age, social group of the owner) to see if there are observable differences in firm size and productivity across firms with different characteristics. Throughout this chapter, we apply frequency weights that are provided by the NSSO to compute descriptive statistics, which is often advocated when estimating population averages from the sample data (Solon et al. 2013).[1]

One important concern about firms in the informal sector is that they pay less wages to their workers than firms in the formal sector (National Commission for Enterprises in the Unorganized Sector [NCEUS] 2009). We look at differences in wages paid to workers by specific characteristics of firms like firm type, ownership, social group of owner(s), and firm size. Simple wage equations are also estimated to determine which of the characteristics of firms matter in explaining these variations in the wages paid to workers.

Finally, we examine one specific issue that has attracted a great deal of interest in Indian academic and policy circles in recent times—the increasing practice of subcontracting of certain activities and the supply of inputs by the formal sector firms to the informal sector firms (Moreno-Monroy et al. 2012; Sahu 2010; Uchikawa 2011). The chapter addresses the nature of interlinkages between informal and formal sector firms and the determinants of these interlinkages in the final section of this chapter.

---

[1] We do not use sample weights when estimating causal effects between variables. See Appendix A2 for a detailed discussion on the pros and cons associated with the use of weights in estimations.

Evolution of Firm Size and Firm Productivity

The evolution of firm size is first examined based on the type of enterprise—OAME, NDME, and DME—with all-India unit-level data, then by state and by industry. We then look at firm size and firm labour productivity by ownership and location of the firm.

Aggregate Trends

Figure 4.1 presents trends in the average size of the firm belonging to all the three enterprise types over the period 2000–1 to 2010–11. We use number of workers to represent firm size. The figure shows a marginal increase in the size of an average DME over time. On the other hand, the average size of a firm in the OAME and NDME categories has marginally declined. The number of workers employed by an average DME in the informal sector increased from 10 workers in 2000–1 to over 11 workers in 2010–11. This increase in size is primarily aided by the substantial increase in the size of DME in the rural segment of

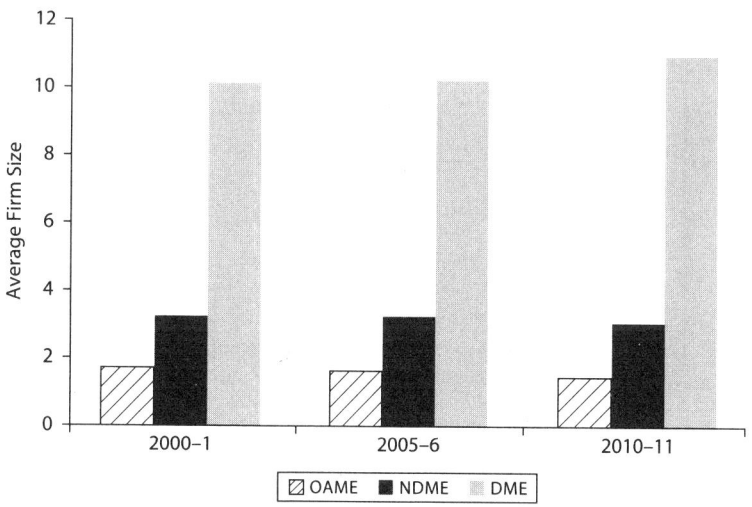

Figure 4.1   Firm Size by Enterprise Type: 2000–1 to 2010–11
Source: Authors' computations based on NSSO data.

the informal manufacturing sector (Figure 4.2). Estimates suggest that the average size of workforce in a DME in the rural sector rose from 12 workers in 2000–1 to 14 workers in 2010–11. On the other hand, the average size of a DME in urban areas witnessed only a marginal increase over the period 2000–1 to 2010–11. Comparison of firm size based on its location in rural and urban areas also shows that there has not been any significant change in the size of an average firm in the OAME and NDME categories in both the rural and urban areas.

We next examine histograms of frequency of firms and firm productivity across different size classes for the years 2000–1, 2005–6, and 2010–11. Looking at the number of firms in each size category first, it can be seen that the number of firms in the smallest size category with 1–2 workers (mostly OAMEs) and in the largest size categories with 16–19 workers and 20 workers and above, has been increasing over time (Figure 4.3). In contrast, the number of firms in the category of 3–5 workers (mostly NDMEs) has witnessed a substantial decline. With respect to firms in the category of 6–9 workers and 10–15 workers,

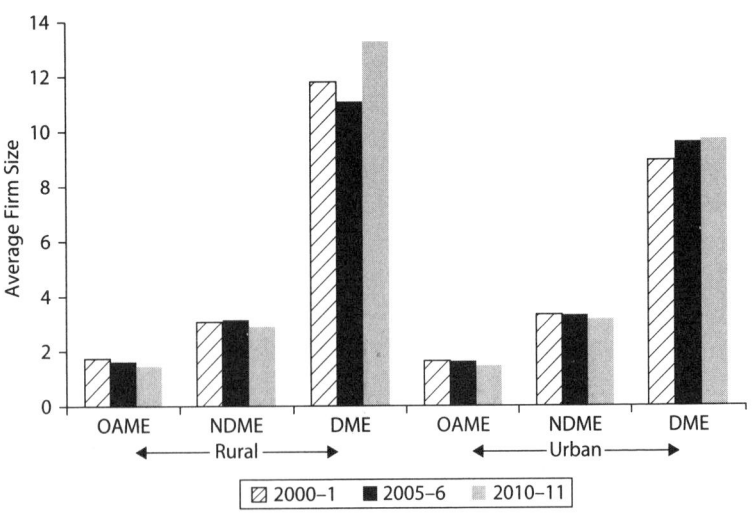

Figure 4.2 Firm Size by Enterprise Type and Sector: 2000–1 – 2010–11
Source: Authors' computations based on NSSO data.

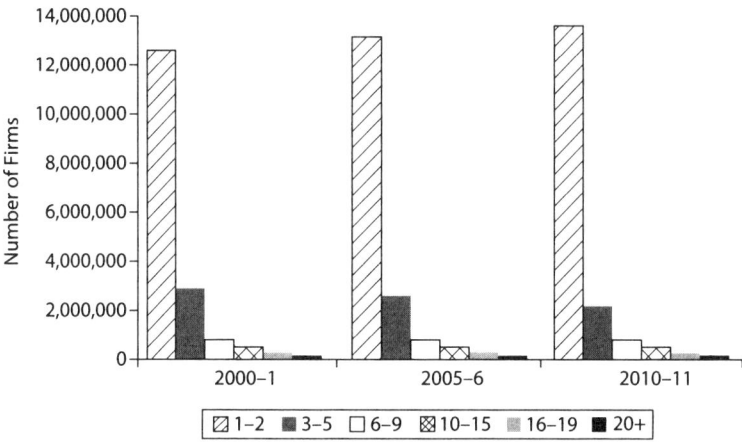

Figure 4.3 Histogram of Frequency of Firms for Different Size Classes
Source: Authors' computations based on NSSO data.
Note: Category 1–2 stands for firms employing 1 or 2 workers, category 3–5
stands for firms employing 3, 4, or 5 workers. The remaining categories should be
understood similarly.

there was a decline between 2005–6 and 2010–11. Perhaps this
points us to two possible developments simultaneously happening in
the informal sector: (a) lack of graduation of firms from the status of
being a family firm to a non-family firm employing at least one hired
worker, as is evident from the shrinking size of the average firm in the
informal sector (from 2.15 employees in 2000–1 to 2.02 employees
in 2010–11), and (b) lack of transition of firms from the informal sector to the formal sector, as is evident from the accumulation of firms
in the border categories. Evidence thus points to the transition within
the non-household segment of the informal sector till they reach the
optimum size as defined by the Factories Act. Next, looking at labour
productivity across different size categories (Figure 4.4),[2] it can be

---

[2] As is the general practice in the literature, labour productivity is measured
as the ratio of real gross value added (GVA) to number of workers. Nominal
GVA is deflated here by wholesale price index (WPI) for manufactured products to arrive at the real GVA. Real GVA figures are expressed at 1993–4 prices.

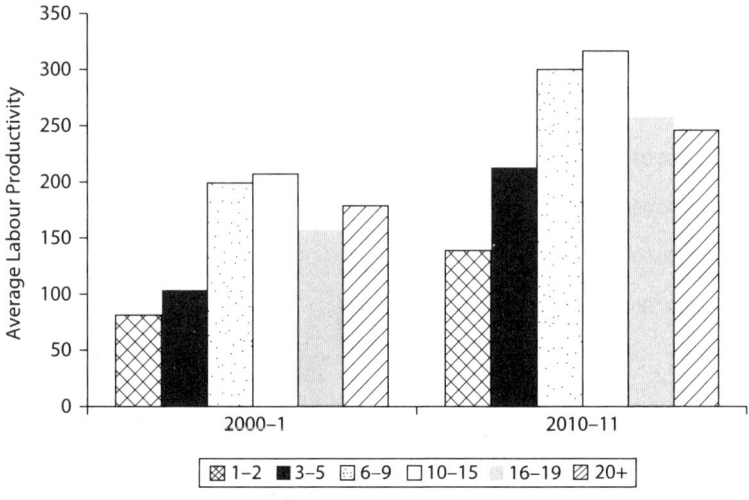

Figure 4.4   Histogram of Firm Labour Productivity (in '00s) for Different
Size Classes: 2000–1 and 2010–11
Source: Authors' computations based on NSSO data.
Note: Category 1–2 stands for firms employing 1 or 2 workers, category 3–5
stands for firms employing 3, 4 or 5 workers. The remaining categories should be
understood similarly.

seen that firm productivity has increased in 2010–11 across all size
categories, relative to 2000–1. The results also suggest the presence of
an inverted-U relationship between firm size and labour productivity.
Firm productivity increased steadily up to the 10–15 workers category
and then declined.

Differences in Firm Size by State and Industry

Next, we look at the changes in the average size of the firm belonging to all three types of enterprises across major states for the period
2000–1 to 2010–11 (Table 4.1). In most states, it is found that the
average firm size has declined in both OAME and NDME types.
With regard to the DMEs, we find that the firm size has increased in
majority of the states. The largest increase in firm size was reported in
Haryana where an average DME employs not less than 17 workers.
In Uttar Pradesh (UP) and Bihar too, an average DME employs

Table 4.1 Firm Size by State, Enterprise Type, and Year

State	OAME			NDME			DME		
	2000–1	2005–6	2010–11	2000–1	2005–6	2010–11	2000–1	2005–6	2010–11
Punjab	1.4	1.4	1.2	3.1	3.2	2.9	9.8	8.4	8.1
Haryana	1.5	1.4	1.4	3.0	3.3	2.9	10.3	9.1	17.0
Rajasthan	1.6	1.4	1.5	3.2	3.3	3.1	8.9	13.5	9.2
Uttar Pradesh	1.8	1.8	1.7	3.1	3.0	3.1	12.7	11.1	15.4
Bihar	1.8	1.7	1.5	3.0	2.8	2.6	11.3	11.4	15.4
Assam	1.6	1.4	1.4	2.9	3.0	2.7	9.1	10.4	9.2
West Bengal	1.8	1.6	1.4	3.2	3.3	3.0	10.0	9.6	11.5
Odisha	2.2	2.0	1.9	2.8	2.9	2.6	8.8	11.8	11.5
Madhya Pradesh	1.7	1.8	1.5	3.3	3.7	3.0	9.9	10.0	9.9
Gujarat	1.6	1.6	1.4	3.5	3.3	3.4	10.4	12.3	11.5
Maharashtra	1.6	1.5	1.4	3.3	3.3	3.2	9.2	9.8	10.1
Andhra Pradesh	1.7	1.5	1.4	3.2	3.3	3.1	9.1	10.1	9.5
Karnataka	1.4	1.4	1.3	3.3	3.2	3.1	9.1	8.4	9.8
Kerala	1.3	1.4	1.2	3.2	3.1	3.0	10.0	9.8	9.8
Tamil Nadu	1.5	1.5	1.3	3.4	3.5	3.1	10.0	10.2	10.4

Source: Authors' calculations based on NSSO data.

15 workers. There are also some states where the size of a DME has witnessed a decline during the same period. For instance Punjab, where an average DME employed about 10 workers in 2000–1, has employed only 8 workers in 2010–11. The size of the average DME seems to be low in Assam and Haryana too, where a DME, on an average, employs 9 workers.

A similar trend can be observed at the industrial level too as was observed at the regional level. The average firm size of both OAME and NDME categories has declined in majority of the industries (Table 4.2). The size of an average OAME has increased only in leather, wood, petroleum, electricals, and motor vehicles industry groups. Similarly, only six industries—leather, petroleum, pharmaceuticals, rubber, non-metallic minerals, and metal products—witnessed an increase in size in the average NDME over the period 2000–1 to 2010–11. On the other hand, the firm size of an average DME has gone up in most of the industry groups in the informal manufacturing sector. The largest increase in firm size was reported in non-metallic minerals and other manufacturing groups. These two industries turned out to be the biggest industry groups in terms of employee size in 2010–11, employing 19 workers on an average. It needs to be noted that brick-making is the key industry within non-metallic minerals group where DMEs are the largest. Metal products and rubber goods are the industries with the lowest DME size in the informal manufacturing sector in 2010–11.

Firm Size and Ownership

In this section we examine whether the firm size differs considerably across different ownership categories. Based on ownership, the firms are divided into three categories, namely (a) male proprietorship, (b) female proprietorship, and (c) partnership. Proprietary firms are those firms where an individual is the sole owner of the enterprise and they mostly operate from the household level. These firms are divided into two based on the gender of the owner: Male proprietorship is a proprietary firm owned by a male and female proprietorship is a proprietary firm owned by a female. The NSSO defines partnership as the 'relation between persons who have agreed to share the profits of a business carried on by all or any one of them acting for

Table 4.2 Firm Size by Industry, Enterprise Type, and Year

Industry	OAME			NDME			DME		
	2000–1	2005–6	2010–11	2000–1	2005–6	2010–11	2000–1	2005–6	2010–11
Food	1.9	1.9	1.6	3.0	3.1	2.8	8.7	9.1	9.0
Beverages	1.9	1.9	1.5	3.1	3.6	2.6	8.5	12.0	8.5
Tobacco	1.5	1.5	1.3	3.7	3.0	3.2	11.5	11.1	11.7
Textiles	1.9	1.8	1.6	3.5	3.5	3.3	9.1	9.6	9.8
Wearing Apparel	1.3	1.2	1.2	2.9	2.9	2.9	8.7	9.0	9.7
Leather	1.6	1.7	1.9	3.4	3.4	3.7	9.1	8.6	8.5
Wood	1.2	1.3	1.3	3.2	3.0	3.0	7.1	7.4	7.6
Paper	2.0	1.8	1.6	3.5	4.0	3.2	8.8	9.1	10.5
Printing	1.8	1.7	1.6	3.3	3.2	3.1	7.9	9.5	8.8
Petroleum	1.8	2.8	3.7	3.6	4.0	4.5	7.1	9.3	9.3
Chemicals	1.5	1.5	1.4	3.7	3.8	3.3	10.8	10.8	9.4
Pharmaceuticals	1.7	2.1	1.5	2.9	2.8	3.6	11.8	12.0	6.9
Rubber	1.5	1.9	1.1	3.4	3.6	3.7	7.6	7.4	7.4
Non-metallic Minerals	2.4	2.3	2.1	3.5	3.7	3.6	16.6	15.4	19.1
Basic Metal	1.6	1.4	1.3	3.6	3.3	3.1	9.9	8.3	9.7
Metal Products	1.8	1.9	1.3	3.4	3.6	3.5	8.5	7.5	7.3
Electronics	1.6	1.0	1.0	4.2	3.8	2.0	8.2	13.0	NA
Electricals	1.6	2.0	2.4	3.9	3.5	2.7	9.5	6.6	10.1
Motor Vehicles	1.6	1.8	2.1	3.5	3.3	3.3	8.7	10.0	10.4
Other Transport	1.7	1.5	1.5	3.7	3.6	3.3	8.6	7.6	8.4
Furniture	1.4	1.4	1.3	3.0	3.1	2.9	8.0	7.5	8.1
Others	1.6	1.5	1.5	3.4	3.1	2.8	11.9	14.3	19.4

Source: Authors' calculations based on NSSO data.

Note: NA = Not Applicable.

all' (NSSO 2002). These partners may be from the same household
or from different households. We pool them together into one category called 'partnership'.[3] The purpose here is to examine whether
the firm size differs across the three ownership categories defined
above. We analyse the difference in firm size across the three types
of enterprises—OAMEs, NDMEs, and DMEs—within each ownership category. In line with the expectations, it is found that the
average firm size of all the three types of enterprise is higher in the
partnership category (Figure 4.5). Though the difference in firm size
between proprietorship and partnership categories is marginal for
OAME and NDME types, the DME size in partnership category is
much higher than that of both proprietary categories. Between male
proprietorship and female proprietorship categories, the average firm

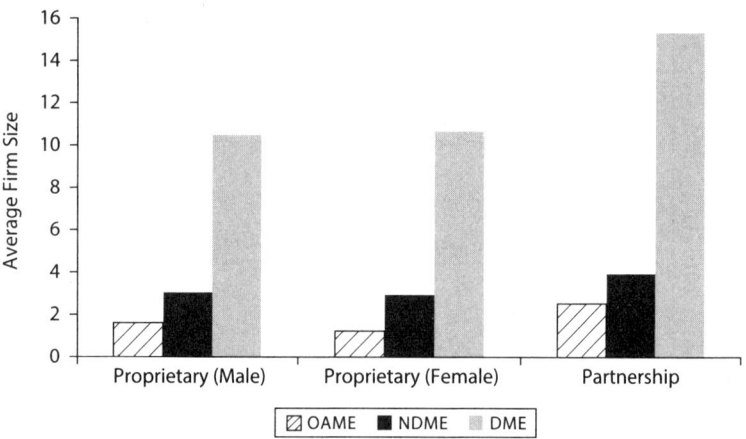

Figure 4.5   Firm Size by Ownership and Enterprise Type: 2010–11
Source: Authors' computations based on NSSO data.
Note: Proprietary (Male) refers to proprietorships with male owners, Proprietary
(Female) refers to proprietorships with female owners, and Partnership stands for
firms that operate on a partnership basis (firms with two or more owners).

[3] It needs to be stated that the units of proprietary and the nature of partnership covered under Annual Survey of Industries (ASI) will not be part of
these categories.

size is relatively smaller for firms owned by females compared to those owned by males, especially among the OAMEs and NDMEs.

There is a clear positive relationship between size and productivity indicating that larger firms are more productive than smaller firms when productivity is examined by the type of enterprise (Figure 4.6). OAMEs are the least productive category of firms in all the ownership categories, followed by NDMEs and DMEs. A comparison across categories reveals that OAMEs and NDMEs are more productive in the male proprietorship category and DMEs are more productive in female proprietorship category.

We also examine the difference in firm size for firms by their location—rural and urban areas (Figure 4.7). The figure makes it evident that across all ownership categories, the average firm size is the highest among the firms located in urban areas. As conjectured, the average firm size is highest in firms that operate on a partnership basis as compared

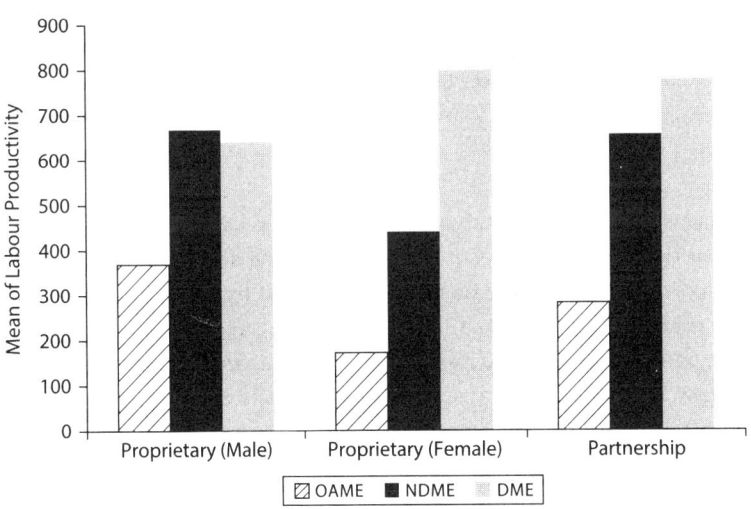

Figure 4.6 Mean Labour Productivity (in '00s) by Ownership and Enterprise Type: 2010–11

Source: Authors' computations based on NSSO data.

Note: Proprietary (Male) refers to proprietorships with male owners, Proprietary (Female) refers to proprietorships with female owners, and Partnership stands for firms that operate on a partnership basis (firms with two or more owners).

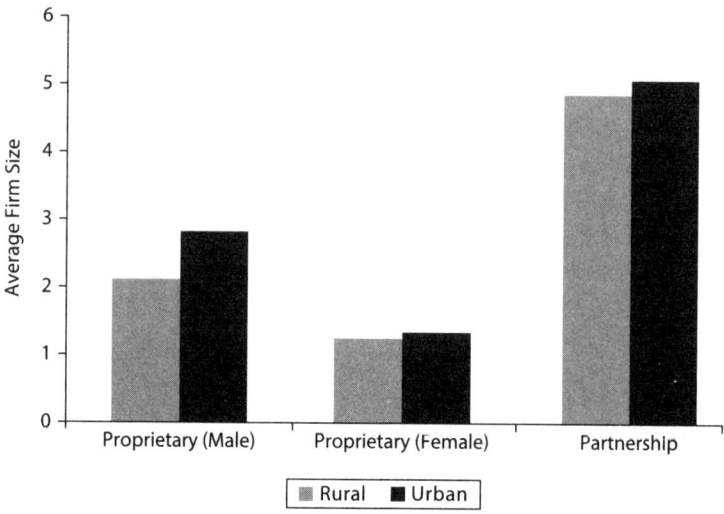

Figure 4.7   Firm Size by Ownership and Sector: 2010–11
Source: Authors' computations based on NSSO data.
Note: Proprietary (Male) refers to proprietorships with male owners, Proprietary (Female) refers to proprietorships with female owners, and Partnership stands for firms that operate on a partnership basis (firms with two or more owners).

to firms that operate at the household level. In case of firms that operate at the household level, it is noticed that the average firm size is the lowest for firms that are owned and operated by the females, both in the rural and urban areas. Our computations suggest that, on an average, partnership firms are more than double in size as male proprietary firms which, in turn, are twice as large as female proprietary firms.

Location and Firm Size

In this section we attempt to understand whether the location of firm operation and the size of the firm are related. Based on location, firms are classified into four categories: (a) firms operating from household premises (WithinHH); (b) firms located outside the household premises and have fixed premises and permanent structures (OH-PERM); (c) firms located outside the household premises but have only temporary structures (OH-TEMP);[4] and (d) firms that shift from market to market, or mobile firms, and those operating as street vendors (STREETVEND). Significant differences are found in firm size between firms operating from household premises and firms located outside the household premises. The average firm size is substantially higher for firms that are located outside the household premises and carry out their operation (OH-PERM and OH-TEMP) as compared to firms that operate from household premises (WithinHH) (Figure 4.8). This is evident across all the types of enterprises and more so for the DMEs. For instance, a DME belonging to the OH-PERM

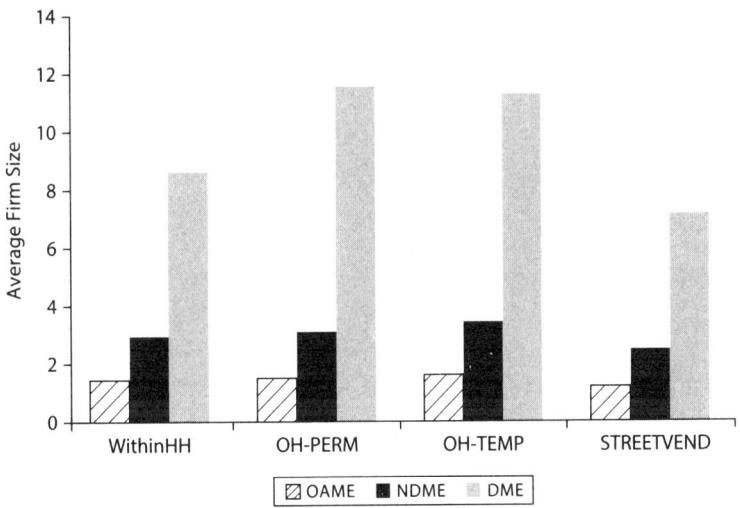

Figure 4.8   Firm Size by Location and Enterprise Type: 2010–11
Source: Authors' computations based on NSSO data.
Note: WithinHH, OH-PERM, OH-TEMP, and STREETVEND stand for firms that operate from within the household, firms with fixed premises and permanent structure, firms with fixed premises but temporary structure, and firms that shift from market to market and street vendors, respectively.

---

[4] The NSSO defines permanent structure as any structure made out of bricks, mud, bamboos, etc., and it cannot be removed as a whole without dismantling. Temporary structures, on the other hand, can be removed from its present location with some effort. Some examples are stalls, kiosks, etc. (NSSO 2002).

category is 1.25 times larger in size than a DME in the WithinHH
category. However, compared to mobile firms and street vendors
(STREETVEND), an average firm belonging to the WithinHH
category is bigger in size in all the three enterprise types (Figure 4.8).

The evidence on the relationship between location of firm and productivity is mixed (Figure 4.9). On the one hand, the results clearly
show that firms that are larger in size have achieved significant gains
in productivity across all types of enterprises. To be more precise,
OH-PERM firms are more productive among all the four categories
of firms, identified on the basis of location.[5] These are a set of firms
that are operating from outside the household premises and are

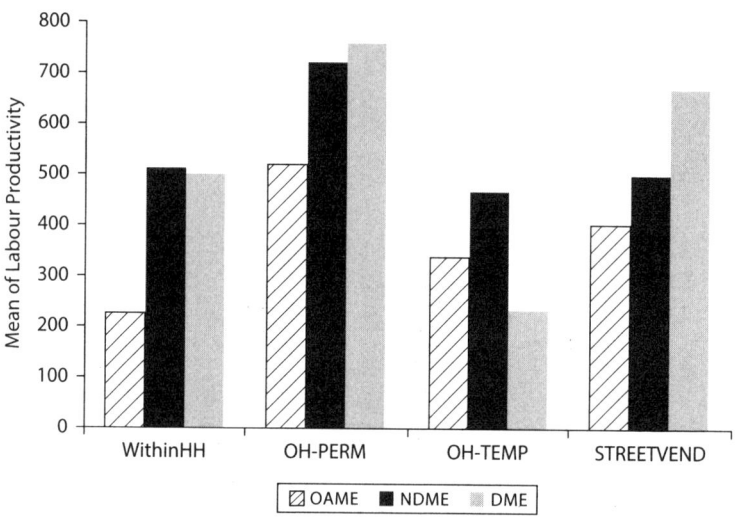

Figure 4.9   Labour Productivity by Location and Enterprise Type: 2010–11
Source: Authors' computations based on NSSO data.
Note: WithinHH, OH-PERM, OH-TEMP, and STREETVEND stand for firms
that operate from within the household, firms with fixed premises and permanent
structure, firms with fixed premises but temporary structure, and firms that shift
from market to market and street vendors, respectively.

[5] Our computations suggest that average productivity of OH-PERM
category in the OAME, NDME, and DME types of enterprises is, respectively,
2.3 times, 1.5 times, and 3.3 times higher than the least productive categories.

with fixed premises and permanent structures. On the contrary, the other category of firms operating from a location that is outside the household premises but with temporary structures (OH-TEMP) is the least productive among the four categories. Does this imply that operating from fixed premises and having a permanent structure is essential for improving growth and productivity? This is not clearly evident from our analysis as STREETVEND, the category in which most firms are without fixed premises, is the second most productive category of firms across all the three types of enterprises.

Also, the rural–urban variation in firm size is analysed across different locational categories of informal sector firms. Figure 4.10 makes it evident that firms located in urban areas are on an average larger in size as compared to those that operate from rural areas for *all* categories except the OH-TEMP category. In OH-TEMP category, rural enterprises are larger in size and the estimates suggest that an

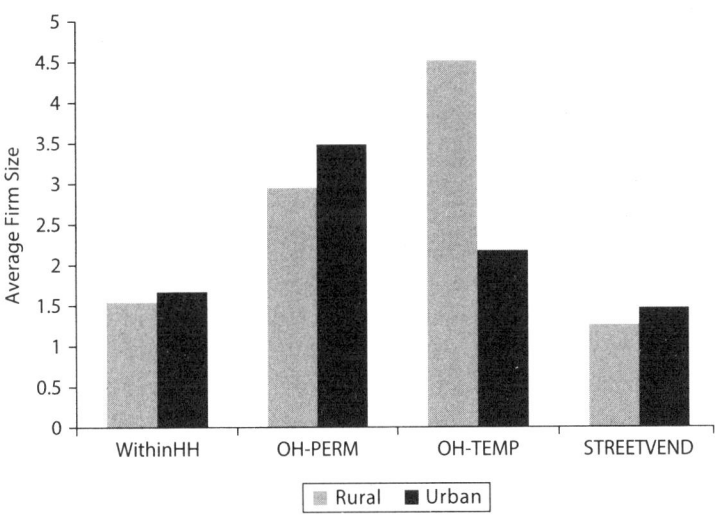

Figure 4.10 Firm Size by Location and Sector: 2010–11
Source: Authors' computations based on NSSO data.
Note: WithinHH, OH-PERM, OH-TEMP, and STREETVEND stand for firms that operate from within the household, firms with fixed premises and permanent structure, firms with fixed premises but temporary structure, and firms that shift from market to market and street vendors, respectively.

average firm in rural areas is two times bigger than an average firm in urban areas.

Sources of Funds

We now look at the sources of external funds for family and non-family firms. An important feature of the changing financial landscape in India has been the decline in the importance of informal sources of finance over time, which fell from 70.8 per cent in 1971 to 39.6 per cent in 1991 as a share of total debt (Tsai 2004). This has been a consequence of the government requirement to banks to lend to small enterprises and agricultural households, as well as the mandated branch expansion policy where the Reserve Bank of India required banks to open branches in rural and semi-urban areas which were under-banked at that time.[6] Table 4.3 shows that informal sector firms are heavily reliant on external funds both from institutional and non-institutional sources, and this is true of both family and non-family firms. In 2010–11, institutional agencies combined provided 60.5 per cent of all loans to family firms, and the corresponding figure for NDMEs and DMEs were 72.7 and 73.5 per cent, respectively (Table 4.3). A large proportion of borrowing from institutional sources was from commercial banks. Informal sector firms also depended on moneylenders and friends and relatives for funds to finance their business-related operations. In 2010–11, moneylenders provided 25.3 per cent of all loans to OAMEs, 16.8 per cent to NDMEs, and 13.3 per cent to DMEs. In the case of loans from friends and relatives, the corresponding figures were 9.6 per cent for OAMEs, 6.3 per cent for NDMEs, and 7.0 for DMEs (Table 4.3). This indicates that family firms were more reliant on funding from non-institutional sources than non-family firms. On the whole, it can be seen that a significant proportion of external funds for informal sector firms emerged from term-lending institutions including commercial banks and other institutional agencies.

---

[6] However, Sen and Ghosh (2005) note that the share of lending to small enterprises in total bank lending to priority sectors may have declined over time.

Table 4.3 Loan Share by Source and Enterprise Type: 2000–1 to 2010–11 (in per cent)

Source of Loan	2000–1			2005–6			2010–11		
	OAME	NDME	DME	OAME	NDME	DME	OAME	NDME	DME
Institutional agencies such as central- and state-level term lending institutions, government and commercial banks	60.4	69.7	70.1	47.7	57.9	58.6	58.9	69.8	72.5
Other institutional agencies	2.3	2.6	4.7	4.3	5.7	7.1	1.6	2.9	1.0
Money lenders	21.0	11.3	9.5	16.5	12.9	10.0	25.3	16.8	13.3
Business partner(s)	0.2	2.3	2.4	2.2	2.1	7.2	0.1	0.3	2.7
Suppliers / contractors	2.6	1.9	2.9	2.0	2.0	2.2	2.5	2.8	1.0
Friends and relatives	12.1	10.8	7.4	21.0	10.6	8.2	9.6	6.3	7.0
Others	1.4	1.4	3.1	6.2	8.9	6.7	2.1	1.0	2.6
Total	100.0	100.0	100.0	100.0	100.0	100.0	100.0	100.0	100.0

Source: Authors' calculations based on NSSO data.

Note: Loans advanced by institutions/agencies such as Khadi and Village Industries Commission, Life Insurance Corporation, provident fund, and chit fund are included under the category 'other institutional agencies'.

Capital Intensity

It is also clearly evident from the analysis that the amount of capital employed per unit of labour input[7] increases with the size of the firm in the informal sector. Figure 4.11 clearly shows that capital–labour ratio (CLR) is higher for NDMEs and DMEs than for OAMEs. It is also found that there has been a consistent increase in CLR in all the types of enterprises over the period 2000–1 to 2010–11. During this period, the CLR increased the fastest in the OAMEs (3.3 times), followed by the NDMEs (2.6 times) and the DMEs (2.1 times). Interestingly, for the terminal year of our analysis, that is, 2010–11, the CLR for the NDMEs was marginally higher than that of the DMEs. Overall, we find a consistent increase in CLR for all the three types of enterprises between 2000–1 and 2010–11. This may considerably explain the observed increase in labour productivity that was noted earlier in the chapter. Further disaggregation of fixed capital investment into investment in

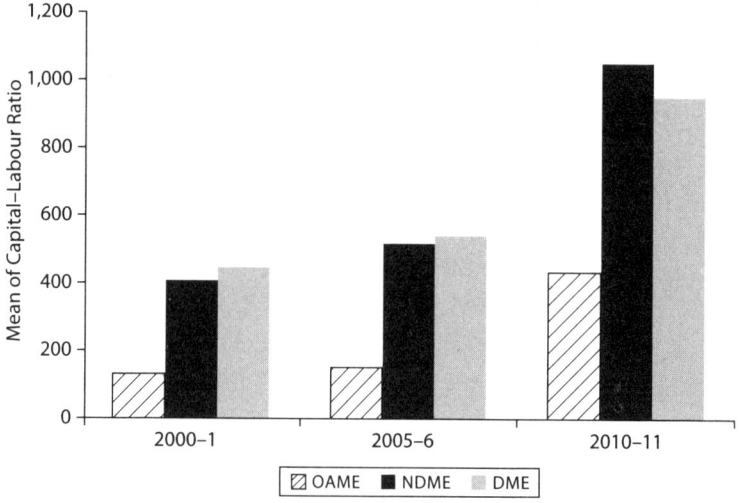

Figure 4.11   Capital–Labour Ratio (in '00s) by Enterprise Type and Year: 2000–1 to 2010–11
Source: Authors' computations based on NSSO data.

---

[7] We also use capital–labour ratio and capital intensity in this study to indicate capital employed per unit of labour input.

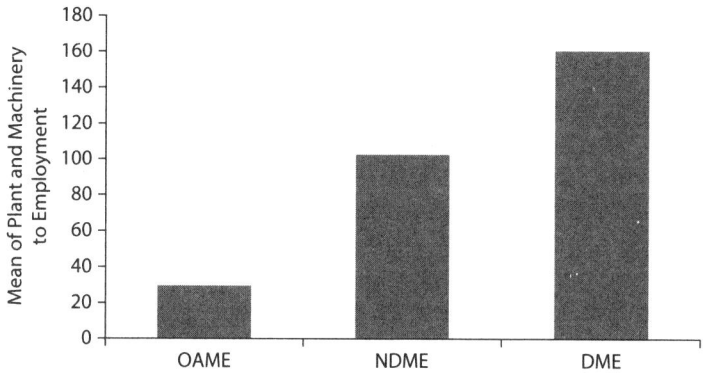

Figure 4.12   Mean Plant and Machinery to Employment by Enterprise Type (in '00s): 2010–11
Source: Authors' computations based on NSSO data.

plant and machinery and investment in land and buildings yields very interesting results. Results show that DMEs are more intensive in plant and machinery (Figure 4.12) and that NDMEs are more intensive in structures investment (Figure 4.13).

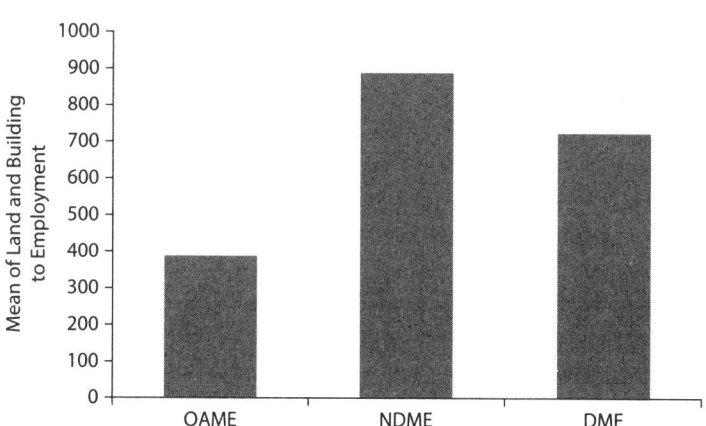

Figure 4.13   Mean Land and Building to Employment by Enterprise Type (in '00s): 2010–11
Source: Authors' computations based on NSSO data.

Firm's Age

We now examine whether the age of the enterprise is correlated with firm size. The available evidence points to a negative relationship between age and growth of the firm (Sleuwaegen and Goedhuys 2002). In the case of India too, a negative association between age and firm growth is reported by Deshpande and Sharma (2013). In the latest round for the period 2010–11, the NSSO reports the year of initial operation of firms they surveyed. The age of the firms is arrived at based on the numbers of years since commencement of its operation. The analysis here does not show the age of the enterprise as a significant factor influencing firm size in the informal sector. If age has an influence on size, then the average age should increase with firm size. As is evident from Figure 4.14, the average age of the enterprise does not show any significant difference across the different types of enterprises. We also examine whether there is any relationship between age and labour productivity. The scatter plot in Figure 4.15 shows absence of any relationship between age and labour productivity in the informal sector in India.

Social Group of the Firm Owner

This section examines the nature of the relationship between the social group of the firm owner and the firm size. An earlier literature has pointed out that enterprises owned by Scheduled Castes (SCs) and Scheduled Tribes (STs) are under-represented in the population of small and medium enterprises, and that they tend to be smaller in size as compared to enterprises owned by other social groups (Deshpande and Sharma 2013; Iyer et al. 2013). The SCs and STs are also over-represented in occupations which have the highest rates of poverty (such as agricultural labour in rural areas and casual workers in urban areas), and there is mixed evidence on the degree of occupational mobility that these social groups have witnessed in recent years, especially in the post-reform period. For example, using quinquennial NSSO employment surveys, Hnatkovska et al. (2012) find significant convergence of occupation and wages of SC and ST groups towards non-SC/ST levels in the period 1983–2005. Similarly, using primary data from UP, Kapur et al. (2010) find clear mobility of SCs from being agricultural labourers to being owners of OAMEs. Gang

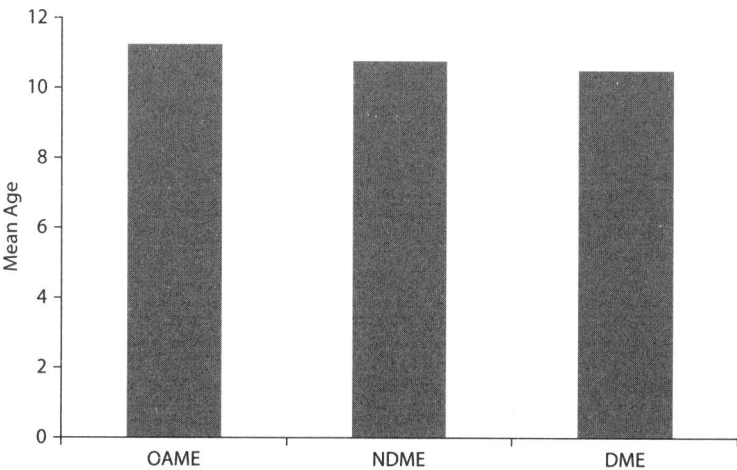

Figure 4.14 Age by Enterprise Type: 2010–11
Source: Authors' computations based on NSSO data.

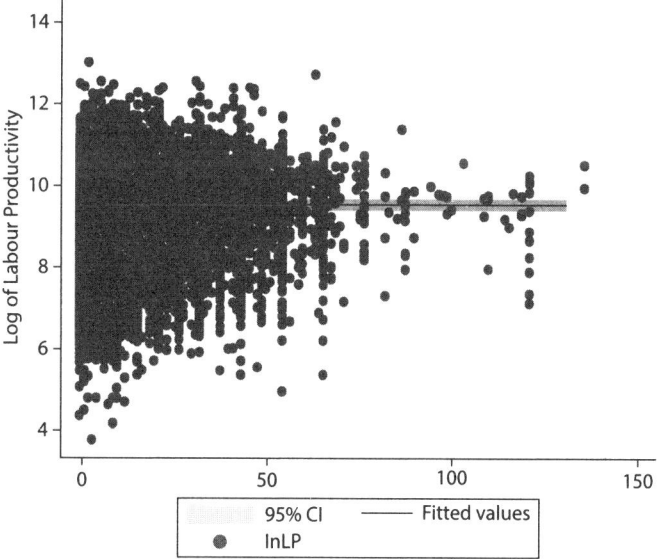

Figure 4.15 Scatter Plot of Labour Productivity by Age: 2010–11
Source: Authors' computations based on NSSO data.
Note: We use logarithm of labour productivity levels (lnLP).

et al. (2012) find evidence of occupational convergence among SCs towards non-SCs/STs, but not STs in rural areas. On the other hand, Thorat and Newman (2012) find that social and economic discrimination significantly restricts the mobility of SCs and their entry into 'non-traditional' occupations.

To investigate whether differences can be observed in firm size and productivity between firms owned by SCs, STs, and other social groups, we use the NSSO's survey for the period 2010–11, which has collected information on the social group of the owner of the enterprise. Using this information, the firms are classified into four: (a) firms owned by those belonging to the general category; (b) firms owned by Other Backward Classes (OBCs); (c) firms owned by SCs; and (d) firms owned by STs. The results with regard to the relationship between the social group of the owner and the firm size are in line with the expectations. The average size of the firm is higher for firms that are owned by those who belong to the general and ST categories, followed by firms owned by OBCs and SCs in the DME category, with very little difference in the size of the OAME and NDME categories across social groups (Figure 4.16). With respect to labour productivity, firms owned by the general and OBC social groups are more productive than firms owned by SC and ST across all three types of enterprises. The fact that ST-owned firms are not as productive as those owned by the general category social group, even though both sets of firms are of the same size on an average, suggests that there are other constraints to productivity that are not linked to size for the ST-owned firms (Figure 4.17). Overall, the evidence presented here shows very clear differences in firm size and productivity, with the SCs (and STs, in the case of productivity) being the most disadvantaged, followed by the OBCs, and with the firms owned by the general category group (forward castes, along with non Hindus who are also non SC, ST and OBC) being the largest in size and being the most productive.

Education of Owner and Firm Size

Previous studies on informal sector firms for other developing countries find that firms with better educated owners tend to improve in

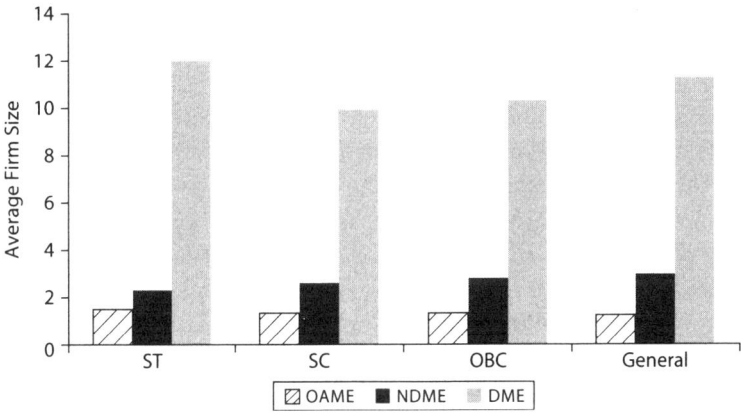

Figure 4.16   Firm Size by Enterprise Type and Caste: 2010–11
Source: Authors' computations based on NSSO data.
Note: SC, ST, and OBC stand for scheduled caste, scheduled tribe, and other backward classes, respectively. General denotes those who do not belong to SC, ST, and OBC.

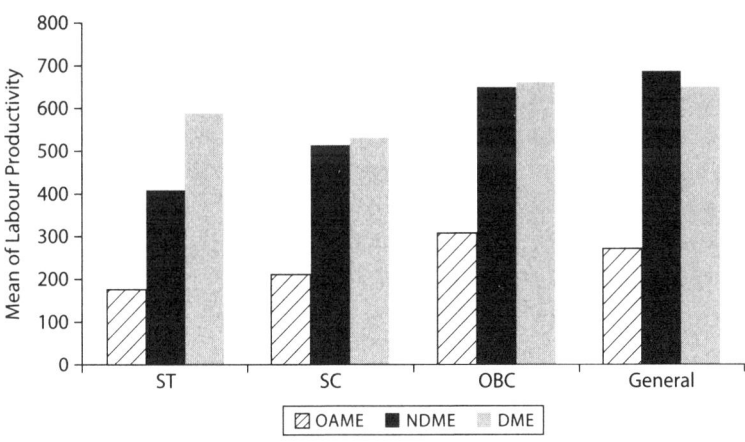

Figure 4.17   Labour Productivity by Enterprise Type and Caste: 2010–11
Source: Authors' computations based on NSSO data.
Note: SC, ST, and OBC stand for scheduled caste, scheduled tribe, and other backward classes, respectively. General denotes those who do not belong to SC, ST, and OBC.

size and productivity as compared to firms with less educated owners (Sonobe et al. 2011). Is this also the case in India? This relationship is examined using the 62nd Round of NSSO surveys on the unorganized manufacturing sector for the period 2005–6, which provides information on the educational qualification of the owner of the firms surveyed. Based on the educational qualification of the owners, the firms are divided into four: (a) firms whose owners who are not educated; (b) firms whose owners are educated up to the primary level; (c) firms whose owners are educated up to the higher secondary level; and (d) firms whose owners have a postgraduate degree and above. We first examine the relationship between firm size and educational qualification of the owner and find that average size of the firm increases with the education qualification of the owner. Figure 4.18 shows that firms that are owned by those with postgraduate degree and above are larger in size as compared to

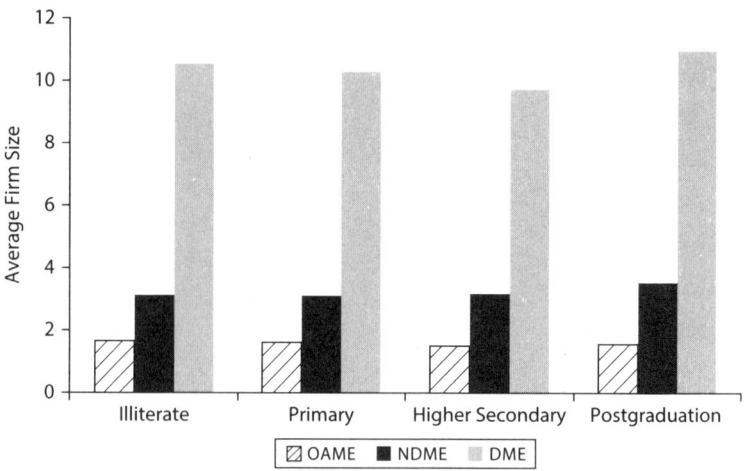

Figure 4.18 Firm Size by Education and Enterprise Type: 2005–6
Source: Authors' computations based on NSSO data.
Note: Illiterate stands for firm owners who are not educated, primary stands for owners who are educated up to primary level, higher secondary refers to owners who have educated up to higher secondary level, and postgraduation refers to owners with postgraduation and above.

other categories. Interestingly, it is found that the next category in terms of size is firms owned by the illiterates. Evidence can be clearly seen in favour of returns to education across OAMEs, NDMEs, and DMEs when the educational qualification of the owner is related with labour productivity (Figure 4.19). Labour productivity is considerably higher for firms run by owners having postgraduate degree and above. This finding is consistent across all types of enterprise in the informal sector.

Wages, Firm Size, and Productivity

How do wages paid to workers differ by the types of firms? Do wages differ by firm ownership and social group of the owner? And, are the most productive firms paying the highest wages? We address

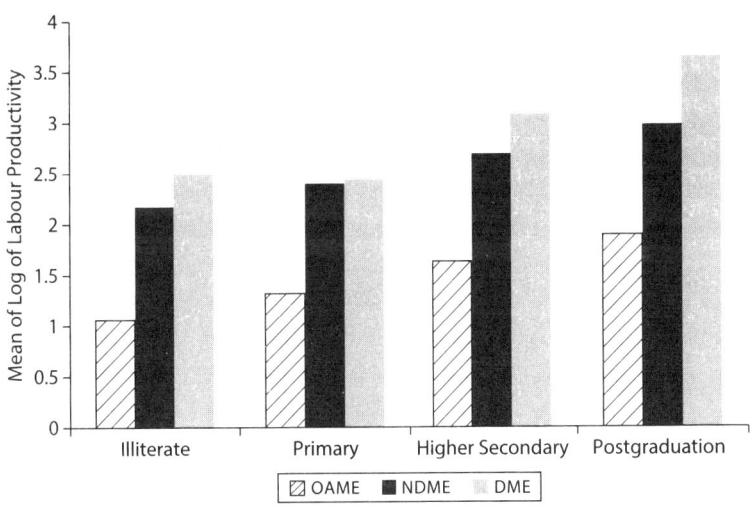

Figure 4.19   Labour Productivity by Education and Enterprise Type: 2005–6
Source: Authors' computations based on NSSO data.
Note: Illiterate stands for firm owners who are not educated, primary stands for owners who are educated up to primary level, higher secondary refers to owners who have educated up to higher secondary level, and postgraduation refers to owners with postgraduation and above.

these questions here. The measure of wages here includes wages and salaries payable in cash or in kind and excludes the value of social contributions paid by the employer.[8] We use real wages, which are obtained by deflating nominal wages with consumer price index (CPI) for industrial workers at 1993–4 prices. Clear evidence can be found for the fact that DMEs pay the highest wages, followed by NDMEs, and then OAMEs. In fact, DMEs pay more than 14 times the wages paid in OAMEs and about two times more than the wages paid in NDMEs, thereby indicating how important it is for firms to move from OAMEs to DMEs in order to increase the living conditions of the workers employed in these enterprises (Figure 4.20). It is also seen that wages paid by partnership firms are much higher than those paid by firms owned solely by female and male proprietors (Figure 4.21). In line with the expectations, male proprietorship firms pay higher wages than female proprietorship firms. Looking at the

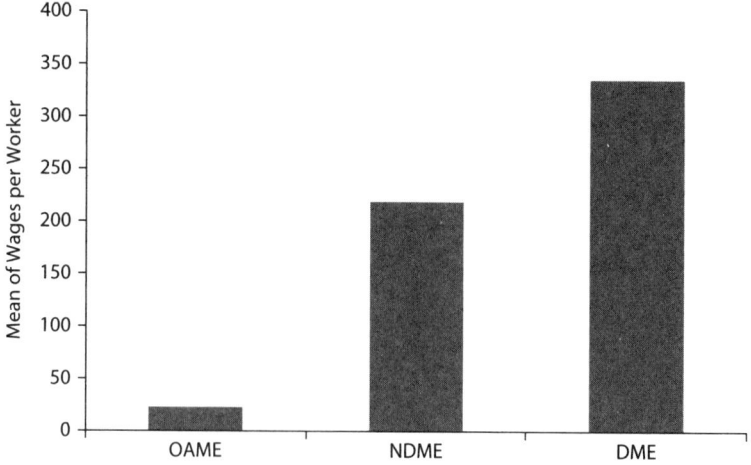

Figure 4.20   Wages per Worker by Enterprise Type: 2010–11
Source: Authors' computations based on NSSO data.

[8] The caveat here is that OAMEs mostly use family labour, and so these include only wages and benefits for working owners.

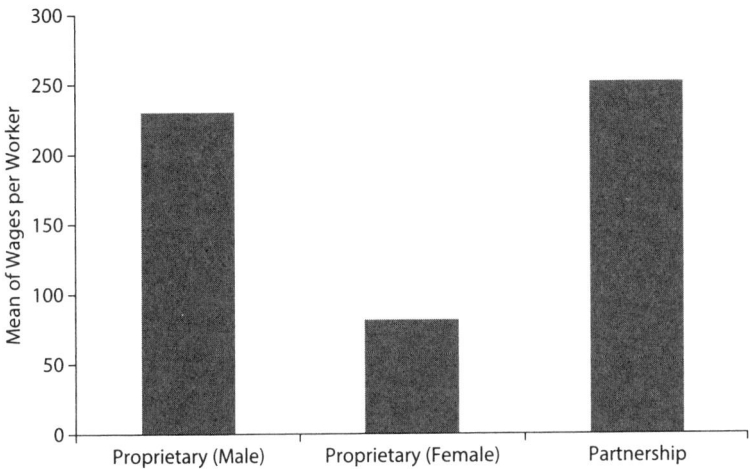

Figure 4.21   Wages per Worker by Ownership Type: 2010–11
Source: Authors' computations based on NSSO data.
Note: Proprietary (Male) refers to proprietorships with male owners, Proprietary
(Female) refers to proprietorships with female owners, and Partnership stands for
firms that operate on a partnership basis (meaning firms with two or more owners).

wages paid by the type of the firm and the social group of owner, we
found that for DMEs, firms owned by the OBCs pays the highest wages,
followed by firms owned by STs, firms owned by general category social
group, and firms owned by SCs, in that order. This is a somewhat surprising finding, as it has already been observed that DMEs owned by
the general category group are the most productive. The correlation
between the wages paid and the social position of the owner is more
for NDMEs, with firms owned by OBCs and the general category
social group paying higher wages than those owned by STs and SCs
(Figure 4.22). However, in the case of OAMEs, where much of the
wages are own payments to firm owners, there is weak correlation
between wages and the relative position of the social group of the
firm owner in the caste hierarchy.

  Finally, evidence is found for clear positive relationships between
wages paid to workers and firm productivity, and wages paid to workers
and firm size (Figures 4.23 and 4.24). In fact, the relationship between
wages and firm productivity is particularly strong, indicating the

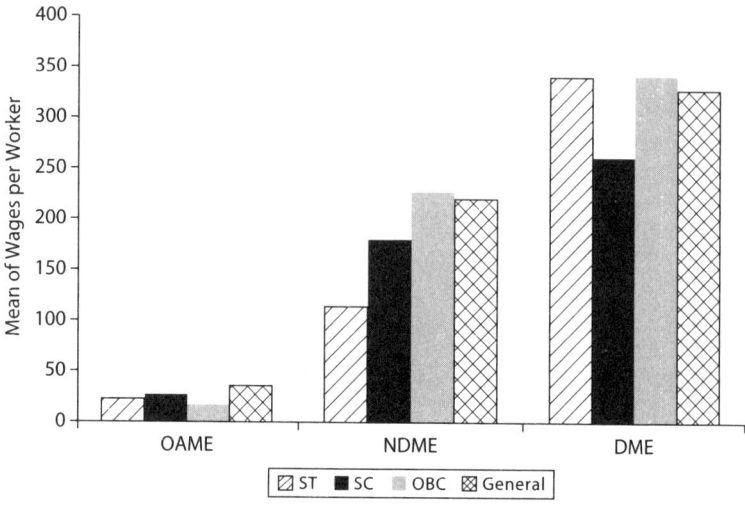

Figure 4.22 Wages per Worker by Caste and Enterprise Type: 2010–11
Source: Authors' computations based on NSSO data.
Note: SC, ST, and OBC stand for scheduled caste, scheduled tribe, and other
backward classes, respectively. General denotes those who do not belong to SC, ST,
and OBC.

importance of improving firm productivity in the Indian informal sector as a means to improve the living standards of the workers employed
in the informal sector.

We end our discussion of wages paid to workers and its relationship
with certain firm characteristics with a simple multivariate regression
analysis of the correlates of wages across different firms in the Indian
informal manufacturing sector. Our dependent variable is firm-level
wages per worker, and we include the firm size, the social group of
the owner, the gender of the owner, and the location of the firm as
the explanatory variables on the right hand side of the regression
function. We anticipate a positive relationship between the size of
the firm and wages paid to the worker. To be specific, it is expected
that the wages per worker increases with the size of the firm. Two
proxies are included to represent firm size. Model 1 includes, two
enterprise-type dummy variables, NDME and DME, with the
residual category being OAME. In this case, the coefficient values

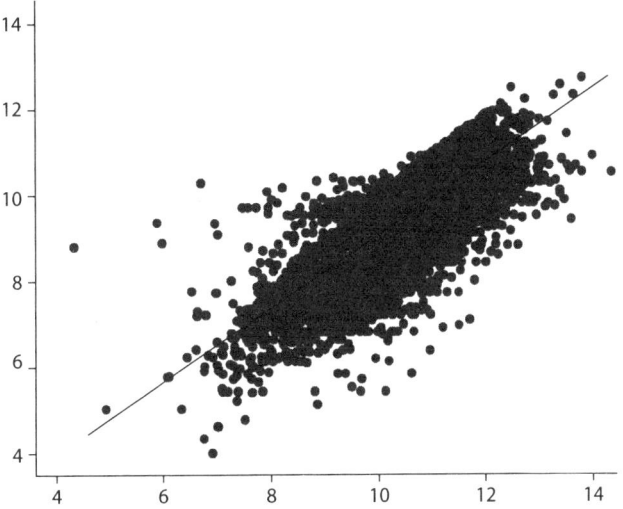

Figure 4.23 Scatter Plot of Relationship between Wages per Worker and Labour Productivity:, 2010–11
Source: Authors' computations based on NSSO data.

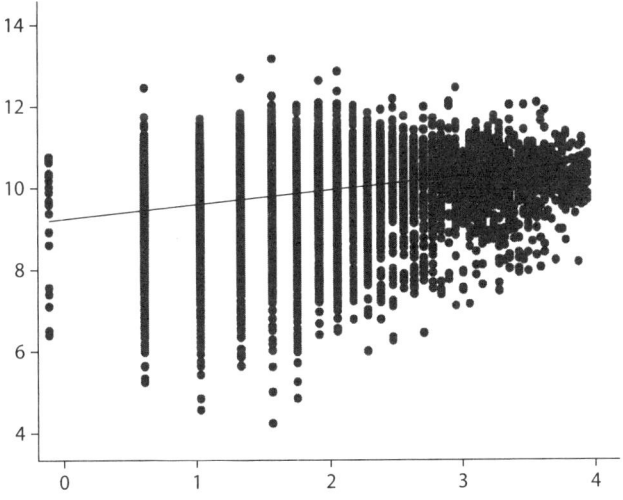

Figure 4.24 Scatter Plot of Relationship between Wages per Worker and Firm Size: 2010–11
Source: Authors' computations based on NSSO data.

of DME and NDME are expected to be positive and significant, and that of DME to be higher than NDME. In Model 2, the enterprise-type dummies are replaced with log of number of workers. In this case too, the coefficient value of firm size is anticipated to be positive and significant. Three dummy variables—SC, ST, and OBC—are introduced to capture the effect of the social group of the owner on wages per worker, with the general category social group being the residual category. As observed in the earlier descriptive analysis, it is expected that the workers in firms with owners belonging to the general category will have higher wages than in firms with owners from OBC, SC, and ST categories, and therefore the coefficients of OBC, SC, and ST are expected to be negative and significant. The variable FEMALE is also introduced to understand the effect of the firm owner's gender on wages per worker. Based on our earlier discussion, the coefficient of FEMALE is anticipated to be negative and significant. To examine the role of location of the firm on wages per worker, three dummy variables are included—OH-PERM, OH-TEMP, and STREETVEND—with WithinHH as the residual category. Our conjecture is that the workers in firms with fixed premises and permanent structures will have higher wages as compared to workers in other categories.

Some firm-specific control variables that are likely to affect the effect of the main variables on wages per worker are also included. These control variables are SECTOR, LINKAGE, FEMALE, REGIS, ASSISTANCE, AGE, MIDGRADEDU, and URBAN. The NSSO surveys report whether the firms are located in rural or urban areas. SECTOR takes the value 1 if the firm is located in urban areas, and 0 if it is located in rural areas. The inclusion of SECTOR is expected to capture differences among firms in terms of access to better infrastructure, and larger markets for skilled labour, raw materials and outputs, and the effect of these on wages per worker. In its surveys, the NSSO asks the firms whether they work solely for a contractor (that is, whether it sells all its output to the contractor, who usually, in this tied arrangement, supplies it with inputs). We name this variable LINKAGE and it is coded as 1 if these firms work for a contractor and 0 if they do not. The conjecture is that the firms that work for contractors are more likely to pay higher wages as they may be needing workers with specialized skills. We argue that being registered under an act/authority could help the firm's owner–manager to access and secure a range of financial resources, which could reflect in higher wages. The variable REGIS, which takes the value 1 if they report that they have registered under any act and 0 if they have not registered under any act, control for this possibility. A positive relationship is hypothesized between REGIS and wages per worker. The variable ASSISTANCE takes the value 1 if the firm received any assistance from the government towards training and marketing and 0 if they state that they did not receive any such assistance. It is expected that any such type of assistance will be positively associated with wages per worker.

We also include some district-level controls such as the level of urbanization in the district as measured by the share of urban population in the total population (URBAN) and the proportion of individuals educated at secondary level and above (MIDGRADEDU). We expected that a higher level of urbanization in a district and a higher level of human capital as measured by high MIDGRADEDU would have a positive effect on wages per worker. We use industry-specific effects to capture the possibilities that wages per worker in larger size enterprises would be likely to be higher in industries with economies of scale such as metal, chemicals, and automobiles.

Our results are reported in Table 4.4. Strikingly, we find across all two models that wages per worker increases with firm size. This is found to be valid irrespective of whether the enterprise dummies (NDME and DME) or log of number of workers is used as proxy for firm size. As expected, the results clearly showed that social group of the firm owner is an important determinant of wages per worker for firms in the informal sector. The coefficients of SC and ST variables were negative and significant, suggesting that workers in firms with owners from SC and ST social groups are paid wages lower than in firms with owners from OBC and general category social groups. Our computations suggest that workers in firms headed by those from SC and ST social groups would be paid 13 and 28 per cent lower than the workers in firms with owners from general category (based on Model 1). On the other hand, the coefficient of OBC is positive and significant, suggesting that wages per worker is higher in firms with owners from OBCs as compared to firms headed by owners from the general category social group. There is also evidence that location of the firm is a significant

Table 4.4   Correlates of Wages per Worker: 2010–11

Variables	Model 1	Model 2
Dependant Variable: Log of Wages per Worker		
NDME	0.1888***	
	(0.0391)	
DME	0.5470***	
	(0.0403)	
Size		0.2583***
		(0.0072)
SC	−0.1327***	−0.1124***
	(0.0168)	(0.0165)
ST	−0.2822***	−0.2533***
	(0.0368)	(0.0369)
OBC	0.0470***	0.0575***
	(0.0085)	(0.0084)
OH-PERM	0.2305***	0.2162***
	(0.0106)	(0.0105)
OH-TEMP	−0.2610***	−0.2338***
	(0.0320)	(0.0319)
STREETVEND	0.0324	0.0434
	(0.0402)	(0.0397)
FEMALE	−0.1917***	−0.1812***
	(0.0207)	(0.0204)
Firm-specific Control Variables		
SECTOR	0.1103***	0.1259***
	(0.0085)	(0.0084)
LINKAGE	−0.0056	−0.0094
	(0.0158)	(0.0156)
REGIS	0.2772***	0.2649***
	(0.0087)	(0.0086)
ASSISTANCE	0.0669***	0.0623***
	(0.0210)	(0.0211)
AGE	−0.0045	−0.0049
	(0.0046)	(0.0046)
District-specific Control Variables		
MIDGRADEDU	1.1940***	1.1186***
	(0.0352)	(0.0360)

Urban	0.1239***	0.1273***
	(0.0099)	(0.0097)
Constant	8.4626***	8.4096***
	(0.2024)	(0.2106)
Industry Dummy	Y	Y
N	29661	29661
F	266.07	272.60
R^2	0.2566	0.2671

Source: Authors' calculations based on NSSO data.

Notes: (a) Figures in parentheses are robust standard errors;

     (b) *** indicate significance at minimum 1 per cent.

factor influencing wages paid to workers in informal sector firms. In line with the expectations, workers in firms that operated from fixed premises and had a permanent structure received higher wages as compared to firms that operated from within the household and firms that have a temporary structure. We find that the wage rate of workers in OH-PERM firms was 23 per cent higher than that in WithinHH firms. The negative and significant coefficient of OH-TEMP indicates that workers in OH-TEMP firms were paid wages lower than workers in firms operating from within the household. We also examined whether the gender of the owner plays any crucial role in influencing wages per worker in the sector. The estimations clearly suggest that there is a difference in wages rate between workers in firms with male owners and in firms with female owners. The variable FEMALE that stands for the gender of the owner has a negative and significant coefficient indicating that wage rate is lower for workers in female-headed firms as compared to workers in male-headed firms. Workers in a female-headed firm are paid 19 per cent less wages than what they would have earned if they were in a male-headed firm. The control variables are having the expected signs. We find that wages are higher in urban firms, firm that are registered, firms that received any type of assistance, and firms that are located in districts that are urbanized and have higher level of human capital.

We also perform a similar regression analysis of the correlates of firm productivity to see whether the correlates of wages differ

Table 4.5   Correlates of Labour Productivity: 2010–11

Variable	Model 1
Dependent Variable: Log of Labour Productivity	
NDME	0.2298***
	(0.0342)
DME	0.1579***
	(0.0355)
SC	–0.1089***
	(0.0147)
ST	–0.1719***
	(0.0332)
OBC	0.0403***
	(0.0078)
OH-PERM	0.2074***
	(0.0094)
OH-TEMP	–0.2462***
	(0.0296)
STREETVEND	–0.0646*
	(0.0336)
FEMALE	–0.2074***
	(0.0190)
Firm-specific Control Variables	
SECTOR	0.1706***
	(0.0076)
LINKAGE	–0.1541***
	(0.0151)
REGIS	0.2673***
	(0.0078)
ASSISTANCE	0.0918***
	(0.0237)
AGE	–0.0059
	(0.0042)
District-specific Control Variables	
MIDGRADEDU	0.5975***
	(0.0323)

URBAN	0.1415***
	(0.0090)
Constant	9.9604***
	(0.2235)
Industry Dummy	Y
N	29661
F	191.45
R^2	0.2170

Source: Authors' calculations based on NSSO data.

Notes: (a) Figures in parentheses are robust standard errors;

     (b) *** indicate significance at minimum 1 per cent level.

significantly from the correlates of firm productivity. We present our results in Table 4.5 and they unambiguously confirm that the sign, significance, and direction of correlates of firm productivity are as same as observed for wages. It was found that large firms (NDMEs and DMEs) are more productive than smaller firms (OAMEs); labour productivity is relatively higher for firms headed by those from the general category social group (but wages per worker in OBC-headed firms are actually higher than in firms headed by members of the general category social group); workers in firms that are operating from fixed premises and having a permanent structure are more productive than workers in firms that are operating from within the household and firms that have a temporary structure (the former is 20 per cent more productive than the latter); and female-headed firms are 20 per cent less productive than male-headed firms. Interestingly, it is found that firms which have entered into subcontracting relationship (LINKAGE = 1) are less productive than firms which have not.

We also find that productivity is higher for urban firms, firms that are registered, firms that received any type of assistance, and firms that are located in districts that are urbanized and have a higher level of human capital (as captured by MIDGRADEDU). The analysis suggests that the most effective way to increase the wages of informal workers is to increase the productivity of the enterprises they work in, and that the larger these enterprises are, the more productive they are. Government schemes that provide assistance to informal enterprises to invest in permanent structures are also important in increasing their productivity and, thereby, the wages of the workers they employ. However, our analysis also shows that there are social and economic barriers to informal enterprises in increasing their productivity—controlling for other factors, enterprises owned by members of disadvantaged social groups such as the SC and ST, and female-owned enterprises are less productive than those headed by the OBC and general category social groups, and by males. Given that the highest incidence of poverty is among the SCs and the STs, the existence of barriers to the growth of firms that are owned by these social groups is a matter of major policy concern. Furthermore, gender-related differences in the productivity of firms suggest that female entrepreneurs may be disadvantaged in their access to output and input markets relative to male entrepreneurs. This again suggests that public policy interventions may be needed to address the disadvantages that female entrepreneurs face in the informal manufacturing sector in India.

Interlinkages between Informal and Formal Sector Firms

There is now an emerging literature which looks at the determinants of outsourcing by multinationals and the determinants of subcontracting by family and non-family firms in developed countries (Feenstra and Hanson 2005; Memili et al. 2011). Surprisingly, little is known about the determinants of subcontracting of firms in India. Yet, there is growing evidence of increasing use of informal sector firms by formal sector firms as providers of specialized inputs, and as a source of cheap labour (Ghani et al. 2013). The NSSO surveys ask firms in the informal sector whether they are engaged in any subcontracting activity. We use this information to gain some insights on the variation in subcontracting across different firm types, and the possible determinants of subcontracting by informal sector firms in India. Figure 4.25 shows that the majority of informal sector firms in India do not have any linkage or subcontracting relationship with formal sector firms (here, the variable LINKAGE is coded 1 if the firm in question states that it has a linkage with a formal firm and coded 0 if it states that it does not). However, OAMEs are more likely to be engaged in this relationship than NDMEs and DMEs. Interestingly, firms which are in subcontracting relationship are less productive than

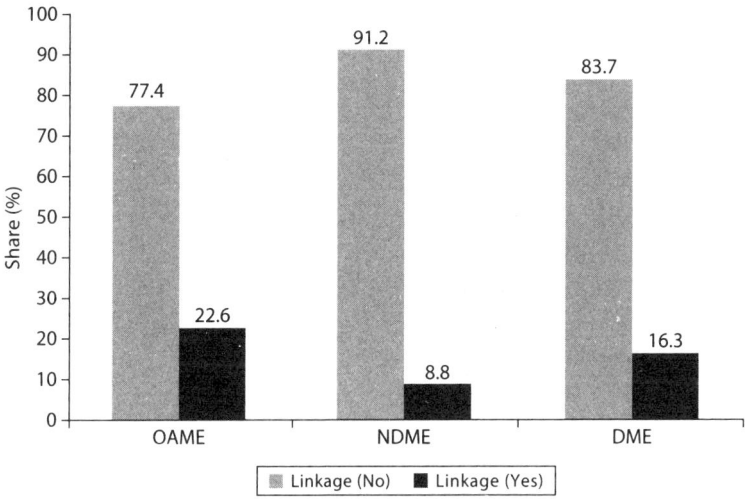

Figure 4.25 Linkage by Enterprise Type: 2010–11
Source: Authors' computations based on NSSO data.

those which are not, and this is true for all three types of firms (see Figure 4.26). This provides some preliminary evidence that subcontracting has not been of substantial benefit to the informal sector firms which have entered into such a relationship. To get a sense of the factors that determine whether a firm enters into a subcontracting relationship or not, we ran a probit regression with the variable Linkage on the left hand side, and the following variables on the right hand side: firm size (NDME and DME, with OAME being the residual category), social group (SC, ST, and OBC, with the general category social group being the residual category), location of the firm (OH-PERM, OH-TEMP, and STREETVEND, with WithinHH being the residual category), the gender of the owner (FEMALE = 1 for female-headed firms), SECTOR, REGIS, ASSISTANCE, PMLAB, MIDGRADEDU, and URBAN. All these variables have been defined before expect PMLAB. PMLAB stands for ratio of investment in plant and machinery to labour. As mentioned before, the expectation is that the DMEs and the NDMEs are more likely to be engaged in subcontracting relationships than OAMEs. By introducing dummy variables

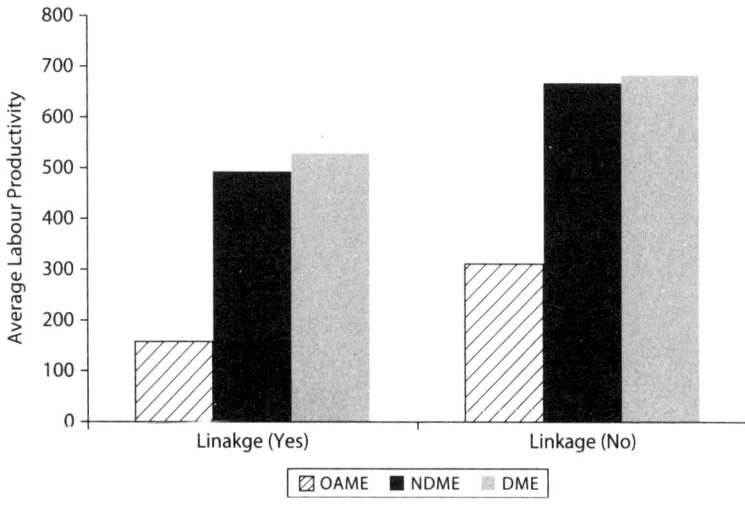

Figure 4.26   Labour Productivity (in '00s) by Enterprise Type and Linkage: 2010–11
Source: Authors' computations based on NSSO data.

for social groups, we aimed to see whether the social group of the owner played any crucial role in the decision of the firm owner to establish subcontracting relationship with firms. We also looked at the relationship between location of firms and their decision to build sub-contracting relationships with other firms. We also examine whether subcontracting relationships are higher among firms with fixed premises and permanent structures as compared to other categories of firms. We included the variable FEMALE to ascertain whether subcontracting relationships are more evident among male-headed firms or female-headed firms. We also test whether subcontracting relationships are higher among urban firms, firms that are registered, firms that receive any type of assistance, and firms that are located in districts with higher level of human capital.

The results are presented in Table 4.6. As anticipated, the coeffi-cients of NDME and DME are positive and significant, indicating that bigger firms (NDMEs and DMEs) are more likely to be engaged in sub-contracting relationships than smaller firms (OAMEs) after taking into

Table 4.6 Probit Regression—Determinants of Subcontracting: 2010–11

Variable	Coefficients
Dependant Variable: LINKAGE	
NDME	0.2339***
	(0.0209)
DME	0.5055***
	(0.0278)
SC	–0.0496**
	(0.0251)
ST	–0.5303***
	(0.0587)
OBC	–0.0625***
	(0.0162)
OH-PERM	–0.4140***
	(0.0200)
OH-TEMP	–0.8299***
	(0.0840)
STREETVEND	–0.4246***
	(0.0918)
SECTOR	–0.0225
	(0.0155)
FEMALE	0.1447***
	(0.0193)
REGIS	0.0608***
	(0.0208)
ASSISTANCE	–0.1387***
	(0.0437)
PMLAB	0.0001***
	(0.0000)
MIDGRADEDU	0.0497
	(0.0732)
URBAN	0.0964***
	(0.0190)
Constant	–6.3997***
	(0.2946)
Industry Dummy	Yes

(*Contd.*)

Table **4.6**   (*Contd.*)

Variable	Coefficients
Dependant Variable: LINKAGE	
N	88352
LR chi^2	15,192.39
Prob > chi^2	0.0000
Pseudo R^2	0.2988

Source: Authors' calculations based on NSSO data.
Notes: (a) Figures in parentheses are robust standard errors;
     (b) *** indicate significance at minimum 1 per cent level.

account all other factors. Comparing the magnitude of the coefficients of NDME and DME, we found that within the bigger enterprises, DMEs are more likely to be engaged in subcontracting relationships than NDMEs. For formal sector enterprises which are engaged in subcontracting relationships with informal sector firms, it is more likely that they will seek out the larger enterprises in the informal sector, who tend to be more established and would be able to invest in the specific assets that are needed to produce customized goods for the formal sector (Berry et al. 2002). The results clearly showed that the social group of the owner does matter in forging subcontracting relationships with other firms. We found that the subcontracting relationships are more evident among firms that are owned by those who belong to the general category social group. This may simply be a consequence of the fact that firms owned by the general category social group tend to be more productive, as was found earlier. The estimations also show that subcontracting relationships are more evident among firms that operate from within household premises. This is a surprising finding, and it may reflect the increasing use of home-based workers engaged in contractual relationships with large retailers in industries, such as garments where there has been an expansion of small-scale power loom workshops in recent years (Breman 2010; Carswell and De Neve 2013). This may also explain why it is found that female-headed firms are more successful in building subcontracting relationships with other firms as compared to male-headed firms, since most of the workers in home-based power loom workshops tend to be women (De Neve 2005). The results with regard to REGIS, URBAN, and PMLAB are on expected lines, which shows that firms that are registered, firms that are located in districts that are urbanized are more likely to enter into subcontracting relationships with other firms. This may reflect the fact that registered informal sector firms located in urbanized districts are easier to identify for formal sector firms to subcontract with. Moreover, formal sector firms which subcontract with informal sector firms are more likely to be found in more urbanized districts. Finally, we found that firms with higher capital labour ratios are engage in greater subcontracting relationships. Firms with higher levels of capital intensity would be more able to produce specialized inputs for the formal sector (Ghani et al. 2013). The findings suggest that the determinants of subcontracting are varied, and that both home-based enterprises and larger firms in the informal sector are likely to enter into subcontracting relationships more. However, as we saw in our discussion on the correlates of labour productivity, firms that enter into a subcontracting relationship are actually less productive than firms which do not enter into such a relationship. This suggests that the subcontracting relationship may not necessarily be beneficial to the informal sector firms in India, and is different to what has been observed in other developing countries such as Indonesia, where subcontracting seems to confer technology and upgrade benefits to the informal firm (see Berry et al. 2002).

☆   ☆   ☆

This chapter presents some stylized facts about firms in the Indian informal manufacturing sector, using unit-level record from the NSSO surveys of unorganized enterprises from 2000–1 to 2010–11. We first examined the evolution of firm size across the three different categories of firms in the Indian informal manufacturing sector—OAMEs, NDMEs, and DMEs—as well as across regions and product groups. We then made an attempt to understand whether there are observable differences in firm size and productivity across firms of different characteristics. Next, we tried to identify the firm characteristics that are most important in explaining variations in wages paid to workers in the Indian informal manufacturing sector. We also investigated the nature of interlinkages between informal and formal sector firms, and which are the factors that determine these interlinkages among firms in the sector.

The results point to a downward shift in the size of the average informal firm in the Indian manufacturing sector over time. We find average firm size declining in both OAMEs and NDMEs, and increasing in DMEs. Across ownership categories, firm size was considerably higher in firms that operate on a partnership basis as compared to firms that operate at the household level. Firms that operate from outside the household premises are found to be bigger in size as compared to firms that operate from within the household. In terms of labour productivity, there is an apparent inverted-U relationship between firm size and firm performance: productivity increases to large size till a certain point before stagnating or declining. Across the types of enterprises, OAMEs are the least productive, followed by NDMEs and DMEs. It is also found that productivity is the highest among firms that operate from fixed premises and have permanent structures.

The attempt here to understand the correlates of wages and labour productivity reveals that firm size, gender, and social group of the firm owner and location of the firm are important determinants of wages and labour productivity in the informal manufacturing sector. Our analysis clearly suggests that the most effective way to increase the wages of informal workers is to increase the productivity of the enterprises they work in, and that the larger these enterprises are, the more productive they are. However, the analysis also shows that there are social and economic barriers to informal enterprises in increasing their productivity—controlling for other factors, enterprises owned by members of disadvantaged social groups such as the SCs and STs, and female-owned enterprises are less productive than those headed by the OBCs and the general category social groups and by males. This suggests that targeted government programmes towards these groups may help in reducing the disparities in the wages of the workers employed in these enterprises with other informal workers.

Finally, the exploratory analysis of the nature of interlinkages between informal and formal sector firms indicates that both home-based enterprises and larger firms in the informal sector are likely to subcontract more, and that firms that enter into a subcontracting relationship are actually less productive than firms which do not enter into such a relationship. This suggests that entering into a subcontracting relationship is not necessarily a positive outcome for the firm in question. This may reflect the lack of investment that formal sector firms make in the informal sector firms—who supply inputs and raw materials to them—as well as the asymmetrical bargaining power that formal sector firms have in negotiating contracts that are not necessarily beneficial to informal sector firms in subcontracting relationships with formal sector firms.

5

THE PERFORMANCE OF INFORMAL MANUFACTURING FIRMS

A key objective of the economic reforms of 1991 was to increase productivity in the Indian manufacturing sector. While there is a substantial literature on the evolution of productivity in the Indian formal manufacturing sector before and after reforms (Kathuria et al. 2013), relatively, little is known about the evolution of productivity in the Indian informal manufacturing sector. In this chapter, we describe the patterns and trends in productivity in the Indian informal manufacturing sector by comparing them with the formal manufacturing sector. We also examine the behaviour of productivity of different types of firms within the informal sector, and also look at the regional evolution of productivity.

As per the conventional wisdom about the informal manufacturing sector, firms in this sector are generally less productive than firms in the formal manufacturing sector (Dabla-Norris et al. 2005). Under this view, since firms in the informal sector tend to remain small to escape the attention of government inspectors, they are not able to reap economies of scale, nor have access to credit from formal financial institutions to expand operations as they are not registered with government authorities. This view often underscores the policy concern about a burgeoning informal sector in the face of a shrinking or stagnant formal sector and is the basis of the oft-repeated policy recommendation that entry of firms from the informal to the formal sector should be eased and that the overall policy aim with respect to the informal sector should be to reduce its size over time (World Bank 2005). However, this view is not without its critics, who argue that informal firms may well be more efficient than formal firms and this could be the reason why the informal sector does not seem to contract in size with economic growth and rapid modernization of the economy (De Soto 1989). Under this view, informal firms are inherently more entrepreneurial and dynamic than formal firms as they are unlikely to face the high degree of regulations faced by formal firms.

There has been little systematic analysis of efficiency differentials between informal and formal manufacturing firms which can provide support to either of the above two propositions.[1] This chapter estimates the efficiency of informal and formal manufacturing firms, paying particular attention to the effect of economic reforms on the efficiency levels of informal and formal firms.[2] The rest of the chapter is in five sections. The first section presents the overall trends in productivity in the informal and formal sectors. The second section looks at performance within the informal sector. The third section discusses the methodology and empirical specification used to estimate efficiency of firms in formal and informal sectors. The fourth section presents the results on the estimates of efficiency of informal and formal firms and the effect of economic reforms on these efficiency levels. The final section concludes the analysis.

Overall Trends: Informal and Formal Sectors

We report the trends in labour productivity which is measured as the ratio of real gross value added (GVA) to number of workers, in the formal and informal sectors for the period 1984–5 to 2005–6 in Table 5.1.[3] It is clearly evident from the table that labour productivity in both the formal and informal sectors witnessed a consistent increase during the

---

[1] The number of empirical studies that have investigated whether small firms are more efficient than larger firms have been limited (see Taymaz 2005; Yang and Chen 2009). However, these studies do not investigate the difference in efficiency between informal and formal firms.

[2] Appendix 5A at the end of this chapter presents a discussion on the construction of variables.

[3] The data for the period 2010–11 is omitted from the analysis due to the lack of strict comparability across types of enterprises for this period.

Table 5.1 Levels and Growth of Labour Productivity: Formal Sector and Informal Sector

Year	Levels		Growth	
	Formal Sector	Informal Sector	Formal Sector	Informal Sector
1984–5	64,699	7,358	–	–
1989–90	89,702	7,944	6.8	1.5
1994–5	122,748	8,400	6.5	1.1
2000–1	157,572	10,718	4.3	4.1
2005–6	235,028	18,619	8.3	11.7

Source: Authors' estimates based on NSSO and ASI data sets.

Note: Average annual growth rates are reported. The growth rates have been estimated using $\left(\dfrac{Y_t}{Y_0}\right)^{\left(\frac{1}{n}\right)} - 1$.

period 1984–2006. While labour productivity increased by 6.3 per cent over the period of two decades in the formal sector, the informal sector reported an increase of only 4.5 per cent. Till recently, the rate of increase in labour productivity was always higher for the formal firms as compared to the informal firms. However, for the recent period 2000–6, the rate of increase in labour productivity for informal firms surpassed the growth for formal firms. Productivity growth was the strongest in this period for both the sectors, increasing at an annual rate of 8.3 per cent in the formal sector and 11.7 per cent in the informal sector.

Another important observation is with regard to the gap in labour productivity of formal and informal sectors. We find that there has been a significant widening of the gap in labour productivity between formal and informal sectors over the 20-year period under consideration (Figure 5.1). In 1984–5, the output per worker in the formal sector was 8.8 times higher than the output per worker in the informal sector. By 2000–1, the gap in productivity went up to 14.7 times. However, we find a small drop in the gap for the recent period 2005–6, when the difference in labour productivity between formal and informal sectors declined to 12.6 per cent. This decline is a result of the faster growth of labour productivity in the informal sector vis-à-vis the formal sector.

Considerable differences are also observed in labour productivity levels across different types of enterprises in the informal sector. This is very

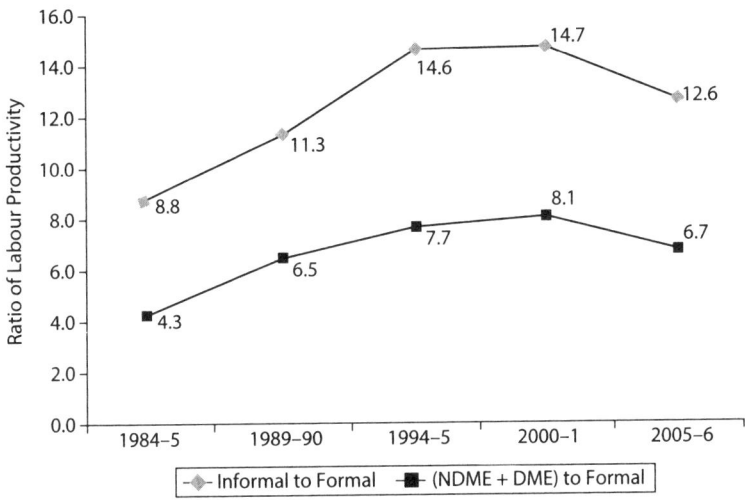

Figure 5.1   Ratio of Labour Productivity: 1984–5 to 2005–6
Source: Authors' estimates based on NSSO and ASI data sets.

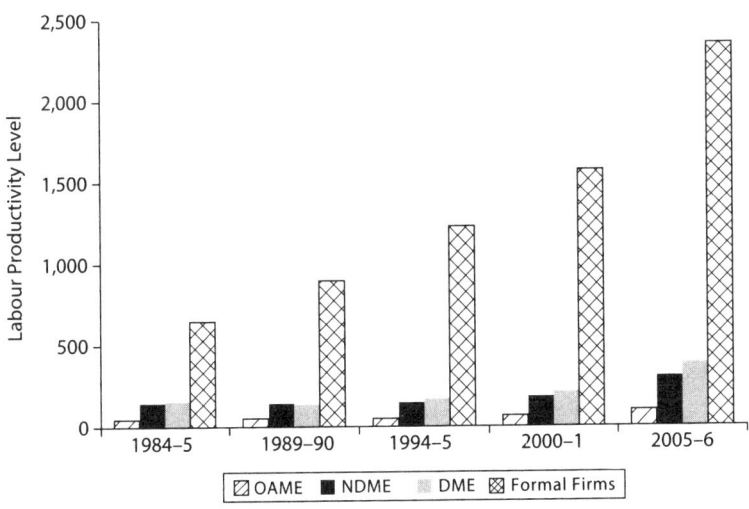

Figure 5.2   Labour Productivity Levels by Enterprise Type (in '00 Rupees):
1984–5 to 2005–6
Source: Authors' estimates based on NSSO and ASI data sets.

much evident from Figure 5.2, which shows that firms that employ only family labour (OAMEs) are the least productive in the informal sector. On the other hand, non-household enterprises that employ both hired and family labour (NDMEs and DMEs) reported higher levels of labour productivity. Even within the non-family firms, the larger firms (DMEs) are more productive vis-à-vis smaller firms (NDMEs). These differences notwithstanding, labour productivity in all the three types of enterprises has witnessed a steady increase over the two decades. However, this consistent growth in labour productivity has not altered the differences in labour productivity levels between the types of enterprises.

We do not find any significant changes in the gap in productivity levels between the three types of enterprises during the period 1984–2006 (Figure 5.3). In 2005–6, the output per worker by the DMEs was four times higher than that of the OAMEs and about 1.5 times higher than that of the NDMEs. The labour productivity in the NDMEs, on the other hand, was about three times higher than that in the OAMEs. Between 1984–5 and 2005–6, the gap in labour productivity between NDMEs and DMEs remained more or less same while the gap between NDMEs and OAMEs increased marginally. Interestingly, the gap in

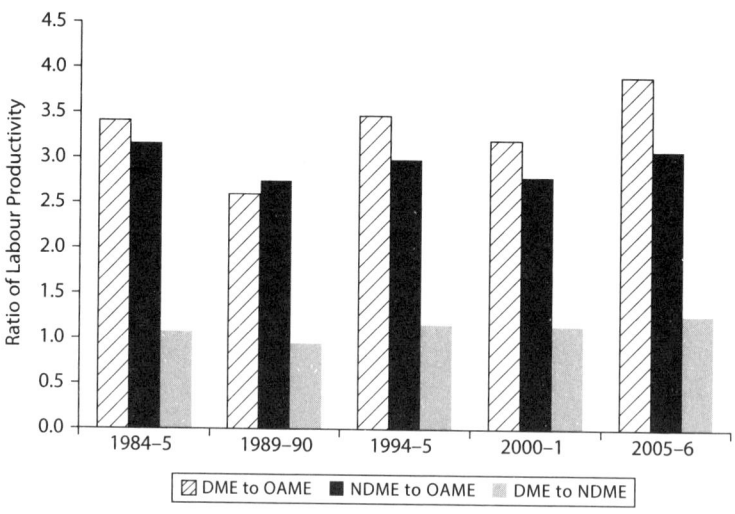

Figure 5.3　Ratio of Labour Productivity across Different Size Groups in the Informal Manufacturing Sector: 1984–5 to 2005–6
Source: Authors' computations based on NSSO data.

labour productivity between DMEs and OAMEs witnessed a slight decline during the 20-year period.

It is thus very much evident from the analysis that the significantly lower productivity of family firms is pulling down the overall productivity of the informal manufacturing sector in India.

Performance within the Informal Sector

In this section, we intend to capture the regional and industry-level variations in labour productivity over the period 1984–5 to 2005–6. Our analysis is confined to 15 major states at the regional level. We find that the aggregate picture masks the interstate variation in the movement of labour productivity. Not even in a single state has there been a consistent increase in labour productivity over time (Figure 5.4). Significant variation is observed in labour productivity across the

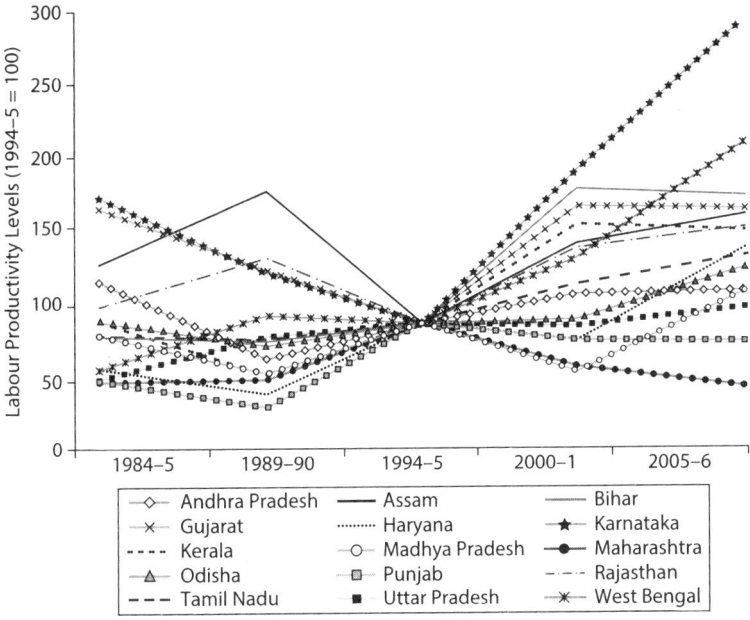

Figure 5.4 Labour Productivity in the Informal Manufacturing Sector across Indian States: 1984–5 to 2005–6
Source: Authors' computations based on NSSO data.
Note: Base Year: 1994–5 = 100.

Indian states. Labour productivity levels are the highest in the two most industrialized states of the country—Gujarat and Maharashtra. While Maharashtra witnessed significant gains in labour productivity between 1984–5 and 2005–6, there has been hardly any change in labour productivity in the informal sector of Gujarat over the same period. Labour productivity witnessed significant gains in Haryana as well. On the other hand, low labour productivity levels are reported in economically backward states such as Bihar, Odisha, and Uttar Pradesh (UP). It is also found that these states have not registered significant gains in labour productivity over the period 1984–5 to 2005–6. The computations suggest that labour productivity in Odisha is 10 times lower than that of Maharashtra, the state with highest level of labour productivity.

Turning to the growth in labour productivity, it exhibited considerable variation across the states. Table 5.2 shows that all states except Bihar, Gujarat, and Kerala registered a positive growth in labour productivity in the period 1984–5 to 2005–6. The output per worker grew the fastest in Maharashtra, followed by Haryana and West Bengal (WB). The changes in labour productivity across selected states for two sub-periods, 1984–5 to 1994–5 and 1994–5 to 2005–6, are also reported in Table 5.2. This decomposition would help us to capture the role of reforms on improving labour productivity as the latter sub-period coincided with the key reform measures carried out in the industrial sector since 1991. We find that the reform measures appeared to have had a positive impact on labour productivity levels. Most of the states have experienced spectacular acceleration in the rate of growth of labour productivity in the period corresponding to reforms. The prominent states among them were Karnataka and Maharashtra. The labour productivity grew at a rate of 9.5 per cent per annum and 6.6 per cent per annum in Karnataka and Maharashtra, respectively, in the post-reform period. In 7 out of 15 states, the direction of productivity change reversed from productivity decline in the pre-reform period to productivity growth in the post-reform period. In Haryana, Madhya Pradesh (MP), Maharashtra, Tamil Nadu (TN), and WB, there was an acceleration in the rate of productivity growth in the post-reform period. On the other hand, Bihar and Punjab reported decline in labour productivity in the second sub-period. For UP, labour productivity declined but remained positive. Thus, overall evidence

Table 5.2 Changes in Labour Productivity in the Informal Manufacturing Sector (in per cent)

State	1984–95	1995–2006	1984–2006
Andhra Pradesh	–0.1	3.8	1.9
Assam	–2.8	4.3	0.8
Bihar	3.8	–3.7	–0.2
Gujarat	–4.8	4.5	–0.1
Haryana	2.8	3.2	3.0
Karnataka	–5.1	9.5	2.3
Kerala	–2.1	1.5	–0.2
Madhya Pradesh	0.7	1.5	1.1
Maharashtra	2.8	6.6	4.8
Odisha	–0.1	2.4	1.2
Punjab	3.7	–1.0	1.2
Rajasthan	–1.0	3.9	1.5
Tamil Nadu	0.7	2.9	1.8
Uttar Pradesh	3.6	0.8	2.1
West Bengal	0.7	4.9	2.9

Source: Authors' computations based on NSSO data.

Note: Average annual growth rates are reported. The growth rates have been estimated using $\left(\dfrac{Y_t}{Y_0}\right)^{\left(\frac{1}{n}\right)} - 1$.

points to reforms generating significant gains in labour productivity in majority of the states.

Despite these significant gains in labour productivity, the difference in levels across types of enterprises is considerably high in majority of the states (Figure 5.5). As observed at the all-India level, output per worker is the lowest for the OAMEs and the highest for the DMEs. It is also found that the gap in productivity levels between the OAMEs and DMEs is higher than the national average (four times) in five states—Bihar, Karnataka, MP, Odisha, and WB. This possibly explains the existence of low overall labour productivity levels in these five states. It is also observed that the gap in labour productivity levels is considerably lower in the industrialized states of Gujarat and Maharashtra.

We also examine the growth of labour productivity across these enterprise types in the selected states. This would help us to find out

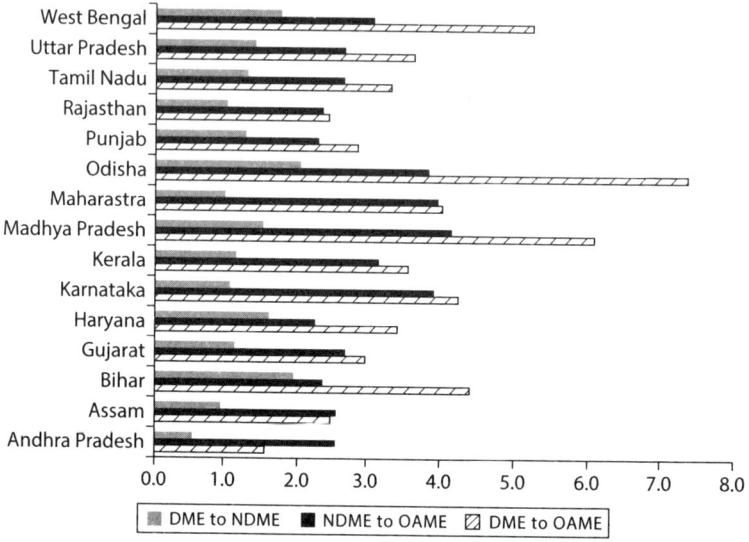

Figure 5.5 Ratios of Labour Productivity in the Informal Manufacturing
Sector, by State: 2005–6
Source: Authors' computations based on NSSO data.

whether the observed improvement in labour productivity over the
last two decades has been driven by any specific type of enterprise.
No evidence is found to confirm that any particular type of enterprise
is driving the growth of labour productivity across the Indian states
(Figure 5.6). For instance, in Maharashtra and WB—the states with
largest productivity gains—OAMEs, NDMEs, and DMEs experienced
uniform gains in labour productivity. In Haryana, another state with
the highest labour growth in productivity, it is the OAMEs that have
propelled the overall growth of labour productivity. On the contrary,
the OAMEs have largely driven the negative growth of labour productivity in Bihar, Gujarat, and Kerala. While DMEs suffered a decline in
labour productivity in five states, NDMEs reported a decline in labour
productivity only in two states. On the other hand, OAMEs suffered a
decline in labour productivity in five states.

Having mapped out the regional variations in labour productivity
levels and growth, we now move on to examine trends in productivity
across industries and by the type of enterprise. The levels in labour

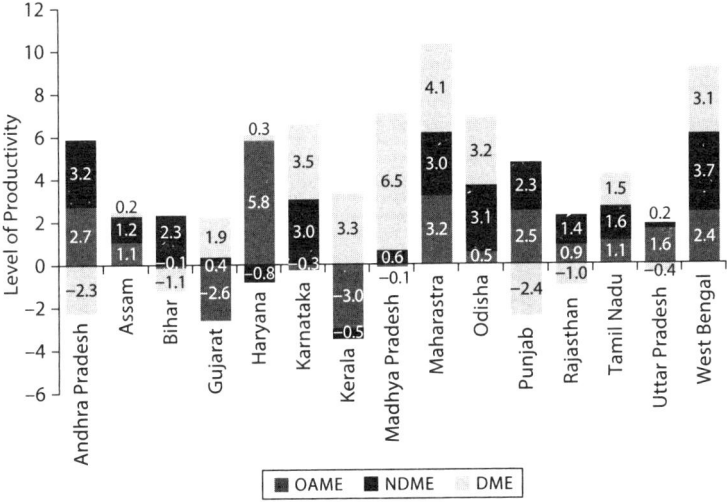

Figure 5.6 Changes in the Level of Productivity in the Informal Manufacturing Sector across States by Enterprise Type: 1984–5 to 2005–6 (in per cent)
Source: Authors' computations based on NSSO data.

productivity for 14 industries for the period 1984–5 to 2005–6 are reported in Table 5.3. The estimates suggest that there exists considerable inter-industry variation in labour productivity levels. As evident from Table 5.3, the output per worker is the lowest in beverages industry and the highest in basic metals industry in 2005–6. The computations suggest that, on average, labour in basic metal industry is 10 times more productive than that in the beverages industry. We also find that labour productivity levels are the highest in industries that are more capital intensive in nature. Basic metal, transport equipment and parts, and metal products, the most capital-intensive industries in the sector, are the ones with the highest output per worker in the sector. When we look at the trends in levels of labour productivity over the last two decades, a consistent increase in labour productivity—a trend evident at the all-India level—was observed only in four industry groups, viz., cotton products, textile products, non-metallic minerals, and other manufacturing goods. In all other industries, labour productivity witnessed a fluctuating trend across the five time periods.

Table 5.3   Labour Productivity Levels by Industry, Informal Sector: 1984–5 to 2005–6

Industry	1984–5	1989–90	1994–5	2000–1	2005–6
Food Products	7,044	8,471	7,874	9,676	18,001
Beverages	4,783	3,800	4,297	4,213	5,834
Cotton Products	4,319	6,821	7,784	10,423	19,835
Textiles	6,061	6,273	6,636	10,828	15,587
Wood Products	8,948	8,318	6,847	6,518	16,563
Paper Products	16,154	18,530	16,144	17,662	30,524
Leather Products	11,835	7,360	12,512	16,354	26,171
Chemicals	17,985	11,486	9,808	11,102	15,073
Rubber Products	9,102	21,681	22,835	21,374	24,692
Non-metallic Minerals	4,307	5,399	6,464	11,438	16,592
Basic Metals	21,725	5,613	22,894	28,861	58,308
Metal Products	19,744	14,734	17,568	22,247	37,817
Transport Equipment and Parts	101,057	22,707	23,296	27,990	44,535
Other Manufacturing Products	5,915	9,092	9,830	15,178	33,032
All	7,358	7,944	8,400	10,718	18,619

Source: Authors' computations based on NSSO data.

Despite this fluctuating trend, our computations suggest that labour productivity grew between 1984–5 and 2005–6 in most of the industries. In 12 out of 14 industries, labour productivity grew in this period. The output per labour declined only in chemicals and transport equipment and parts. The fastest increase in labour productivity was observed in cotton products, non-metallic minerals, and other manufacturing goods. In Table 5.4, we report the growth rates for the two sub-periods, 1984–5 to 1994–5 and 1994–5 to 2005–6. In 1984–5 to 1994–5, the output per worker witnessed a decline in six industries, whereas no industry reported a decline in labour productivity in the second sub-period—1994–5 to 2005–6. We also find that all industries, except rubber products, have registered considerable gains in labour productivity in the second sub-period following the reforms. Labour productivity grew at a rate of over 8 per cent in cotton products, textile products, wood products, non-metallic minerals, basic metals, and other manufacturing goods in this period. The results also suggest that all the types of enterprises have contributed to the rise in labour productivity in this period (Table 5.5). In most of the industries, gains in labour productivity in the post-reform period are similar across OAMEs, NDMEs, and DMEs. In beverages and basic metals, it is the DMEs that seem to have driven the growth of labour productivity in the post-reform period.

Table 5.4 Period-wise Changes in Labour Productivity across Industries: Informal Manufacturing Sector (in per cent)

Industry	1984–95	1995–2006	1984–2006
Food Products	1.12	7.81	4.6
Beverages	−1.07	2.82	1.0
Cotton Products	6.07	8.88	7.5
Textiles	0.91	8.07	4.6
Wood Products	−2.64	8.36	3.0
Paper Products	−0.01	5.96	3.1
Leather Products	0.56	6.94	3.9
Chemicals	−5.88	3.98	−0.8
Rubber Products	9.63	0.71	4.9
Non-metallic Minerals	4.14	8.95	6.6
Basic Metals	0.53	8.87	4.8
Metal Products	−1.16	7.22	3.1
Transport Equipment and Parts	−13.65	6.07	−3.8
Other Manufacturing Products	5.21	11.65	8.5
Total	−3.08	6.86	3.6

Source: Authors' computations based on NSSO data.
Note: Average annual growth rates are reported. The growth rates have been estimated using $\left(\dfrac{Y_t}{Y_0}\right)^{\left(1/n\right)} - 1$.

Table 5.5 Industry-wise Changes in Labour Productivity across Enterprise Types in Informal Manufacturing Sector (in per cent)

Industry	Labour Productivity								
	1984–95			1995–2006			1984–2006		
	OAME	NDME	DME	OAME	NDME	DME	OAME	NDME	DME
Food Products	3.0	-0.4	-1.2	6.9	6.7	8.1	5.0	3.3	3.6
Beverages	-1.2	4.6	0.3	2.7	5.5	16.7	0.8	5.0	8.6
Cotton Products	3.9	0.6	2.5	8.9	6.7	7.9	6.5	3.7	5.3
Textiles	-3.4	-1.0	3.8	11.3	10.2	8.3	4.0	4.7	6.1
Wood Products	-3.9	-0.1	-1.6	7.6	6.1	9.0	1.9	3.1	3.8
Paper Products	5.2	-1.0	1.4	3.3	5.6	7.8	4.2	2.4	4.7
Leather Products	-0.1	0.7	-3.9	6.0	7.9	4.3	3.1	4.4	0.3
Chemicals	-1.4	-0.1	-4.8	1.9	7.6	6.5	0.3	3.9	0.9
Rubber Products	12.7	-1.9	7.4	0.7	-0.4	2.4	6.2	-1.1	4.7
Non-metallic Minerals	1.7	4.1	6.1	5.3	10.1	7.5	3.6	7.2	6.8
Basic Metals	5.9	0.9	1.0	0.5	1.9	10.1	3.0	1.4	5.7
Metal Products	0.4	-5.6	-2.2	5.7	5.5	8.9	3.1	0.0	3.4
Transport Equipment and Parts	-2.7	-19.0	-11.0	5.7	3.7	5.8	1.6	-7.8	-2.6
Other Manufacturing Products	2.9	5.2	8.4	10.7	12.3	5.7	6.9	8.9	6.9
Total	1.4	-6.2	-1.5	5.3	6.2	7.8	3.6	2.8	4.2

Source: Authors' computations based on NSSO data.
Note: Average annual growth rates are reported. The growth rates have been estimated using $\left(\frac{Y_t}{Y_0}\right)^{\left(\frac{1}{n}\right)} - 1$.

Trends in the Efficiency of Informal and Formal Firms in the Post-reform Period

Technical efficiency (TE) captures the extent to which firms in the manufacturing sector are producing the maximum possible output, for a given bundle of inputs, in a given industry. Improvements in TE of the average firm thus imply a higher level of output being produced, on average, for a given level of inputs in that industry (Kumbhakar and Lovell 2000). This section examines the trends in the TE of firms in the formal and informal sectors. We use stochastic frontier analysis (SFA) to estimate firm efficiency.[4] The standard approach to SFA is the one proposed by Aigner et al. (1977), but it does not account for the selection bias—that is, if being located in the formal sector is not by chance but by choice, the comparison of efficiency levels of formal and informal firms without addressing the endogeneity of firm location may yield biased results. It is, therefore, important to correct the selection bias in firm location in the informal or formal manufacturing sector in the estimation of TE.

The conventional approach to addressing selection bias—the Heckman's (1976) two-step method—is not appropriate for models that are non-linear in nature. Greene (2006) proposed an internally consistent method of incorporating 'sample selection' into an SFA framework. Greene's methodology is followed here in estimating a stochastic frontier model for the firms in the sample for correcting the selection bias (see Greene 2006 and 2010 for further details on the methodology). The methodology involves two stages: In the first stage, we estimate a probit equation, which models the selection of firms into the informal and formal sectors; and in the second stage, estimates for the production function and for TE are obtained, conditioned on the sample selection.

Econometric Methodology

Greene (2006) proposes the following analytical approach to correct the selection bias:

---

[4] For an early application of SFA to the estimation of firm efficiency in developing countries, see Taymaz and Saatci (1997).

$$d^* = \alpha'z + w, \qquad d = 1, d^* > 0, \tag{5.1}$$
$$y = \beta'x + v - u, \tag{5.2}$$
$$u = |U|, \text{ with } U \sim N\left[0, \sigma_u^2\right],$$
$$(v, w) \sim \text{bivariate normal with }\left[(0,0), (\sigma_u^2, \rho\sigma_v, 1)\right],$$
$$(y, x) \text{ only observed when } d = 2,$$

where d is a probit selection equation (with its adoption depending on a host of price and non-price factors) and y is the stochastic frontier function, specified only for the adopting firms. In the present case, the equation selection is whether to formalize or continue working in the informal sector based on several institutional factors. Then, a stochastic frontier function is estimated for only those firms which decide to be in the formal sector.[5]

The estimation, thus, is divided into two parts. For the selected observations, $d = 1$, conditioned on v, the joint density for y and d is the products of the marginals as conditioned on v, where y and d are independent:

$$f(y, d = 1 | x, z, v) = f(y | x, v)\,\text{prob}\,(d = 1 | z, v).$$

This is the second part. For the first part,

$$y | x, v = (\beta'x + \sigma_v v) - \sigma_u u,$$

where u is the truncation at zero of a standard normal variable, as is done in estimating stochastic production frontier.
Therefore, the joint conditional density is given by:

$$f(y, d = 1 | x, z, v) = \frac{2}{\sigma_u}\,\varnothing\left(\frac{(\beta'x + \sigma_v v) - y}{\sigma_u}\right)\varphi\left(\frac{\alpha'z + \rho v}{\sqrt{1 - \sigma^2}}\right). \tag{5.3}$$

The unconditional density is obtained by integrating v out of equation 5.3. The integral does not exist in a closed form, and hence Greene (2006) proposes computation by simulation. The final simulated log likelihood is given by:

---

[5] Correspondingly, the probit selection equation for informal firms is re-estimated, where the adoption decision is to be in the informal sector. Once decided/selected, stochastic frontier estimates are only estimated for those firms that decide to be in the informal sector.

$$logL_s = \sum_i log \frac{1}{R} \sum_{r=1}^{R} \left\{ d_i \left[\frac{2}{\sigma_u} \oslash \left(\frac{\beta'x + \sigma_v v_{ir} - y}{\sigma_u} \right) \varphi \left(\frac{\alpha'z + \rho v_{ir}}{\sqrt{1 - \sigma^2}} \right) \right] \right.$$

$$\left. + \left(1 - d_i \right) \left[\varphi \left(\frac{-\alpha'z + \rho v_{ir}}{\sqrt{1 - \sigma^2}} \right) \right] \right\}. \tag{5.4}$$

The model is estimated using NLOGIT version 4.[6]

Empirical Specification

In the first stage, we estimate a probit equation which models the selection of firms into the informal and formal sectors, and in the second stage, we obtain estimates for the production function and for TE, which are conditioned on the sample selection.

First Stage of Analysis

We assume that firms can choose between being in the formal or informal sector subject to a set of variables that capture the benefits and costs of formalization. The decision of the ith firm to be in the formal sector is described by an unobservable selection criterion function, F^*, that is postulated to be a function of variables that determine the benefits and costs of formalization. The model is specified as:

$$F^* = \alpha Z_i + w_i, \tag{5.5}$$

where Z is a vector of variables explaining the decision to formalize, α is a vector of parameters, and w_i is the white noise error term.

The selection criterion F^* is not observed. Instead, a dummy variable F is observed, which takes the value of one for formal sector firms, and zero for informal sector firms. Therefore, $F = 1$, if $F^* = \alpha Z_i + w_i \geq 0$; and otherwise, $F = 0$.

---

[6] NLOGIT is a suite of programs for estimating discrete choice models that are built around the logit and multinomial logit form (Greene 2007). NLOGIT began in 1996 with the development of the nested logit command, originally an extension of the multinomial logit model. This is now the only generally available package that contains panel data (repeated measures) versions of this model, in random effects and autoregressive forms (for details, see Greene 2007).

To obtain the set of explanatory variables which determine the benefits and costs of formalization, we draw from recent theoretical literature on why firms formalize. We also exploit the fact that there are important differences in institutions relating to labour regulation, access to credit, and the provision of infrastructure across Indian states and over time.

Since labour laws are both within the jurisdiction of the state and the central governments, the Industrial Development and Regulation Act has been extensively amended by state governments during the post-Independence period. Besley and Burgess (2004) have coded each state amendment to labour laws as neutral, pro-worker, or pro-employer for the period 1947–97. We extended the Besley–Burgess variable till 2005 and then normalized it between 0 and 1, such that the more pro-worker labour law amendments in a state would result in lower value for that state. We would expect that more pro-employer labour law amendments (LABOUR LAWS) as seen by a higher value of our variable would have a positive effect on the firm's decision to formalize.

Access to priority sector lending depended a great deal on the level of financial development in a given state, and this differed from state to state and across time (Burgess and Pande 2005). We capture differential access to organized sector credit for small and medium enterprises across Indian states and over time by the share of bank lending going to priority sectors (PRIORITY SECTOR LENDING) for 1989–90, 1994–5, 2000–1, and 2005–6. We expect that with higher lending going to the priority sector, including small firms, more informal firms are likely to formalize.

The third variable to explain the decision of a firm to formalize is the provision of a productive public good to formal sector firms which creates a strong incentive to formalize (Dessy and Pallage 2003). We take electricity to be the public good that has been found to be a binding constraint for formal manufacturing growth in India (World Bank 2004). Indian states have differed widely in their ability to provide electricity to manufacturing firms, partly due to the very different performances of state electricity boards, who are the main agencies responsible for transmission and distribution across the Indian states (Krueger and Chinoy 2002; Panagariya 2008). Following Bond and Malik (2007), the electricity constraint is measured on a firm's decision to formalize by the transmission and distribution losses (T&D losses) of electricity as percentage of total energy availability at the state level (in short, T&D LOSSES). The T&D losses are a suitable proxy for electricity infrastructure, because the higher the losses are in a given state, the higher the probability that firms will have operational problems with electricity, and the greater the disincentive for firms to move from the informal to the formal sector to take advantage of access to electricity in the state.

We estimate probit model of the following type:

$$F = f(\text{LABOUR LAWS, PRIORITY SECTOR LENDING,}$$
$$\text{T\&D LOSSES}), \tag{5.6}$$

where F is 1 if the firm is in the formal sector, 0 otherwise. It is expected that the signs of LABOUR LAWS and PRIORITY SECTOR LENDING will be positive while the sign of T&D LOSSES will be negative.

The probit equation for each industry is estimated separately, but it is estimated in a combined manner for all four years.[7] We explain below why we estimate the probit model separately for each industry.

Second Stage of Analysis

The production behaviour of formal and informal sector firms is modelled using a simple Cobb–Douglas function. Thus, we have:

$$lnY_{iT} = \beta_0 + \beta_1 lnK_{iT} + \beta_2 lnL_{iT} + (v_{iT} - u_{iT}), \tag{5.7}$$

where $T = 1989{-}90, 1994{-}5, 2000{-}1,$ and $2005{-}6$ and i is the firm. Y is gross value added, K is capital stock, L is labour, and βs are the parameters to be estimated. The v_{iT}s are random variables independent of the u_{iT}s and purport to capture the random shocks that are beyond the control of firms. The u_{iT}s capture TE and are the combined outcome of non-price and organizational factors that constrains

---

[7] Estimating the selection equation for the pooled firm-level data implies that we are assuming that the effects of labour laws, priority sector lending, and T&D losses on the firm's formalization decision are the same across the years. We also estimated selection equations year by year and found no significant change in our results, indicating that the effect of these variables on the firm's location choice is uniform over time (the results are available on request).

a firm from achieving their maximum possible output from the given set of inputs and technology. The u_is are non-negative and assumed to be identically distributed at truncations at 0, $u = |U|$ with $U \sim N$ [0, $\sigma^2 u$]. Technical efficiency (here TE_i) is measured as the ratio of the observed output (y_i) of the firm to the potential output $(\hat{y})$ derived by the frontier function, $TE_{iT} = \dfrac{Y_{iT}}{\hat{Y}_T}$, where TE_{iT} is technical efficiency for firm i in year T.

Instead of estimating the same production function for the entire set of firms, irrespective of industry, equation 5.7 is estimated industry by industry and for each of the two groups—formal and informal —separately, at the National Industrial Classification (NIC) two-digit industry level (broadly corresponding to the International Standard Industrial Classification of All Economic Activities [ISIC] three-digit level of industrial classification used by the United Nations Industrial Development Organization [UNIDO]). There are 22 industries in our data set. By estimating the production function separately for formal and informal firms at the industry level, we not only allow the parameters for capital and labour in the firm-level production function to differ across industries, but also across the two groups. This is a reasonable assumption to make when (a) the industries differ so widely in their production technology and in characteristics relating to export orientation and market structure (for example, leather versus electrical machinery); and (b) even within the same industry, production coefficients may be different for labour-intensive informal firms and capital-intensive formal firms.

Results

Efficiency Comparison: Formal vs Informal Firms

Figure 5.7 shows the kernel density plots of efficiency of informal and formal manufacturing firms for 1989–90, 1994–5, 2000–1, and 2005–6. We observe that the efficiency distribution for formal firms is generally to the right of that for informal firms for all the years. There has been a rightward shift of both the efficiency distributions over time, indicating higher efficiency gains for both the formal and informal firms over time. Figure 5.8 also presents kernel density plots of changes in absolute TE for formal and informal firms for selected industries. We observe that absolute efficiency levels of firms in the formal and informal sector show a clear improvement over time in these industries.

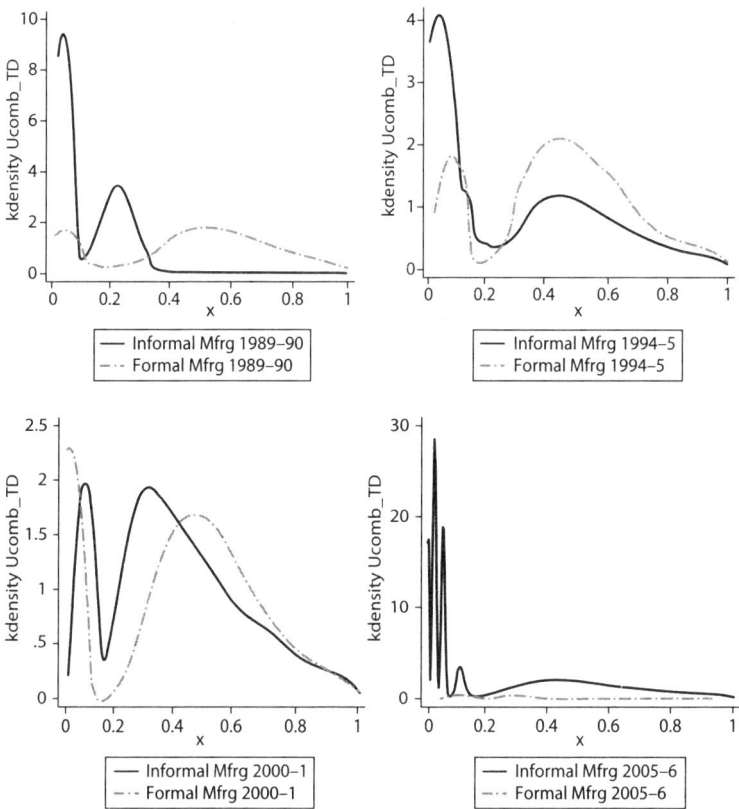

Figure 5.7   Kernel Density Plots Showing Year-wise Changes in Efficiency: Informal Manufacturing vs Formal Manufacturing Firms
Source: Authors' estimates based on NSSO and ASI data sets.
Note: Mfrg = Manufacturing.

What Have Been the Effects of Reforms on Efficiency of Informal and Formal Firms?

Our interest in this chapter is also to investigate the effect of economic reforms of the 1990s on the efficiency levels of the formal and informal sectors. We are specifically interested in examining whether the product-market reforms initiated in the Indian economy have played any role in widening the gap in efficiency levels of formal and informal sector firms. This is an important issue to be examined as the reforms with respect to the industrial sector were intended to free the sector

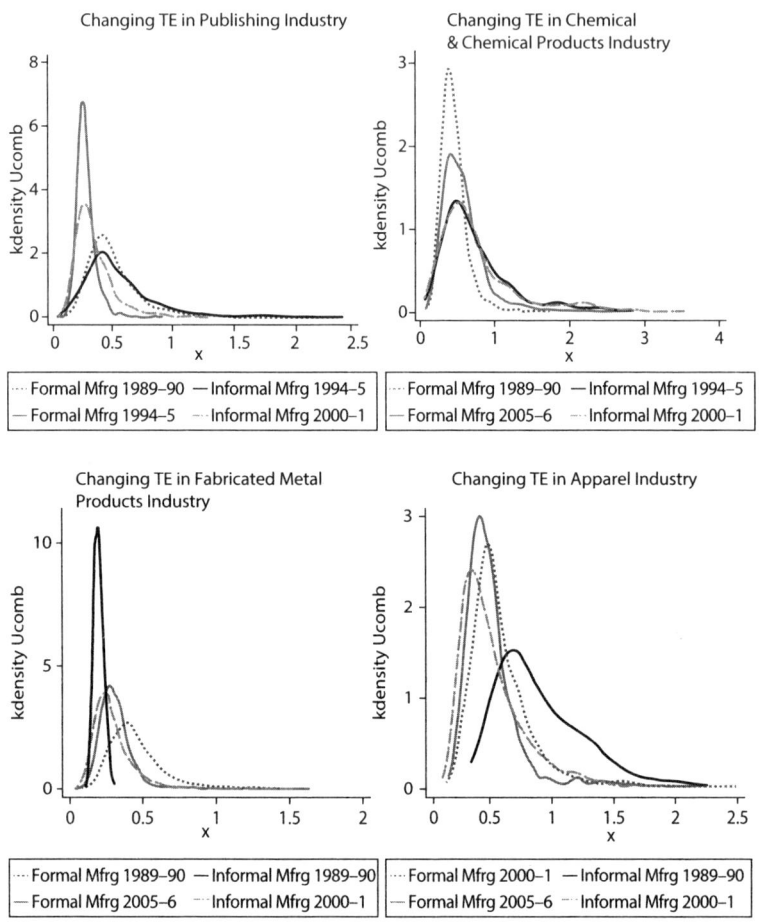

Figure 5.8 Kernel Density Plots Showing Changes in Absolute Technical Efficiency for Selected Industries—Formal and Informal Firms
Source: Authors' estimates based on NSSO and ASI data sets.
Note: Mfrg = Manufacturing.

from barriers to entry and from other restrictions to expansion, diversification and modification, so as to improve its efficiency, productivity, and competitiveness.

We construct a composite variable (REFORM) that captures the key sets of product-market reforms enacted in India since the late

1980s, which are delicensing, dereservation, and trade reforms, and examine its effect on efficiency differentials between formal and informal firms, and also examine the effects of each of the product-market reforms on these differentials separately. To be specific, our attempt here is to find the answers for the following questions: (a) Which sets of firms are more efficient—formal or informal? (b) Have the reforms had a positive impact on efficiency levels in both the sectors? (c) Have the reforms led to a widening of efficiency gap between formal and informal forms?

For this, firm-specific TE scores are regressed on the composite index of reforms (REFORM) and a variable representing firm location (FORMAL). The following specification is estimated:

$$TE_{ijt} = \alpha + \beta_1 FORMAL_{ijt} + \beta_2 REFORM_{ijt} + \delta_j + \gamma_t + \varepsilon_{ijt}, \qquad (5.8)$$

where TE_{ijt} is TE of firm i, in industry j, and year t, and FORMAL is a dummy for firm location which takes the value one if the firm is in the formal sector, and zero if the firm is in the informal sector. δ_j is the industry-fixed effects, γ_t is the year effects, and ε_{ijt} is the error term. If β_2 is greater than zero (and statistically significant), we would conclude that product-market reforms have led to an increase in efficiency for both the formal and informal sectors. Similarly, if β_1 is greater than zero and statistically significant, we would conclude that formal firms are more efficient than informal firms, and vice versa if β_1 is less than zero.

To find out whether the efficiency differential has widened with the advent of reforms, we introduce an interaction term, FORMAL* REFORM, where we interact the reform variable, REFORM, with the FORMAL variable. The revised model takes the following form:

$$TE_{ijt} = \alpha + \beta_1 FORMAL_{ijt} + \beta_2 REFORM_{ijt} + \beta_3 FORMAL * REFORM_{ijt}$$
$$+ \delta_j + \gamma_t + \varepsilon_{ijt}. \qquad (5.9)$$

The coefficient β_3 measures the differential impact of reforms on formal and informal firms. A positive and statistically significant β_3 (along with a positive and statistically significant β_2) would indicate that reforms have led to a greater increase in efficiency for formal firms vis-à-vis informal firms indicating a further widening of efficiency gap between the two sectors in Indian manufacturing sector. A negative and statistically significant β_3 would imply just the reverse. It should be noted that in equation 5.9, the effect of FORMAL on technical efficiency is given by the expression, $\beta_1 + \beta_3$REFORM. Even if β_1 is negative, $\beta_1 + \beta_3$REFORM can be positive if the β_3REFORM is positive and greater than β_1, when evaluating the expression at the mean value of REFORM. We estimate the equations 5.8 and 5.9 by using ordinary least squares. To consider into account the facts that efficiency may be impacted by macroeconomic shocks and cyclical factors, and that firm efficiency may be correlated with unobserved industry characteristics, we include year and industry fixed effects in all the regressions.

Construction of the 'Reform' Variable

The major product-market reforms that have occurred in the Indian economy since the mid-1980s were the withdrawal of the requirement of a license that firms require if they wish to produce in a given industry (DELICENSE), the dereservation of products earlier earmarked only for small-scale and informal producers (DERESERVE), and trade reforms in the form of cuts in import tariffs (TARIFF). We construct the DELICENSE variable as the total number of four-digit industries delicensed in a year to that of the total number of four-digit industries in the sector. The DERESERVE variable represents the ratio of cumulative number of products deserved in respective two-digit industries to that of the total reserved products in these industries. The ratios of tariffs are obtained from the trade and industrial output data of the World Bank Trade Database (Nicita and Olarreaga 2006).

Using the data for these three product-market reforms, a composite index of reform (REFORM) is constructed by assigning equal weights for all the three reforms. The composite measure, which is a weighted index of these three reforms, thus is given by:

$$\text{REFORM}_{jt} = \sum_{i=1}^{3} W_i \, \text{REFORM}_{ijt},$$

where W_i is the weight for each of the product-market reform variables. We assume esqual weights for each of the three product-market reform variables (that is $W_i = 0.33$). In order to ensure that higher values of the reform variables imply greater reforms, we reconstruct our tariff reform variable as 100 – Current Tariff. This modification reconciles the direction of tariff reform with the other two reforms. A high value of

REFORM thus indicates a greater extent of reforms and a lower value indicates more restrictions, and thus less reforms.

Figure 5.9 presents the trends in this composite reform variable for the period 1989–2005. It is clearly evident from the figure that the progress of reform is not uniform and that it varies significantly across industries. Industries like tobacco, minerals, and transport equipment and parts are far behind textiles, apparels, leather, office machinery, publishing, and basic metals in these reforms.

Table 5.6 presents the estimates of equations 5.8 and 5.9. Column 1 presents the results on the effects of reforms and firm location in the

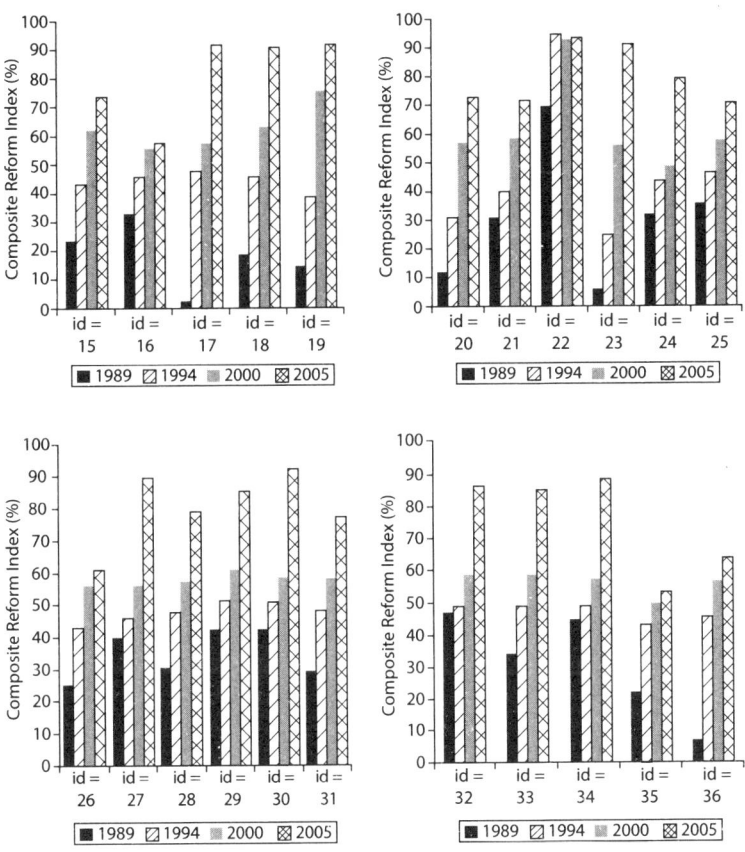

Figure 5.9 Industry-wise Trends of Composite Reform Variable (REFORM)
Source: Authors' computations based on NSSO data.
Note: Industry IDs (based on NIC 1998) are in Table A1.5 of Appendix A1.

Table 5.6 Impact of Reforms on Technical Efficiency in Indian Manufacturing

Variable	Dependent Variable: Absolute Technical Efficiency							
	Model 1 (1)	Model 2 (2)	Model 3 (3)	Model 4 (4)	Model 5 (5)	Model 6 (6)	Model 7 (7)	Model 8 (8)
FORMAL	0.220*** (0.00191)	0.220*** (0.00192)	0.230*** (0.00192)	0.228*** (0.00196)	−0.175*** (0.00401)	−0.0746*** (0.00456)	0.131*** (0.00232)	0.401*** (0.00404)
REFORM	0.00539*** (0.000107)				0.00345*** (0.000101)			
DELICENSE		0.00237*** (6.38e-05)				0.00125*** (6.03e-05)		
DERESERVE			0.00255*** (5.89e-05)				−0.000126** (6.29e-05)	
TARIFF				0.000476*** (0.000119)				0.00150*** (0.0 00112)
FORMAL *REFORM					0.00736*** (6.23e-05)			
FORMAL *DELICENSE						0.00349*** (5.17e-05)		
FORMAL *DERESERVE							0.0411*** (4.46e-05)	
FORMAL *TARIFF								−0.00365*** (7.83e-05)
Constant	0.353*** (0.00326)	0.373*** (0.00314)	0.441*** (0.00302)	0.412*** (0.0103)	0.556*** (0.00338)	0.515*** (0.00320)	0.522*** (0.00313)	0.406*** (0.0101)
Ind. Dummy	Yes	Yes	Yes	Yes	Yes	Yes	Yes	Yes
Year Dummy	Yes	Yes	Yes	Yes	Yes	Yes	Yes	Yes
Number of Observations	174,736	174,736	174,736	174,736	174,736	174,736	174,736	174,736
R^2	0.249	0.246	0.246	0.239	0.286	0.259	0.278	0.246

Source: Authors' estimates based on NSSO and ASI data sets.

Note: *** and ** indicate significance at minimum 1 per cent and 5 per cent levels, respectively; figures in parenthesis are standard errors.

formal sector on technical efficiency and column 5 presents the results with the interaction term included. The estimates clearly suggest that formal firms are more efficient than informal firms as the coefficient of the FORMAL dummy is positive and statistically significant at one per cent level (column 1). The computations based on the coefficient value of FORMAL indicate that the efficiency level of formal firms is 17.69 per cent higher than that of informal firms. Our results also show that firms in both formal and informal sectors have gained in efficiency in the post-reform period. This is evident from the positive and statistically significant coefficient of the REFORM variable in column 1. Based on the coefficient value of the REFORM variable, we find that the gains in efficiency due to the reforms have been 28.4 per cent.

We report the estimates for equation 5.9 in column 5. It is found that the coefficient on the interaction term FORMAL*REFORM is positive and statistically significant. This suggests that the economic reforms have led to an increase in the efficiency gap between formal and informal firms in the Indian manufacturing sector. At the mean value of technical efficiency (0.43), the calculations show that reforms have increased the efficiency of formal firms by 50.1 per cent vis-à-vis informal firms. The results thus suggests that both the formal firms and the informal firms have gained in efficiency in the post-reform period, but these gains are significantly larger for the formal firms vis-à-vis the informal firms. An additional 10 per cent reform (from the mean value) would have increased efficiency of formal firms by 4.5 per cent, while the increase would have been only 2.5 per cent for informal firms.

The effect of each product-market reform on efficiency, and on efficiency gap between formal and informal sectors are also examined here. Each reform variable is entered sequentially rather than including all of them at the same time in equation 5.9. Columns 2 to 4 in Table 5.6 present the results for delicensing, dereservation, and tariff reform variables, respectively. It is found that delicensing and dereservation have had a discernible positive impact on technical efficiency, while tariff reform has had a negative effect.[8] The results indicate that additional delicensing and dereservation reforms to the tune of

---

[8] We also used weighted tariff instead of simple tariff as a measure of trade reforms. Our results did not change, indicating the robustness of the results to different measures of tariffs.

10 per cent from their mean values would have resulted in a 2.9 per cent and a 0.93 per cent increase in efficiency of Indian manufacturing firms. On the other hand, a reduction in tariffs by 10 per cent would have reduced efficiency of Indian manufacturing firms by 0.41 per cent, though the magnitude is relatively small compared to the other two sets of reforms.

To see how individual reforms have influenced the efficiency gap, we introduce the interaction of the three reform variables with FORMAL one by one. Columns 6 to 8 of Table 5.6 report the results. We find that the interaction between delicensing and formal (FORMAL*DELICENSE) and between dereservation and formal (FORMAL*DERESERVE) is positive and significant, while the interaction between tariff cuts and formal (FORMAL*TARIFF) is negative and significant. This suggests that all three reforms have contributed to the increase in efficiency differentials between formal and informal firms. In the case of tariff reforms, though we observe a decline in efficiency for the overall manufacturing sector, formal firms have gained in efficiency by 0.17 per cent.

We find that an additional 10 per cent delicensing would have increased efficiency of formal firms by 3.5 per cent and of informal firms by only 1.7 per cent. A 10 per cent tariff reduction, on the other hand, would have resulted in formal firms gaining in efficiency by 0.3 per cent, whereas it would have resulted in efficiency decline for informal firms by 1.5 per cent. Lastly, additional dereservation of 10 per cent would have resulted in an increase in efficiency of formal firms by 0.7 per cent, but would have led to a decline in the efficiency of informal firms marginally by 0.05 per cent.

✿   ✿   ✿

This chapter investigated the effect of economic reforms on the efficiency of informal and formal firms. At first, we compared the productivity performance of the formal and informal segments of the Indian manufacturing sector, both at the national and the sub-national level for the period 1984–2005. It was found that labour productivity witnessed a consistent increase in both the formal and informal manufacturing segments. However, the rate of increase was faster for the formal firms as compared to the informal firms. This has resulted in significant widening of the gap in labour productivity between formal and informal sectors over the period 1984–2005. Further, it was also observed that the consistent growth in labour productivity in the informal sector has not altered the differences in the levels labour productivity amongst the types of enterprises within the sector. The computations showed that the largest firms in the sector were four times more productive than the smallest firms in the sector. It is thus very much evident from the analysis that the significantly lower productivity of family firms is pulling down the overall productivity of the informal manufacturing sector in India. At the regional level, overall evidence points to reforms generating significant gains in labour productivity in majority of the states. Our estimates also points to considerable inter-industry variation in labour productivity levels. Despite these differences, we noticed that all industries except rubber products have recorded considerable gains in labour productivity in the period following reforms.

Next, we looked at the evolution of productivity within the informal manufacturing sector. We found that economic reforms have had an unambiguous positive effect on absolute levels of technical efficiency in the entire manufacturing sector (both informal and formal sectors combined). While average efficiency levels in both the informal and the formal manufacturing sectors have increased, the increase has been more for the formal firms. It was also found that economic reforms have increased the efficiency differentials between the more efficient formal firms and the less efficient informal firms in Indian manufacturing, and that all three product-market reforms have contributed to greater dualism in the manufacturing sector in the post-reform period.

The findings have important implications for the effects of economic reforms on pro-poor growth in India. While economic reforms can have strong positive effects on overall efficiency in the manufacturing sector, the widening gap between the productivity of formal and informal firms in manufacturing will make it difficult for informal firms to compete in external and domestic markets that are increasingly integrated. Given the large presence of unskilled and semi-skilled workers in the workforce of the informal sector, such a process of dualistic development may act as a significant obstacle for the poverty-reducing and employment-creating impact of economic growth.

Appendix 5A: Construction of Variables

The construction of *Real Gross Value Added* and *Employment* was already discussed in Chapter 3.

Fixed Capital Stock

The measurement of capital input is rather problematic, and has been a controversial topic in theoretical as well as empirical literature. There is no universally accepted method for its measurement and, as a result, several methods have been employed to estimate capital stock. In many studies, the capital unit is treated as a stock measured by the book value of fixed assets (Ray 2002) while in others it is considered as a flow, measured by the sum of rent, repairs, and depreciation expenses. In some other cases, perpetual inventory method has been adopted for the construction of a capital stock series from annual investment data. In this case, it is assumed that the flow of capital services is proportional to the stock of capital (Ahluwalia 1991; Balakrishnan and Pushpangadan 1994; Trivedi 2004; Trivedi et al. 2000). It is essential to point out that each of these measures has its shortcomings. The book value method has three limitations. First, the use of this 'lumpy' capital data may underestimate or overestimate the amount of capital expenditure (Mahadevan 2002). Second, the physical stock of machinery and equipment may not be truly represented by the book value (Ray 2002). Third, it does not address the question of capacity utilization (Kumar 2006). According to Ray (2002), perpetual inventory method also does not address the question of capacity utilization. The flow measure may be criticized on the ground that the depreciation charges in the financial accounts may be unrelated to the actual wear and tear of hardware (Ray 2002).

Despite its limitations, most studies in the unorganized manufacturing sector in India have used book value of total fixed assets owned by the unit on the closing date of the accounting year to represent capital input (Rani and Unni 2004; Unni et al. 2001). Fixed assets include land, buildings and other constructions, plant and machinery, transport equipment and parts, tools, and other fixed assets that have a normal economic life of more than one year from the date of acquisition. Salim and Kalirajan (1999) and Hossain and Karunaratne (2004) argue that the use of gross figures to represent the capital stock can be justified in the case of developing countries such as India in general, and unorganized manufacturing sector in particular, on the ground that capital stocks are more often used at approximately constant levels of efficiency for a period far beyond the accounting life measured by normal depreciation until they are eventually discarded or sold for scrap. In essence, the value of old machine may decline, but it need not lead to any decline in the current services of the capital equipment. Due to the absence of data on fixed capital stock formation at the state level or industry level, the present study used gross fixed capital stock formation by unregistered manufacturing sector at the all-India level to deflate fixed capital stock in the unorganized manufacturing sector. The values are expressed in 1993–4 prices.

6

THE DETERMINANTS OF FIRM TRANSITION

We have already established in previous chapters that there are clear productivity differences between Own Account Manufacturing Enterprises (OAMEs), Non-directory Manufacturing Enterprises (NDMEs), and Directory Manufacturing Enterprises (DMEs). At the same time, we also observed that the predominant type of firms in the informal manufacturing sector in India is the OAMEs, which forms the bulk of employment in the informal economy. This is common to what is observed in other developing countries (Gollin 2008).[1] The majority of OAMEs (very small, household enterprises) are not able to grow in size and make the transition to NDMEs and DMEs (larger enterprises that employ non-family wage labour) (De Neve 2005; Woodruff 2012).[2]

What can explain as to why some OAMEs can make the transition to NDMEs and DMEs and others cannot? As we noted in Chapter 1, the determinants of firm growth in the informal sector of India and other developing countries remain less understood, with much of previous literature focusing on firm growth in the formal sector (Gang 1992; Shanmugam and Bhaduri 2002; Variyam and Kraybill 1992).

[1] In contrast, as Gollin (2008) notes, small enterprises play a small role in advanced market economies.

[2] As Breman (2010: 99) notes, the movement of self-employed workers in family-run firms to owner–managers of firms which employ wage labour 'turns out to be anything but exceptional'.

A wide set of factors have been seen as constraints to the growth of small firms such as lack of access to external finance (Gulyani and Talukdar 2010; Mead and Liedholm 1998; Rijkers et al. 2010), the lack of capabilities in small firms that allow them to compete with large firms (Arend 2014; Schmitz 1982), the lack of access to networks and locational disadvantages (Mead 1984; Rijkers et al. 2010; Schmitz and Nadvi 1999), human capital (Burki and Terrell 1998; Nafziger and Terrell 1996), and infrastructural constraints (Aterido et al. 2011). In this chapter, we assess the role of financial constraints, firm capabilities, locational and geographical factors, and infrastructure and human capital in explaining the transition of firms in the informal sector from small, family-run firms to larger firms employing wage labour.

The rest of the chapter is divided as follows: The next section provides a brief discussion of the literature on the possible determinants of firm transition in the informal sector. The second section discusses the data, describes the econometric methodology, and also discusses the empirical specification. The third section provides an array of descriptive statistics and presents the results of the empirical analysis. The last section concludes the analysis.

Related Literature

A considerable body of research has focused on examining the factors that drive the growth of small firms in the manufacturing sector (see Davidsson et al. [2005]; Nichter and Goldmark [2009] for a review of these studies). These studies have highlighted broadly four important factors influencing the growth and performance of small firms: (a) access to finance, (b) firm capabilities, (c) locational and geographical factors, and (d) the contextual factors (such as infrastructure development, level of human capital, investment climate, and business environment). Our attempt here is to provide a brief review of select studies that examined the role of finance, firm capabilities, locational and geographical factors, and infrastructure and human capital on a firm's growth.

Access to Finance

The access to and cost of finance is one of the factors that determines the ability of a firm to grow (Binks and Ennew 1996; Oliveira and

Fortunato 2006). Available evidence points to a positive relationship between increased access to finance and the firm's growth (Demirgüç-Kunt and Maksimovic 1998; Rajan and Zingales 1998). Firms that face financial constraints are less likely to invest in fixed assets (Ojha et al. 2010; Winker 1999) and they also lack the capabilities to innovate (Winker 1999). There is also evidence to show that access to finance and the firm's size (measured by number of workers) move in the same direction (Aterido and Hallward-Driemeier 2008).

The effect of financial constraints on the firm's growth varies across firms of different sizes. There is evidence that the effect is stronger on smaller firms (Beck et al. 2005) as small firms are financially more constrained than larger firms (Beck 2007; Beck et al. 2008; Beck and Demirgüç-Kunt 2006; Kuntchev et al. 2012). The presence of greater financial constraints thus exerts a negative influence on the growth of small firms (Oliveira and Fortunato 2006).[3] Beck et al. (2008) estimate that financial constraints reduce firm growth by 6 percentage points, on average, for large firms, but by 10 percentage points in the case of small firms.

While there are studies that have established the clear role for financial constraints on entrepreneurial start-ups, the significance of finance for the subsequent growth and performance of small firms has been more controversial. Brown et al. (2005) show that small firms that have access to credit grow more rapidly. Catao et al. (2009) find that financial deepening shifts the composition away from self-employment towards larger firms. Woodruff and Zenteno (2007) also show evidence of the high importance of access to credit in Mexico, measured by remittances, in microenterprise development. On the other hand, there are also studies that highlight the less important role of financial constraints on firm growth. For instance, Daniels and Mead (1998), Johnson et al. (2002), and McPherson and Rous (2010) do not find compelling evidence to show that access to formal credit is a significant factor influencing firm growth. Like any other factors, it is likely that access to finance could be a necessary but not a sufficient condition for small firm growth (Nichter and Goldmark 2009).

---

[3] In the enterprise survey by the World Bank, 35 per cent of the small firms consider cost of finance as a major growth constraint and 30 per cent consider access to finance as a major growth constraint (Beck 2007).

Firms' Capabilities

Many studies have tried to understand the role of firm capabilities on growth. In the resource-based view of firm capabilities, where the firm is not just an administrative unit but a collection of productive resources (Penrose 1959), the capabilities of the managers of firms (which, in the case of the informal firms, are also the owners) are important to attain competitive advantage and for the expansion of the firm. Studies have used different indicators to represent firm capabilities. Indicators, such as investment in R&D or purchase of specialized machinery, which are used in previous studies are less applicable as measures of firm capabilities in the informal sector (Sher and Yang 2005; Yang and Huang 2005). A key source of information on technology and marketing for owners of informal firms is other firms, often in the formal sector, with whom they have subcontracting arrangements (Berry et al. 2002). Lall (1980) and Hill (1985) consider subcontracting as a means by which technological improvements are transmitted from the large-scale sector to the small-scale sector. Subcontracting helps firms gain in generating productive employment and higher incomes (Yasuda 2005). In a study on Italian industry, Giunta et al. (2012) notice that subcontracting, when coupled with the propensity to innovate, turns out to be a determinant of firm growth. However, in the case of Japan, Kimura (2002) shows that subcontracting is negatively related to firm size, sales, and technological capability. Another indicator of firm capabilities in the informal sector context is the maintenance of accounts by the manager—the maintenance of accounts by a small, informal firm may allow the owner/manager of the firm to access external finance through the presentation of these accounts to bank managers, and help overcome the constraints to its expansion. The registration of firms under a given act or authority of the government also provides a proxy for the firm capabilities, as registered firms are able to access specialized training and acquire knowledge than non-registered firms. Sharma (2014) finds that registration leads to 32 per cent gain in sales per employee and 56 per cent gain in value added per employee for firms in the small-scale sector.

Location and Geographical Factors

There exists substantial evidence on the positive role of locational and geographical factors on firm growth. Previous studies have employed different indicators to capture the effect of location on the growth of small firms. Some studies argue that urban location is associated with faster growth of firms. Bigsten and Gebreeyesus (2007) and Liedholm and Mead (1999) find that urban enterprises typically grow more rapidly than their rural counterparts. Voulgaris et al. (2003) show that small and medium-sized enterprises (SMEs), which are located in big cities, behave differently from firms located in the periphery with regard to factors related to growth. North and Smallbone (2000), however, argue that the typical rural–urban classification masks the significant variations between different types of rural areas. Keeble et al. (1992) observe that firms in accessible (rather than remote) rural areas compared favourably with firms in urban areas. In another study, Keeble and Tyler (1995) conclude that accessible rural firms are more dynamic, innovative, and technologically focused than their counterparts in either urban or remote rural locations.

Some studies have used measures of market accessibility such as access to transport and distance, cost, and travel time to the main market as proxies for location, and have examined their impact on firm growth. Shiferaw et al. (2013) find a positive relationship between the quality of transport facility and enterprise performance in Ethiopia. Their results clearly show that improvements in travel distance and having the area accessible within an hour's drive from a town where firms are located significantly influence performance of firms. The positive productivity effects of market accessibility for firms are also found for Spain (Holl 2012), the UK (Rice et al. 2006), and India (Lall et al. 2004). However, Hoogstra and Dijk (2004) and Almeida and Carneiro (2005) observe that access to transport is not a significant factor that influences a firm's growth. In general, location is a key variable influencing a firm's growth, although the specific effects may vary at the country level.

Infrastructure and Human Capital

There is ample evidence in the literature to show that infrastructure is critical to firm growth as it helps the firm to get connected to core economic activities and to access additional productive activities. Better infrastructure also helps firms to overcome the bottleneck of locating in backward areas by reducing the costs of production in remotely accessible regions. Bigsten and Gebreeyesus (2007) find that better access to infrastructure boosts firms' growth in Ethiopia. Dollar et al. (2005) also demonstrated a strong association between a firm's growth and its infrastructural quality. They argue that firms with better access to electricity have higher levels of productivity and grow faster. A similar finding is also arrived at by Rijkers et al. (2010), who show that firms which use electricity are more productive than firms which do not. In another study, using road accessibility as an indicator of infrastructure, Shiferaw et al. (2013) find that improved road infrastructure has a favourable impact on the entry patterns as better road access increases a town's attractiveness for manufacturing firms. The significant role of better road infrastructure on production for manufacturing firms is also highlighted by Stephen (1997).

There is overwhelming evidence at the firm level that human capital embodied in the owner of a firm or its workers (generally measured as education, age, or experience) promotes firm growth (McPherson and Rous 2010; Mead and Liedholm 1998; van der Sluis et al. 2005). McPherson and Rous (2010) estimate that the firms in which the typical worker has had formal training have average annual growth rates that are about 2.3 percentage points higher than other firms. Parker (1994) found that enterprises with workers trained formally at vocational schools show significantly higher growth than those enterprises with untrained workers.

Empirical Strategy

The focus of the chapter is to analyse the factors that explain the transition of firms across the entire continuum of the firm size in the informal manufacturing sector. In other words, we look into the factors that explain the transition of OAMEs to NDMEs and then to DMEs. Such a transition also implies that the firm is growing in size from OAMEs (with no wage labourers) to NDMEs (with 1–5 workers), and then to DMEs (with 6–9 workers). Such a transition would also help in improving the overall productivity of the manufacturing sector as lack of upward mobility of firms is argued to be a major hindrance affecting productivity of manufacturing sectors of developing countries (Gollin 2008).

Our data is in the form of repeated cross-sections, and not in panel form, as the National Sample Survey Office (NSSO) does not reveal the identity of the firm/plant in the unit-level data, and the same firms may not be surveyed in each round. The lack of availability of panel data that can follow a firm over time and examine its mobility across the three categories is a limitation of the analysis here. However, given the rigorous sample survey methods used by the NSSO to ensure the representativeness of the unit-level data of the informal manufacturing sectors, and the relative consistency of these methods over time, the repeated cross-sections can be seen as a close approximation of the panel data that we ideally would have liked to use in our analysis.

Our analysis is based on the unit-level data for three years: 2000–1, 2005–6, and 2010–11. The choice of time period is governed by the fact that the data on some of the firm specific variables used in the analysis are only available for these years.[4] For our unit-level data, we had 294,736 firms in the pooled data set, across 22 industries, 364 districts, 15 major Indian states, and the three years.[5]

Data on district-level variables are obtained from the 2001 Census of India.

The Econometric Model

We use econometric analysis to formally test the role of financial constraint, firm capabilities, locational and geographical factors, and infrastructural and human capital variables in influencing the upward progression of firms in the informal sector in India. An ordered logit model is used to capture the firm transition in the informal sector.[6] The dependent variable is e, which is an ordered categorical variable ranging from 1 to 3 (1 = OAME, 2 = NDME, and 3 = DME) denoting the type

---

[4] The unit-level data set for the year 1994–5 does not provide information for the variables CAPSHOR, CONTRACT, ASSISTANCE, ACMAINT, REGIS, and ELEC.

[5] The 15 states included are Andhra Pradesh (AP), Assam, Bihar, Gujarat, Haryana, Karnataka, Kerala, Madhya Pradesh (MP), Maharashtra, Odisha, Punjab, Rajasthan, Tamil Nadu (TN), Uttar Pradesh (UP), and West Bengal (WB). It is important to note here that the AP was bifurcated into two states—Telangana and AP—in 2014. As the period for this study ends in 2010–11, we use the data for the combined AP.

[6] The model would explain the probabilities of a unit falling in the three types of enterprises.

of the firm. We assume here that there is a latent variable e^* given by the following expression:

$$e^*_{j,i,d,t} = \alpha_0 + \alpha_1 \text{FIN}_{j,i,d,t} + \sum_{k>1} \beta_k \text{FCAP}_{j,i,d,t} + \sum_{l>1} \mu_l \text{LOC}_{d,t} + \sum_{p>1} \varphi_p \text{INF}_{d,t}$$
$$+ \lambda_m \text{STATUS}_{j,i,d,t} + \gamma_i + \delta_t + \varepsilon_{j,i,d,t}, \tag{6.1}$$

where the subscripts denote: j for firm, i for industry, d for district, and t for time.

The variable FIN is our measure of financial constraints that a particular firm faces. A direct measure is used to capture the firm's financial constraints. The NSSO asks the firms in its surveys if they have faced any constraint on its borrowing in the last year. We denote this variable as CAPSHOR and code this variable as 1 if the firm faces a constraint and 0 if it does not. We expect that α_1 would be less than zero if access to finance acts as a constraint on firm transition.

FCAP is a vector of factors representing firm capabilities. The NSSO asks the firms in its surveys whether they work solely for a contractor (that is, they sells all their output to the contractor, who usually, in this tied arrangement, supplies them with the inputs). We name this variable as LINKAGE and code it as 1 if they work for a contractor and 0 if they do not. We examine whether firms that work for contractors are more likely to scale up their size as well as employ outside workers. Firms that are working in subcontracting relationships may be needing the specialized skills that outside workers bring. The survey also asks the firms whether they receive any assistance from the government towards training and marketing. We label this variable as ASSISTANCE and assign the code 1 if the firms received any assistance and 0 if they did not. If ASSISTANCE increases firms' productivity, it is likely to be positively associated with firm transition in the informal sector. ACMAINT is another variable used, which takes the value of 1 if the firms maintain a regular account and 0 if they do not. Firms that maintain account are likely to be better organized and, therefore, shift to the next size class in the informal sector. The NSSO surveys also ask the firms whether they have registered under any act or authority. Being a part of an act/authority could help the owner–manager to access and secure a range of financial and non-financial resources (information, knowledge, technology, and finance) that are otherwise mostly unavailable to the firms in the informal sector. We denote this variable as REGIS and code it as 1 if they have registered under any act and 0 if they are not. A positive relationship is envisioned between REGIS and firm transition.

The vector LOC contains four variables that encapsulate the locational and geographical features of firms. The four variables are SECTOR, URBAN, TRANSPORT, and DISTANCE. SECTOR is a firm-level attribute intended to capture the benefits that a firm may derive by being located in urban areas. It is expected to capture differences among firms in access to better infrastructure and larger markets for skilled labour, raw materials, and outputs. The NSSO surveys report whether the firms are located in rural or urban areas. SECTOR takes the value of 1 if the firm is located in urban areas and 0 if it is located in rural areas. The expectation is that firms that are located in and around cities and towns (as a large market area) will experience faster expansion in size than their counterparts. URBAN is a district-level measure representing the level of urbanization (measured by the share of urban population in total population) in the district where the firms are located. We surmise that the higher the level of urbanization in a district, the higher will be the firm transition. Two more district-level measures are introduced, TRANSPORT and DISTANCE. TRANSPORT indicates the access to the district in terms of a major transportation link, and it takes the value of 1 if a national highway or a broad gauge line passes through the district and 0 if neither of them passes through the district. DISTANCE signifies the remoteness of the district as captured by the distance of the district from the state capital. We expect that TRANSPORT will have a positive impact on firm transition and DISTANCE will have a negative impact on the same.

INF is a vector that includes infrastructural and human capital variables. Our attempt is to see whether differences in the availability of infrastructure and human capital at the regional level influence the upward progression of firms in the informal sector. Five such variables—namely, ELEC, SHSCSTPOP, PRIMEDU, MIDGRADEDU, and ROADVILLG—are identified. ELEC is a firm-specific factor while other four variables are constructed at the district level. ELEC indicates whether the firm has access to electricity, and it takes the value of 1 if it has access to electricity and 0 if it lacks access to it. SHSCSTPOP represents the proportion of Scheduled Caste (SC) and Scheduled

Tribe (ST) population in total population, PRIMEDU captures the proportion of individuals who are educated at primary level or below, MIDGRADEDU stands for the proportion of individuals educated at secondary level and above, and ROADVILLG represents share of villages with paved approach road in total villages. We expect that higher level of human capital as measured by high MIDGRADEDU and low PRIMEDU would have a positive effect on firm transition.[7] On the other hand, social and economic backwardness as captured by SHSCSTPOP will have a negative effect on firm transition.[8] We also envisage that better provision of infrastructure captured through the availability of power (ELEC) and better roads (ROADVILLG) would positively influence firm transition.

We also introduce a firm-specific control variable, STATUS, which indicates whether the firm has been expanding in the past three years (STATUS takes the value of 1 if the firm has been expanding and 0 if the firm has been stagnant or contracting). This variable captures the demand-side determinants of firm transition—clearly a firm that has seen an increase in its sales is more likely to make the transition from OAME status to NDME status and then to DME status, than a firm which faces a stagnant or contracting market. The variables γ_i are industry-specific fixed effects and δ_t are the year-specific dummies. Industry-specific effects are used to capture the possibilities that firm transition to larger size enterprises would be more likely in industries

[7] Unfortunately, we do not have data on the age of the firm and education of the firm's owner–manager for all three rounds, which does not allow us to include these two variables in the ordered logit regressions. This is a limitation of our econometric analysis as both the age of the firm and firm-specific human capital may play an important role in the firm transition.

[8] India's SCs and STs remain socially excluded from the mainstream due to the persistence of caste and other forms of social discrimination. The incidence of headcount poverty among SCs and STs was, respectively, 21 and 15 percentage points higher than for the rest of the population in 2009–10 (Himanshu and Sen 2014), and SC and ST households are much more likely to face barriers for access to credit and human capital acquisition, and are less likely to be owners–managers of non-family firms than other social groups (Thorat and Newman 2012). Thus, districts with high SC/ST presence are less likely to see the mobility of family firms to non-family firms.

with economies of scale such as metal, chemicals, and automobiles. The year dummies capture the possibility that economy-wide demand shocks may have an impact on the firm transition. The link between the observed and the latent variables is given by:

$$P(e_i = 1 \mid v_i) = \theta(-\alpha_0 - v_i\gamma),$$
$$P(e_i = 2 \mid v_i) = \theta(\mu - \alpha_0 - v_i\gamma) - \theta(-\alpha_0 - v_i\gamma),$$
$$P(e_i = 3 \mid v_i) = 1 - \theta(\mu - \alpha_0 - v_i\gamma),$$

where is $v_i = [\text{FIN}_i, X_i, Z_i], \gamma = [\alpha_1, \beta_k, \lambda_m], \theta$ the logistic distribution function, and μ is the additional intercept that differentiates category 2 firm from category 3 firm. For all probabilities to be positive, μ should be greater than 0.

We estimate the model using the maximum likelihood method. The ordered logit model, however, assumes proportional odds between the different categories, which imply that the relationship between each pair of outcomes is the same for all variables. Therefore, we also test this assumption of proportional odds by comparing the estimates from the ordered logit model with those of the generalized ordered logit model, where not just the intercept but the coefficients also vary by the category of the dependent variable. In all these estimations, we use firms as units of analysis.

Descriptive Statistics and Results

Descriptive Statistics

We begin the empirical analysis by presenting the summary statistics in Table 6.1 for the main dependent and independent variables used in the analysis. In the data set here, an average firm employs more than one worker. Of firm owners, 36.2 per cent report that they face shortage of capital, while only 20 per cent of firms undertake work on a contract basis. Urban enterprises in the data set constitute 55 per cent of total firms surveyed. More than a fifth (23.3 per cent) of firms report that they have access to an electricity connection, while only 7.4 per cent mention that they maintain accounts. Very few firms in the data set receive any assistance towards training and marketing from the government in the period 2001–11. Notably, less than a quarter of firms' owners feel that their firms are expanding. Further, only 24 per cent of

Table 6.1 Summary Statistics: Firm-level Analysis

Variable	N	Mean	SD	Min.	Max.
ENTYP	294,736	1.448988	0.682141	1	3
CAPSHOR	294,736	0.362307	0.480668	0	1
SECTOR	294,736	0.542343	0.498205	0	1
REGIS	294,736	0.232588	0.422482	0	1
CONTRACT	294,736	0.200227	0.400171	0	1
ASSISTANCE	294,736	0.004794	0.069074	0	1
STATUS	294,736	0.226029	0.418259	0	1
ELEC	294,736	0.233097	0.422804	0	1
ACMAINT	294,736	0.073832	0.261498	0	1
URBAN	294,736	0.34537	0.396945	0	1
SHSCSTPOP	294,736	0.231766	0.117352	0.026295	0.942542
PRIMEDU	294,736	0.292051	0.060837	0.14919	1
MIDGRADEDU	294,736	0.261882	0.105644	0.068002	0.964556
DISTANCE	294,736	255.5111	184.2678	0	1010
TRANSPORT	294,736	0.800832	0.399375	0	1
COLLGVILLG	281,606	0.016217	0.028592	0	0.166667

Source: Calculations based on NSSO unit-level data for 2000–1, 2005–6, and 2010–11 and the Census of India for 2001.

firms in the data set report that they have registered under any act or authority. Table 6.1 also reports summary statistics for district-level variables included in the analysis. On average, SCs and STs constitute 23 per cent of the total population at the district level. Average educational attainment is found to be considerably lower at the district level. The percentage of population that has attained pre-primary or primary levels of education is very low at 29 per cent, while the educational attainment beyond secondary level is estimated at 26 per cent. Interestingly, 80 per cent of all districts are connected to a national highway or a broad-gauge railway line.

We also present the firm-level characteristics for three types of enterprises—OAMEs, NDMEs, and DMEs—in Table 6.2. We find little variation across types of enterprises in percentage of firms that are financially constrained. In the data set, urban areas account for more than 60 per cent of NDMEs and DMEs and less than 50 per cent

Table 6.2 Type-wise Characteristics of Firms (Mean Values)

Variable	OAME	NDME	DME
N	194,517	68,105	32,114
(%)	(66.0)	(23.1)	(10.9)
CAPSHOR	0.365289	0.356714	0.356106
SECTOR	0.486456	0.668835	0.612599
REGIS	0.092856	0.428456	0.663574
LINKAGE	0.194122	0.188973	0.261070
ASSISTANCE	0.004838	0.003377	0.007536
STATUS	0.190847	0.281727	0.321013
ELEC	0.187228	0.299493	0.370119
ACMAINT	0.021001	0.097981	0.342623
TRANSPORT	0.781315	0.827296	0.862926
ROADVILG	0.659530	0.723272	0.775610
MIDGRADEDU	0.249531	0.279956	0.298361

Source: Calculations based on NSSO unit-level data for 2000–1, 2005–6, and 2010–11 and the Census of India for 2001.

of OAMEs. Percentage of firms that are registered under any act or authority in the data set increases with the size of the firm. It varies from 9 per cent in the case of OAMEs to a whopping 66 per cent in the case of DMEs. We also observe that larger share of DMEs (26 per cent) engaged in works that are farmed out to them by big firms. Concomitant to the picture at the level of all enterprise types, very few OAMEs, NDMEs, and DMEs receive any training and marketing assistance from the government. More than one-third of DMEs in the data set report that they maintain accounts, while only 10 per cent of NDMEs and 2 per cent of OAMEs claim that they maintain regular accounts. While comparing the access to infrastructure between small and large firms, a clear bias is observed towards large firms. For instance, 37 per cent of DMEs and 30 per cent of NDMEs reported to have electricity access as opposed to 19 per cent of OAMEs. A similar picture can be discerned when access to a major transportation link, availability of better roads, and availability of human capital is considered.

Regression Results

Table 6.3 presents the estimates of ordered logit regression model as in Equation 6.1.[9] In all, we estimate five specifications of Equation 6.1. In model 1, we introduce only the CAPSHOR variable. Model 2 includes industry and year dummies. We then introduce variables representing firm capabilities in Model 3. Locational variables, along with STATUS as control variable, are brought in Model 4. We also include infrastructure and human capital variables in Model 5.

The results unequivocally suggest that credit availability plays a positive role in the upward progression of firms in the informal sector. The coefficient of CAPSHOR variable is negative and significant at the 1 per cent level across all five models implying a negative relationship between financial constraints and firm transition across the continuum of size classes in the informal manufacturing sector in India. This gives credence to the fact that with the easing of financial constraint, a firm is likely to expand and move to the next size classes.

The results with respect to the influence of firm capabilities on the firm transition are in line with the expectation. LINKAGE is positively associated with firm transition. Firms that are under contract are more likely to expand in size, which is quite plausible as these firms will be needing the specialized skills that outside workers bring to perform the tasks assigned by the parent firms. Our conjecture is further strengthened by the fact that relatively a higher share of DMEs work as subcontractors for large firms as compared to OAMEs and NDMEs (Table 6.2). ACMAINT is positively correlated with firm transition, suggesting that the progression of firms to immediate size class is more evident among firms that maintain regular accounts. This result is in line with the finding of Acar (1993) who shows that sound accounting practices is an important factor associated with the firm growth. This could be the reason why accounting practices are more apparent in large firms, while majority of small firms especially those in the household sector tend to neglect the recording aspects of business. As conjectured, REGIS is also positively associated with the firm

---

[9] We also estimated Equation 6.1 for each year and we find that the results are consistent across years. Hence, the results for the pooled sample are being presented.

Table 6.3 Results: Ordered Logistic Regression Estimates

Dependent Variable: ENTYP

Variable	Model 1	Model 2	Model 3	Model 4	Model 5
			Finance		
CAPSHOR	−0.037*	−0.150*	−0.052*	−0.035*	−0.033*
	(0.008)	(0.009)	(0.010)	(0.010)	(0.011)
		Firm Capabilities			
LINKAGE			0.379*	0.312*	0.239*
			(0.012)	(0.012)	(0.013)
ASSISTANCE			0.039	0.098	0.173*
			(0.070)	(0.070)	(0.071)
ACMAINT			1.527*	1.455*	1.400*
			(0.015)	(0.016)	(0.016)
REGIS			1.964*	1.878*	1.795*
			(0.010)	(0.010)	(0.011)
		Locational Variables			
SECTOR				0.306*	0.277*
				(0.009)	(0.009)
URBAN				0.287*	0.210*
				(0.011)	(0.012)
TRANSPORT				0.164*	0.079*
				(0.011)	(0.012)
DISTANCE				−0.0003*	−0.0001*
				(0.0000)	(0.0000)
	Infrastructure and Human Capital Variables				
ELEC					0.653*
					(0.011)
SHSCSTPOP					−0.0001
					(0.0440)
PRIMEDU					−1.096*
					(0.089)
MIDGRADEDU					0.605*
					(0.065)
ROADVILLG					1.045*
					(0.024)
	Other Control Variables				
STATUS				0.453*	0.480*
				(0.010)	(0.010)
Industry Dummy	N	Y	Y	Y	Y
Year Dummy	N	Y	Y	Y	Y

N	294,736	294,736	294,736	294,736	281,606
Pseudo R^2	0.00	0.04	0.17	0.18	0.20
Log Likelihood	−251,788.55	−241,343.33	−207,446.79	−204,836.63	−189,305.88
LR test of proportionality of odds across response categories:					
chi^2	0.53	10,856.35	9,541.14	10,983.51	10,512.41
Prob > chi^2	0.4665	0.0000	0.0000	0.0000	0.0000

Source: Calculations based on NSSO unit-level data for 2000–1, 2005–6, and 2010–11 and the Census of India for 2001.

Note: * significant at 10 per cent level or below.

transition. This shows that firms that are part of an organization or authority or those registered under any act tend to grow in size as against firms that are neither a member of an organization nor are registered under any act. On the other hand, there is very little evidence that assistance provided to firms play a positive role in the upward progression of firms as the coefficient for ASSISTANCE is significant in only one of the estimations. Of course, the raw data would have anticipated this result; very few firms (a meagre 0.4 per cent) in the data set report that they received assistance in the form of training and marketing.

Does location matter for firm transition in the informal sector? The results forcefully point to the significant role that locational and geographical variables play in influencing the transition of firms to larger sizes. The coefficient of SECTOR variable is positive and highly significant in all our estimations, thereby suggesting that upward progression is faster among firms that are located in urban areas, cities, and towns as compared to their counterparts in rural towns and villages. We also find that firms are more likely to make transition across size classes in more urbanized districts. This is clearly evident from the positive and highly significant coefficient of URBAN. This indicates that the demand-side factors are important for firm transition since in the more urbanized districts, there will be greater demand for manufacturing products. Results also indicate that availability of better transport infrastructure at the district level leads to more firms shifting to larger types of enterprises. Access to better transport infrastructure improves market accessibility for small firms, which will have an impact on their average firm size and their subsequent growth (Tybout 2000). We also find significant negative relationship between remoteness of the district (DISTANCE) and the firm transition. The coefficient of DISTANCE variable is significant and negative in all the specifications indicating that graduation of firms to bigger sizes decreases with increase in the distance of the district from the state capital. The results thus suggests that reduction in transport costs captured through lesser distance and better transport infrastructure are very important for firm transition as firms benefit from reduced factor costs, increased access to specialized labour, and general agglomeration economies (Shiferaw et al. 2013). This also affects the firm transition by reducing the importance of spatial proximity to engage in subcontracting and output and input linkages.

The results of our study also confirm the pivotal role of infrastructure and human capital on the firm transition. The coefficient of ELEC that captures the firms' access to electricity is positive and significant indicating that provision of quality electricity is an important dimension of infrastructure affecting firm size expansion in informal sector. Importance of power availability for firm growth has been already highlighted by a number of studies in the literature (Aterido et al. 2011; Kathuria et al. 2013). We find that the share of people with education up to the primary level in total population (PRIMEDU) has a negative influence on the firm transition. This perhaps explains the effect of the constraints emanating from lower levels of human capital on the firm transition. The positive and significant coefficient of MIDGRADEDU confirms the conjecture on the positive role of human capital on firm transition. On the other hand, SHSCSCTPOP, when included in the equation to gauge the effect of social backwardness on firm transition, is not significant, though it gives the expected negative sign.

To lend exact interpretation of the magnitude of change of the explanatory variables on firm transition, we also estimated odds ratios. Figure 6.1 reports the results which are the exponential expression of the coefficients in Table 6.3. Results suggest that the switch in firm's status from being financially constrained to not being financially constrained increases the likelihood that the firm will be a DME or an NDME instead of an OAME. Among the variables representing firm capabilities, REGIS and ACMAINT are the most important variables aiding firm transition. On an average, firms that are registered under any act or authority are 6 times more likely to experience expansion in their size than firms that are neither registered under any act nor are with any authority. Similarly, firms that maintain accounts are 4 times more likely to shift to bigger sizes as compared to firms that do not maintain accounts. When a firm moves from having no contract to the status of having contract, the odds of upward progression of firms improves by about 1.3 times. Among the locational variables, the likelihood of a firm expanding to a bigger size increases by 1.3 times for a unit change in SECTOR (a firm shifting from rural to urban areas) and by 1.2 times for a unit change in URBAN. For a unit change of TRANSPORT, the chance of firm transition in the informal sector goes up by 1.1 times. Among the infrastructure and human capital variables, ROADVILLG, ELEC, and MIDGRADEDU play significant role in influencing firm transition in the informal sector. Figure 6.1 shows that the probability of a firm growing to a larger size improves by 2.8 times, 1.9 times, and

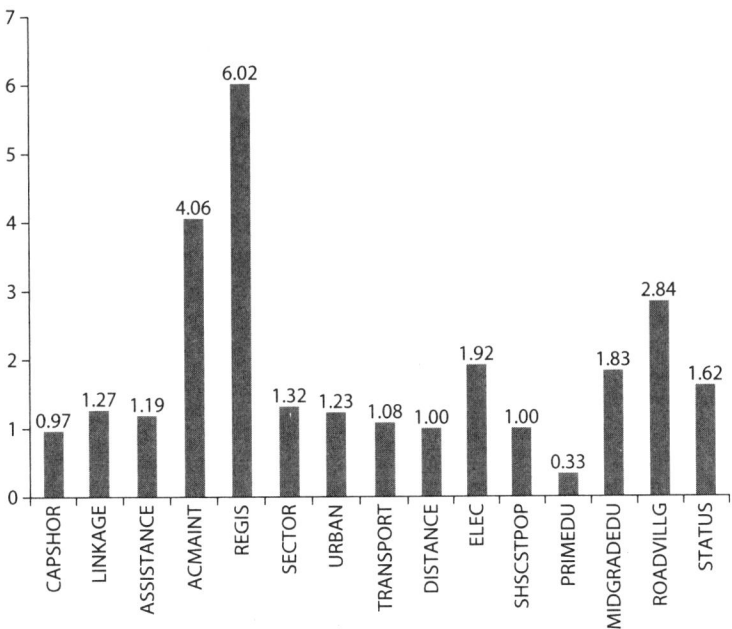

Figure 6.1 Odds Ratios: Ordered Logistic Regression Estimates
Source: Based on Model 5 in Table 6.3.

1.8 times, respectively, for a unit change in ROADVILLG, ELEC (that is, moving from no access to access to electricity), and MIDGRADEDU. In contrast to the evidence in the literature, credit availability seems to play only a lesser role in the transition of firms to larger sizes.

The ordered logit model, however, assumes proportionality of odds between the different categories. In other words, the model assumes that the relationship between each pair of outcomes is the same for all variables. The validity of this assumption is tested for this study and it is found that the proportional odds assumption is rejected at the 5 per cent level (see the bottom row of Table 6.3).[10] Therefore, Equation 6.1 is also estimated using generalized logit regression (GOLOGIT) model that relaxes the proportionality of odds assumption.[11] According to Williams (2006), estimating GOLOGIT model is equivalent to estimating separate binary logit regressions. We report the results in Table 6.4 under two columns for each model (*a* and *b*). For an ordinal dependent variable with three categories (as is in our case), the column under *a* can be interpreted as a binary logit regression where the dependent variable is reordered as 1 versus 2 + 3 (that is, OAMEs versus NDMEs and DMEs). Similarly, the column under *b* can be treated as the results of a binary logit regression where we compare 1 + 2 versus 3 (in other words, comparing OAMEs and NDMEs versus DMEs). The same order of specification is followed in both these estimations as in Table 6.3.

We do not observe a considerable variation in the results with the relaxation of the assumption of proportional odds.[12] The coefficients of variables representing firm capabilities, location, infrastructure, and human capital remain qualitatively similar not only across categories but also compared to the slopes of the ordinary logit model. Only exceptions are SECTOR and DISTANCE whose coefficients switch signs in column *b*. The odds ratios of GOLOGIT model presented

[10] We employed a stata program known as *omodel* to test the proportionality of odds across different categories.

[11] The estimation is performed using stata by using the program, *gologit2*, developed by Williams (2006), that estimates a generalized logistic regression model for an ordinal dependent variable.

[12] The results of the Wald test of proportionality are also very similar to those obtained through *omodel* estimation.

Table 6.4 Results: Generalized Ordered Logistic Regression Estimates

Dependent Variable: ENTYP

Variable	Model 1		Model 2		Model 3		Model 4		Model 5	
	a	b	a	b	a	b	a	b	a	b
Finance										
CAPSHOR	-0.038*	-0.030*	-0.122*	-0.300*	-0.027*	-0.163*	-0.018*	-0.131*	-0.025*	-0.110*
	(0.008)	(0.012)	(0.009)	(0.013)	(0.010)	(0.015)	(0.010)	(0.015)	(0.011)	(0.016)
Firm Capabilities										
LINKAGE					0.358*	0.528*	0.277*	0.472*	0.204*	0.401*
					(0.012)	(0.017)	(0.012)	(0.017)	(0.013)	(0.018)
ASSISTANCE					-0.056	0.199*	0.073	0.026	0.156*	0.053
					(0.067)	(0.076)	(0.068)	(0.080)	(0.069)	(0.082)
ACMAINT					1.481*	1.683*	1.416*	1.631*	1.348*	1.578*
					(0.019)	(0.018)	(0.020)	(0.019)	(0.020)	(0.020)
REGIS					2.031*	1.719*	1.943*	1.672*	1.852*	1.586*
					(0.011)	(0.014)	(0.011)	(0.015)	(0.012)	(0.016)
Locational Variables										
SECTOR							0.408*	-0.067*	0.384*	-0.094*
							(0.010)	(0.015)	(0.010)	(0.015)
URBAN							0.257*	0.364*	0.176*	0.290*
							(0.011)	(0.014)	(0.012)	(0.015)
TRANSPORT							0.167*	0.132*	0.083*	0.058*
							(0.012)	(0.019)	(0.012)	(0.020)
DISTANCE							-0.0004*	-0.0001*	-0.0002*	0.0002*
							(0.0000)	(0.0000)	(0.0000)	(0.0000)

(*Contd.*)

Table 6.4 (Contd.)

Variable	Model 1 a	Model 1 b	Model 2 a	Model 2 b	Model 3 a	Model 3 b	Model 4 a	Model 4 b	Model 5 a	Model 5 b
Infrastructure and Human Capital Variables										
ELEC									0.671* (0.011)	0.598* (0.016)
SHSCSTPOP									0.039 (0.047)	−0.040 (0.072)
PRIMEDU									−1.089* (0.095)	−1.037* (0.136)
MIDGRA-DEDU									0.597* (0.064)	0.907* (0.110)
ROADVILLG									1.024* (0.026)	1.038* (0.040)
Other Control Variables										
STATUS							0.482* (0.011)	0.423* (0.015)	0.503* (0.011)	0.458* (0.016)
Industry Dummy	N		Y		Y		Y		Y	
Year Dummy	N		Y		Y		Y		Y	
N	294,736		294,736		294,736		294,736		281,606	
Pseudo R²	0.00		0.062		0.195		0.211		0.221	
Log Likelihood	−251,788.29		−236,096.96		−202,717.01		−198,783.62		−184,072.36	
Wald test of proportionality										
chi²	0.51		12,156.29		14,523.89		25,125.92		25,798.59	
Prob > chi²	0.4769		0.0000		0.0000		0.0000		0.0000	

Source: Calculations based on NSSO unit level data for 2000–1, 2005–6, and 2010–11 and the Census of India for 2001.

Notes: (a) The column a can be interpreted as a binary logit regression where the dependent variable is reordered as 1 versus 2 + 3 (OAME versus NDME and DME). Column b can be treated as another binary logit regression where we compare 1 + 2 versus 3 (OAME and NDME versus DME).

(b) * significant at 10 per cent level or below.

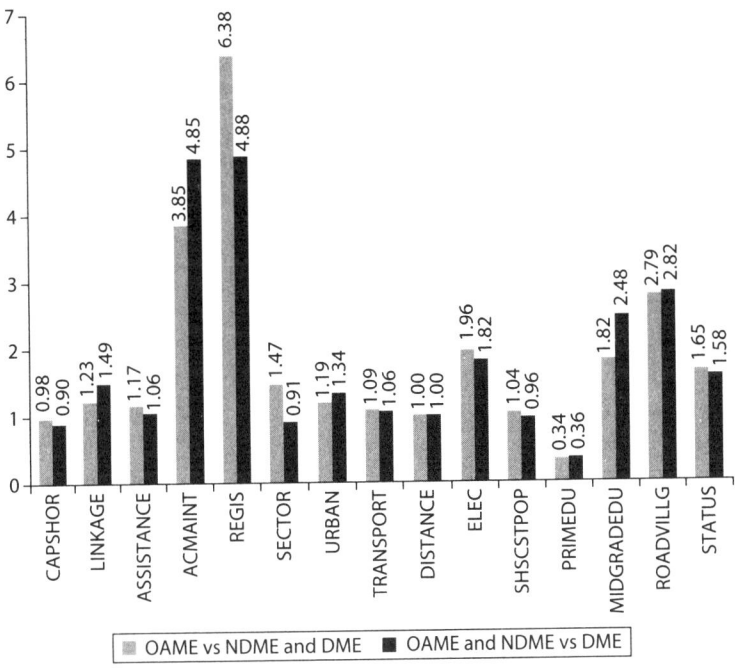

Figure 6.2 Odds Ratios: Generalized Ordered Logistic Regression Estimates
Source: Based on Model 5 in Table 6.3.

in Figure 6.2 indicate that the effect of most of the variables on firm transition is only marginally different across the two categories. There exist significant differences in the influence of ACMAINT, REGIS, and MIDGRADEDU on firm transition between *a* and *b*. As evident from Figure 6.2, a unit change in ACMAINT increases the odds of the occurrence of *b* (switching the status to DME from OAME or NDME) by 4.8 times, while the odds to the occurrence of *a* (shifting from OAME to NDME or DME) increases by only 3.8 times. A relatively faster occurrence of *b* as against *a* is also observed for a unit change in MIDGRADEDU. On the other hand, changes in REGIS will lead to faster occurrence of *a* as compared to *b*. We find that a unit change in REGIS increases the odds of occurrence of *a* by 6.4 times but *b* by only 4.8 times.

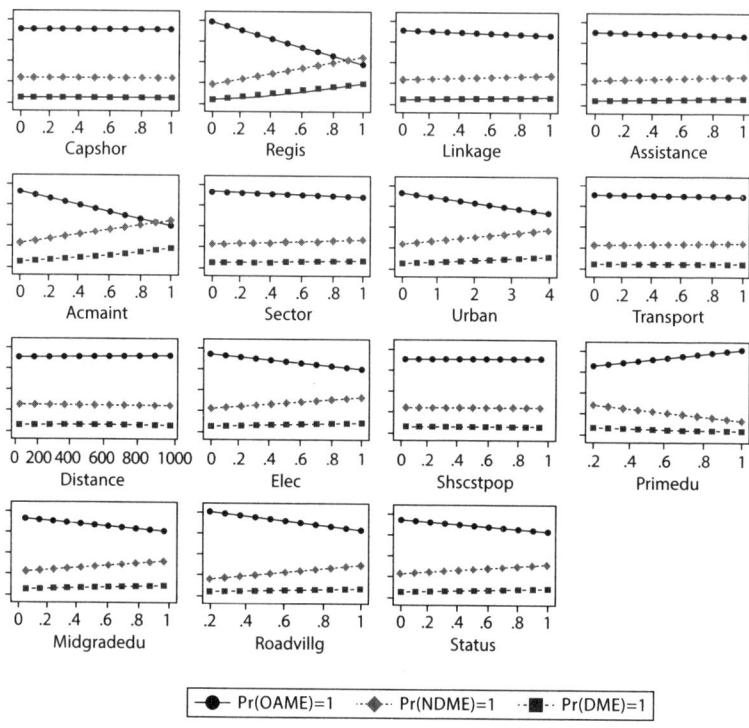

Figure 6.3 Effect on Firm Transition by Enterprise Type
Source: Authors' estimates.

Predicted Probabilities of Firm Transition

Figure 6.3 depicts the predicted probabilities of firm transition due to the changes in the key determinants of firm transition. The figure captures the probability of being in each category changes as a function of each explanatory variable, holding the other variables constant. We used model 5 to estimate the predicted probabilities, where the estimation of the probability of firms graduating to next type of classes (ENTYP) on 15 independent variables (CAPSHOR, REGIS, LINKAGE, ASSISTANCE, ACMAINT, SECTOR, URBAN, TRANSPORT, DISTANCE, ELEC, SHSCSTPOP, PRIMEDU, MIDGRADEDU, ROADVILLG, STATUS) were considered. The coefficients obtained are used to calculate the probability of firm graduation on sample mean values for these independent variables. Figure 6.3 presents the predicted probabilities for each type of enterprise separately.

We find that the predicted probability of being in the OAME category declines with changes in average values of most of the determinants. Among the variables capturing firm capabilities, REGIS and ACMAINT make sizeable effect on the predicted probability of being in the OAME size class. The predicted probability of a firm being in the OAME category declines by more than half (from 80 per cent to 40 per cent) if the firm is registered and is maintaining accounts. A similar change in REGIS and ACMAINT also lead to the predicted probability of being in the NDME category increase from 20 per cent to 40 per cent. A marginal increase in predicted probability is also observed for DME category. Changes in LINKAGE and ASSISTANCE, on the other hand, lead to only marginal changes in the predicted probability of being in these types of enterprises. In the case of locational and geographical variables, the predicted probability of being in the OAME size class decreases, and being in the NDME and DME size classes increases, with increasing urbanization. The predicted probability changes are lower for changes in the values of SECTOR and TRANSPORT. Changes in infrastructural variables such as ELEC and ROADVILLG are also significant in influencing the predicted probability of being in these types of enterprises. A similar change in predicted probabilities is also observed for the changes in the availability of qualified human capital (MIDGRADEDU). Contrary to the evidence in the literature, we do not find that improvements in access to finance significantly influence the predicted probability of being in different size classes in the informal sector.[13] Our findings from the quantitative analysis is supported by the qualitative surveys we have undertaken in the state of Karnataka (see Box 6.1).

---

[13] A limitation of our analysis is that the lack of suitable instrumental variables does not allow us to control for endogeneity of some of our explanatory variables (such as credit constraints and firm capabilities). Thus, our findings should be interpreted with some caution, so that the variables we highlight in our econometric analysis can be seen as correlates of firm transition, and not necessarily causal to firm transition.

Box 6.1:   Understanding the Constraints to Firm Growth

As part of the research on the constraints to firm growth in the Indian informal manufacturing sector, we interviewed owners and managers of informal firms of all size categories—OAMEs, DMEs, and NDMEs—as well as formal enterprises that have recently made the transition from the informal sector. The surveys were conducted in two locations, Bangalore (now Bengaluru) and Hubli, in the state of Karnataka, which has a major share of enterprises in the unorganized manufacturing sector in the traditional industries, and also provides an ideal setting for examining firms in technology-intensive industries. The survey was conducted in two phases. In the first phase, we used close-ended questionnaires to elicit background data on 100 firms—80 informal firms and 20 formal firms. In the second phase, we identified 60 firms for more detailed case studies, 30 from each location, using the background data obtained in the first phase. Semi-structured questionnaires and interviews were used with firm owner–managers to obtain qualitative data on the firms in the second phase. We considered only those firms which are in operation for more than three years.

The interviews provide further support for the findings that is obtained from the quantitative analysis in this chapter. The lack of availability of skilled labour, poor infrastructure, the lack of a market close to the production unit, and difficulty in getting access to credit recurred frequently in the responses of firm owners and managers in the interviews. For example, Shyam,* who runs the manufacturing unit which specializes in manufacture of tool components (an NDME), highlighted the problem of lack of skilled labour; even diploma holders do not have the minimum required skills. Vikram, who owns an ink-manufacturing unit (a DME), when asked about the major hurdles for his business, cited lack of finance and labour shortage. Bhagya, a housewife who runs a small unit that manufactures identity cards for schools (an OAME) mentioned the seasonality of demand and the lack of skilled labour during peak demand times as the main constraints for her firm. Hamid, who runs a business of making photogravure printing rollers (a DME), stated that poor roads and erratic electricity supply were major concerns for his firm. Samarth, a shirt maker, finds it difficult to compete with large formal firms such as Arvind Mills, as he lacks the reputational advantage that these large formal firms have. Gagan Industries, a firm which makes turned components and springs and press components for ordinance factories controlled by the Ministry of Defence (a DME) complained about the level of corruption faced by the firm in terms of bribes paid to labour inspectors. The overall finding from the firm interviews is that no one particular constraint stood out and that different informal firms faced different constraints.

* All names mentioned in this case study are fictitious.

✻   ✻   ✻

This chapter investigates the determinants of firm transition in the informal manufacturing sector, and tries to understand why very few small, family firms (OAMEs), which are the predominant type of firms in the informal sector, fail to make the transition to the larger firms that employ non-family labour (DMEs and NDMEs) in developing economies.

Firm capabilities seem to matter significantly for the firm transition in the informal sector. Among the variables capturing firm capabilities, registration status and account maintenance play a crucial role in the transition of firms to larger sizes. Based on the marginal effects of the estimated generalized ordered logit model (as in Table 6.4), we find that if the status of the firm changes from 'not registered' to 'registered', the probability of the firm being in the NDME category increases by 30 per cent and in the DME category increases by 12.2 per cent, while the probability of firm continuing as OAME reduces by 42 per cent. A firm that switches its status from not maintaining account to one that maintains account increases the probability of being in the NDME and DME categories by 17.3 per cent and 14.6 per cent, respectively, holding all other factors constant. In contrast, it reduces the probability of being in the OAME category by 32 per cent. Firms that are tied through subcontracting arrangements are 4.4 per cent less likely to be an OAME, while the probability of such firms in the NDME and DME categories goes up by 2 per cent.

Relative to firms in rural areas, urban firms have a greater chance of being in the larger-size type in the informal sector. Estimates suggest that the likelihood of an urban firm being in the NDME size class improves by 8 per cent while its continuance as an OAME reduces by 8 per cent. It is also found that firms are less likely to be in the household sector with an increase in urbanization. As the urban population rises relative to the total population, the probability of a firm being in the OAME category decreases by 3.7 per cent while the probability of being in the NDME and DME size classes improves by 2.3 per cent and 1.4 per cent, respectively. These results imply that the size of the market and the availability of a relatively skilled workforce—both factors being captured by the urbanization variables—are important correlates of firm transition.

Our results also suggest that an improvement in infrastructure can significantly accelerate firm transition in the informal sector. We find that the rise in the share of villages with paved approach road in total villages in a district is likely to reduce the probability of firms being in the OAME class type by 21.4 per cent and increase the likelihood of firms being in the NDME and DME size classes by 16.3 per cent and 5.2 per cent, respectively. Providing firms with access to electricity would significantly reduce the chance of firms continuing as OAMEs by 14.9 per cent. On the other hand, electricity access would significantly increase the probability of firms being in the NDME and DME categories by 11.4 per cent and 3.4 per cent, respectively. Our study also confirms the positive role of human capital on firm transition. With the rise in the proportion of individuals educated at secondary level and above in a district, there is likelihood of 12.5 per cent decline in firms being in the OAME category. On the other hand, it significantly enhances the probability of firms being in the NDME and DME category by 8 per cent and 4.5 per cent, respectively.

We find that financial constraints do not contribute significantly to a firm's expansion in the informal sector, as compared to firm capabilities, locational and infrastructural variables, and human capital. This may because firms in the informal sector have access to funds from friends and family and, given their small size, do not need loans of any significant scale to operate. The relatively low importance of financial constraints in explaining firm transition may also be due to the directed lending programme of commercial banks to the priority sector and the role of specialized term-lending institutions such as Small Industries Development Bank of India (SIDBI) in alleviating the financial constraints of small firms.

Overall, the results are in accord with the previous literature in identifying firm capabilities, infrastructure, locational factors and, to a lesser extent, financial constraints as being important in understanding the likelihood of firm transition across the continuum of firms in the Indian informal manufacturing sector.

7

GLOBALIZATION AND ITS EFFECTS

This chapter examines the effect of international trade on manufacturing employment in India. The Indian experience with globalization relating to manufacturing employment is an important one to consider, given the high rates of poverty in the country and the limited possibility of agricultural growth being the driver of poverty declines in many regions of the country (Palmer-Jones and Sen 2003). Furthermore, given the relative abundance of unskilled labour as compared to skilled labour in India, it is pertinent to probe whether India's rapid integration with the world economy, following the trade reforms that were undertaken in the 1980s and 1990s, has led to an increase in employment in the manufacturing sector, especially in the labour-intensive and informal segments of the sector (Wood 1994).

The key question which the chapter sets out to answer is whether this trade integration has created or destroyed jobs in the Indian informal manufacturing sector since the mid-1980s when trade reforms were initiated in India. Since the integration would affect both the formal and informal manufacturing sectors, we compare the effect of trade integration on both informal and formal segments of the manufacturing sector. We employ three approaches in our study—factor content, growth decomposition, and labour demand modelling.

The rest of the chapter is divided as follows: The next section introduces the three empirical methods. The second section discusses the structure and growth of exports and imports in Indian manufacturing. The third, fourth, and fifth sections apply, respectively, the factor content, growth decomposition, and labour demand approaches to Indian industry and trade data. The last section concludes the analysis.

The Methodological Approaches

We employ three commonly used methodological approaches to study the impact of international trade on employment. These are factor content, growth accounting, and labour demand approaches. These three approaches can be used to study the composition, scale, and process effects of trade, respectively.

Factor Content Approach

The factor content approach helps to capture the composition effect of international trade on employment. This approach examines whether a change in the structure of production as a result of greater outward orientation leads to an increase in the labour intensity of production, and hence, overall employment. It does this by computing direct and indirect labour requirements per unit of exports and import substitutes, with indirect labour requirements being calculated using input–output tables. In this chapter, we will only examine the direct labour requirements per unit of exports and import substitutes, as we lack the requisite input–output tables for India for the more recent periods.

Growth Accounting Approach

To capture the scale effect of trade on employment, we use the growth accounting approach. This approach decomposes changes in employment into the effects of changes in domestic demand, exports, imports, and productivity.

Starting from the basic accounting identity that

$$Q_{it} = D_{it} + X_{it} - M_{it}, \tag{7.1}$$

where

D_{it} is domestic absorption of industry i at time t,
Q_{it} is domestic production of industry i at time t,
X_{it} is exports of industry i at time t, and
M_{it} is imports of industry i at time t,

employment can be calculated as

$$L_{it} = l_{it}(D_{it} + X_{it} - M_{it}),$$ (7.2)

where L_{it} is employment in industry i at time t and $l_{it} = L_{it}/Q_{it}$.

Changes in employment between $t = 0$ and $t = 1$ can then be decomposed using the equation:

$$\Delta L_i = l_{i1}(1 - m_{i0})\Delta D_i + l_{i1}\Delta X_i + l_{i1}(m_{i0} - m_{i1})D_{i1} + (\Delta l_i)Q_{i0},$$ (7.3)

where $m_{it} = M_{it}/D_{it}$ and $l_{i1}(1 - m_{i0})\Delta D_i$ measures the impact of changes in domestic demand on employment, $l_{i1}\Delta X_i$ captures the effect of changes in exports on employment, $l_{i1}(m_{i0} - m_{i1})D_{i1}$ quantifies the impact of changes in import penetration on employment and $(\Delta l_i)Q_{i0}$ indicates the effect of productivity changes on employment. This corresponds to a Chenery-type decomposition. This approach assumes that increases in exports create additional employment, while increased import penetration reduces employment.

Labour Demand Modelling

International trade can also lead to changes in the efficiency of labour use within the same industry—the process effect of trade on employment. This can be captured by the estimation of labour demand equations at the industry level, where employment at the industry level is regressed against a number of explanatory variables, derived from a standard labour demand framework.

Consider a standard derived demand for labour equation at the industry level, augmented by a variable that captures the extent of integration of the industry with the world market.

$$L_{it} = \alpha + \beta_1 W_{it} + \beta_2 Q_{it} + \varphi Z_{it},$$ (7.4)

where L_{it} is employment in industry i at time t, W_{it} is real wage in industry i at time t, Q_{it} is real output in industry i at time t, and Z_{it} measures the degree of openness of industry i at time t.

We estimate the equations using the natural logarithms of L, W, and Q, so that the coefficients on W and Q in equation 7.4 can be interpreted as the wage and output elasticities of labour demand.

As is standard in the literature, the degree of openness (Z_{it}) is captured by the import penetration ratio (IM) and the export–output ratio (EO) defined at the industry level (Greenaway et al. 1999; Hine and Wright 1998).[1] The use of these two variables also allows us to separate the effects of import competition from export orientation on the efficiency of labour use. Thus, Equation 7.4 can be rewritten as:

$$L_{it} = \alpha + \beta_1 W_{it} + \beta_2 Q_{it} + \varphi_1 IM_{it} + \varphi_2 EO_{it}. \qquad (7.5)$$

This approach can take into account the indirect impact of trade on employment via trade-induced productivity changes. In fact, since the output variable incorporates the direct effects of changes in exports and imports, the import penetration and export orientation variables capture the indirect effects. We would expect that $\beta_1 < 0$ and $\beta_2 > 0$. The signs of φ_1 and φ_2 are indeterminate as greater import penetration and export orientation can lead to productivity gains and labour shedding. On the other side, this could also result in more employment intensity of production, as firms substitute away from capital to labour (which usually would be the cheaper factor in a labour surplus economy) to compete more effectively in world markets.

Patterns of Trade in Indian Manufacturing

Structure and Growth of Exports and Imports[2]

Manufacturing exports registered a steady increase between 1978 and 2005. In 1978, manufacturing exports were Rs 32 billion, which reached a peak of Rs 2,869 billion in 2005 (Figure 7.1). The growth of manufacturing exports was the strongest in 1978–84, when the annual rate of growth of exports was 25 per cent. Following this, the growth rate declined continuously from the mid-1980s till the late 1990s. The lowest growth of manufacturing exports occurred

[1] We define the import-penetration ratio for a particular industry as the total imports of products in that industry as a ratio of domestic demand (that is, imports + output − exports), and the export-orientation ratio as the ratio of exports to output.

[2] The construction of variables is discussed in Appendix 7A, presented at the end of this chapter.

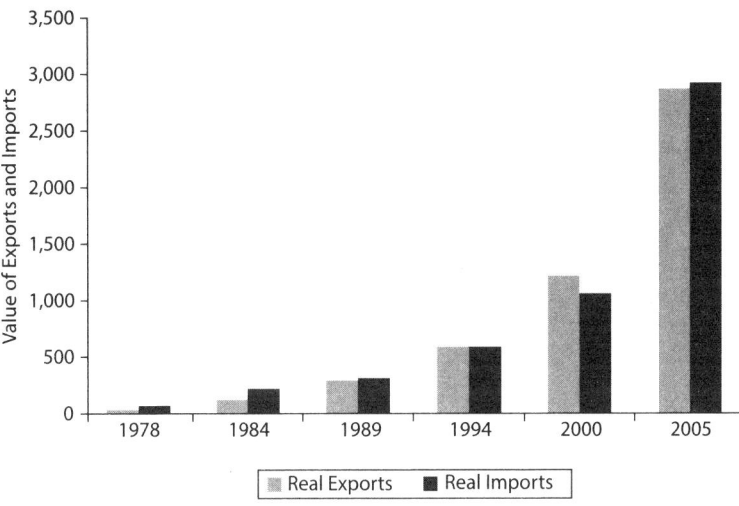

Figure 7.1   Exports and Imports of Manufactured Products: 1978–2005
(in billion)
Source: Authors' calculations based on data from Nicita and Olarreaga (2006).

during the second half of the 1990s, when exports grew at an annual rate of 13 per cent in this period. There was a marginal increase in its growth during the period 2000–5. In this period, exports grew at an annual rate of 19 per cent.

Table 7.1 reports the contribution of each industry in manufacturing exports from India. We notice significant changes in the structure of exports over time. Though cotton products still account for a significant share in the export basket of manufacturing products from India, their importance has declined over time. The export share of industries producing food products, wood products, leather products, basic metals, and transport equipment and parts also fell considerably during this period. Textiles, chemicals, and other manufacturing products have considerably improved their share in total exports of manufacturing products from India during the period 1978–2005.

Manufacturing imports also reported a steady increase in the period 1978–2005 (Figure 7.1). However, the strongest growth in imports

Table 7.1   Structure of Exports in India (in per cent)

Industry	1978	1984	1989	1994	2000	2005
Food Products	13.56	10.79	7.73	7.19	5.82	6.16
Beverages	0.43	0.57	0.19	0.17	0.14	0.29
Cotton Products	23.06	18.86	13.93	15.83	15.35	11.55
Textiles	1.10	10.97	12.96	12.99	13.20	12.45
Wood Products	1.34	0.39	0.18	0.20	0.14	0.24
Paper Products	0.26	0.44	0.29	0.55	0.57	0.79
Leather Products	8.90	12.10	7.57	6.31	4.02	3.31
Chemicals	4.89	7.55	12.31	10.46	10.99	13.42
Rubber Products	3.51	4.73	4.62	4.61	5.78	6.09
Non-metallic Minerals	1.60	0.67	0.75	1.71	1.93	1.74
Basic Metals	10.43	1.38	2.06	3.82	4.15	4.28
Metal Products	5.83	4.48	3.28	3.53	5.14	7.06
Machinery	10.26	7.12	7.12	5.35	7.36	11.48
Transport Equipment and Parts	11.99	3.59	2.58	3.74	2.83	5.82
Other Manufacturing Products	2.83	16.36	24.42	23.55	22.58	15.31

Source: Calculations based on data from Nicita and Olarreaga (2006).

has occurred in the first half of the 1980s and the 2000s, when the annual rates of growth of imports were 21 per cent and 22 per cent, respectively. The growth of manufacturing imports was the lowest in the period 1984–1990, increasing at an annual rate of 7 per cent in this period. Table 7.2 presents breakdown of manufacturing imports into product groups. By 2005, machinery had become the most important item in the import basket, closely followed by chemicals and metal products. The other rapidly growing import item is 'other manufacturing products'. It needs to be stated that chemicals, metal products, and other manufacturing products were essentially non-existent in the late 1970s. Instead, imports were concentrated on manufactures such as food products and rubber products. In essence, capital-intensive goods dominated the manufacturing imports in the early 2000s as compared to the late 1970s.

Table 7.2 Structure of Imports in India (in per cent)

Industry	1978	1984	1989	1994	2000	2005
Food Products	24.03	12.72	3.74	5.74	4.94	2.86
Beverages	0.07	0.02	0.06	0.04	0.03	0.20
Cotton Products	0.11	1.06	1.69	1.69	1.79	2.26
Textiles	0.00	0.00	0.02	0.02	0.07	0.12
Wood Products	0.01	0.05	0.14	0.10	0.13	0.22
Paper Products	5.30	3.88	3.86	2.69	2.57	2.75
Leather Products	0.01	0.09	0.33	0.49	0.50	0.49
Chemicals	2.35	21.63	25.17	21.11	13.03	14.08
Rubber Products	22.20	15.69	11.74	14.88	5.63	3.18
Non-metallic Minerals	3.39	0.69	0.87	0.67	0.67	0.80
Basic Metals	5.89	8.36	9.12	5.48	2.49	4.27
Metal Products	5.35	7.36	8.57	9.42	21.61	11.62
Machinery	17.77	23.10	24.09	21.38	23.72	33.22
Transport Equipment and Parts	12.54	3.50	6.50	5.64	3.08	11.24
Other Manufacturing Products	0.98	1.84	4.10	10.65	19.76	12.69

Source: Calculations based on data from Nicita and Olarreaga (2006).

Factor Content Approach: Main Results

We begin this section by examining the factor intensity of manufacturing exports as a prelude to the factor content calculations.[3] In order to do so, Krause's (1982) International Standard Industrial Classification (ISIC) of manufacturing industries is applied according to their dominant factor input. This distinguishes between natural-resource-intensive, labour-intensive, technology-intensive, and human-capital-intensive industries. The natural resource-intensive industries are further subdivided into agricultural and mineral-based industries. Unskilled-labour-intensive industries are those with the lowest value added per worker. The remaining industries are divided into technology-intensive

---

[3] The study relies on the ISIC definition of manufacturing, which is broader than the Standard International Trade Classification (SITC), and includes processing of many primary products.

and human-capital-intensive industries, with technology-intensive industries being those with a high ratio of research and development (R&D) to value added.

We find that unskilled-labour-intensive commodities are the most important commodities in India's manufacturing exports, comprising 45 per cent of total manufacturing exports in 1996–9 (Figure 7.2).[4] However, while the share of unskilled-labour-intensive commodities in total manufacturing exports has increased over the period 1975–99, the increase has not been substantial; from 37 per cent in 1975–80 to 45 per cent in 1995–9. India's human-capital-intensive

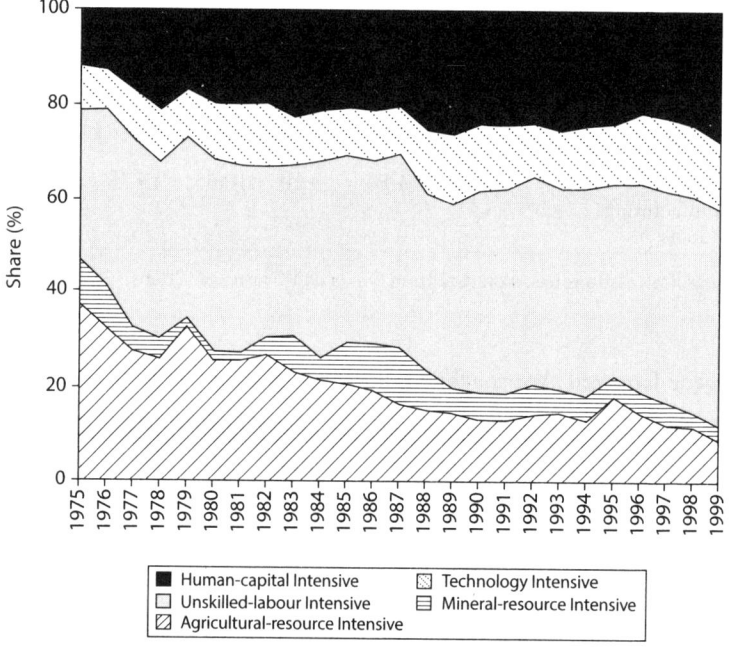

Figure 7.2 Factor Content of India's Manufacturing Exports
Source: Authors' elaboration from Nicita and Olarreaga (2006).

---

[4] The data is obtained from the International Economic Databank of the Australian National University. We do not have access to more recent data than 1999.

and technology-intensive exports have also increased as a share of total manufacturing exports over the period 1975–99 from 10 per cent and 17 per cent in 1975–80 to 15 per cent and 24 per cent in 1996–9, respectively. On the other hand, India's agricultural-resource-intensive exports as a share of total manufacturing exports fell quite dramatically from 31 per cent in 1975–80 to 12 per cent in 1996–9. With respect to imports, technology-intensive exports remained the dominant set of commodities in India's manufacturing import basket, followed by human-capital-intensive goods (Figure 7.3). There has been a marginal increase in the share of human-capital-intensive goods in India's manufacturing imports, with no significant change in the share of technology-intensive imports in total manufacturing imports, in spite of the trade liberalizations of the 1980s and 1990s, which were mostly biased towards import liberalization of capital and intermediate goods.

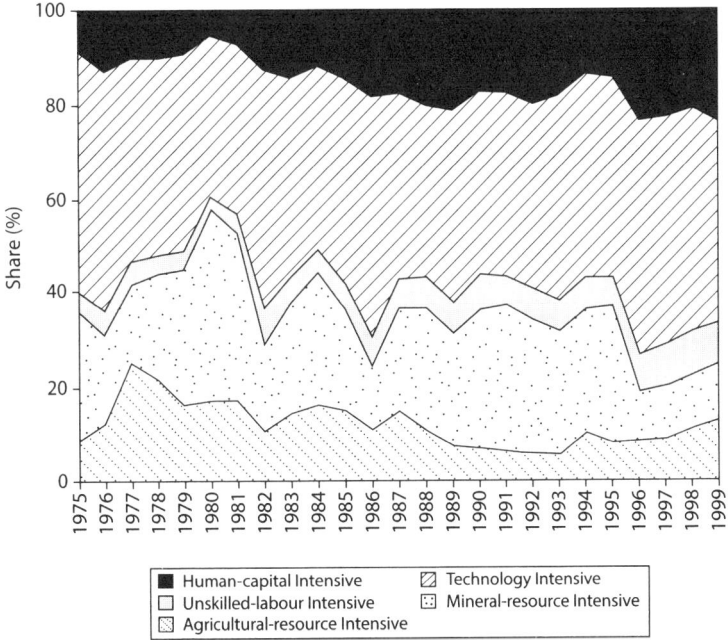

Figure 7.3   Factor Content of India's Manufacturing Imports
Source: Authors' elaboration from Nicita and Olarreaga (2006).

Employment Coefficients of Exports and Import-competing Domestic Production

So far, our discussion has focussed solely on the composition of exports and imports, without explicit computations of their labour intensities. However, in order to examine the impact of trade on employment, the labour intensity of both exports and imports need to be looked at. To do this, we derive employment coefficients at the industry level for the formal and informal manufacturing sectors, separately, and also for the manufacturing sector as a whole, which are then weighted by the share of each industry in exports and imports. The employment coefficients are presented in Figures 7.4, 7.5, and 7.6.[5] It can be seen that the employment coefficients of exports and imports consistently fell over the period in the formal manufacturing sector. As regards the informal manufacturing sector, the employment coefficient of imports has declined throughout the 1980s, remained stagnant during the 1990s, and declined considerably over the period 2000–5. The labour intensity of exports, on the other hand, fluctuated considerably during the period under study. The employment coefficient of exports increased between 1978 and 1985, and then declined during the late 1980s. It went up during the first half of the 1990s, and declined again in the period 1994–2000. As in the case of imports, the employment coefficient of exports has also declined drastically during the first half of the 2000s. The employment coefficients of exports and imports for the total manufacturing sector more or less followed a similar trend as observed in the informal manufacturing sector. Moreover, the difference between the employment coefficient of exports and that of imports has narrowed over time in both the sectors. The findings thus suggest that a unit increase in manufacturing exports matched by an identical increase in manufacturing imports will lead a smaller positive effect on employment in 2000–5 as compared to 1984–9.

To understand what explains the phenomenon of falling employment intensity of exports during a period when India attempted to re-align its trade regime in line with its own comparative advantage in

---

[5] To compute the employment coefficients, we use employment per real gross output than employment per real gross value added as the export and import figures are in gross terms.

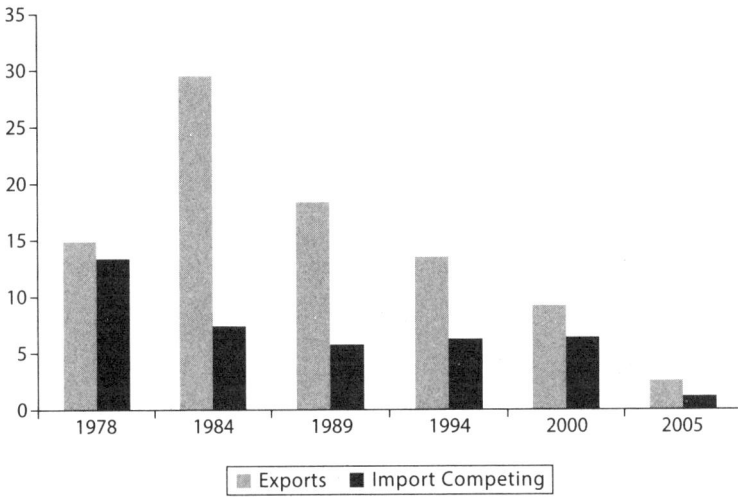

Figure 7.4   Employment Coefficients of Exports and Import-competing
Production: Total Manufacturing Sector
Source: Authors' calculations using NSSO and ASI Industry data sets and Nicita and
Olarreaga (2006).

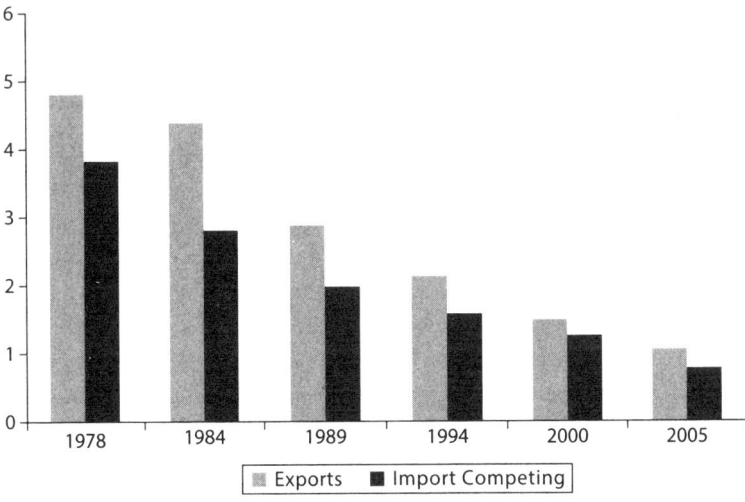

Figure 7.5   Employment Coefficients of Exports and Import-competing
Production: Formal Manufacturing Sector
Source: Authors' calculation from ASI data sets and Nicita and Olarreaga (2006).

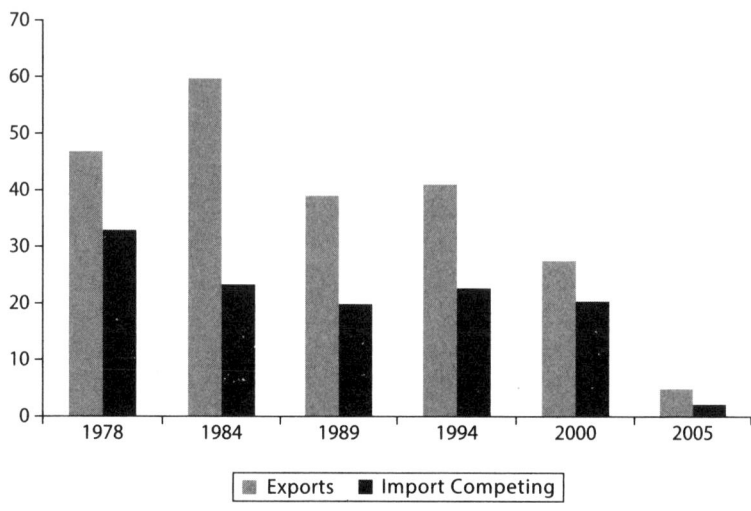

Figure 7.6   Employment Coefficients of Exports and Import-competing
Production: Informal Manufacturing Sector
Source: Authors' calculation from NSSO data sets and Nicita and Olarreaga (2006).

unskilled-labour-intensive commodities, we look at the changes in the
contribution of four sets of commodities which compose the bulk of
India's manufacturing exports. These are cotton products (ISIC code
321), textiles (ISIC code 322), chemicals (ISIC code 351 + 352), and
other manufacturing products (principally jewellery, sporting goods,
and toys) (ISIC code 385 + 390) comprising 13.5 per cent, 12.8 per
cent, 12.2 per cent, and 18.9 per cent, respectively, of total manufacturing exports in 2000–5. These four sets of commodities can contribute to
changes in the overall employment coefficient either by a change in their
own individual employment coefficients or by a change in their share of
total manufacturing exports. We scale the employment coefficients and
export shares for food products, cotton products, textiles, chemicals, and
other manufacturing products to 100 for the year 1978. We then look at
the contribution of these commodities to changes in employment coefficient in the formal and informal manufacturing sectors. The results are
presented in Figures 7.7 to 7.14. The employment coefficients for all
sets of commodities declined over the period 1984–2005 in the formal
manufacturing sector. As regards the informal manufacturing sector,

Figure 7.7   Contribution of Cotton Products to the Change in Employment
Coefficient: Formal Manufacturing Sector
Source: Authors' calculation from ASI data sets and Nicita and Olarreaga (2006).

Figure 7.8   Contribution of Cotton Products to the Change in Employment
Coefficient: Informal Manufacturing Sector
Source: Authors' calculation from NSSO data sets and Nicita and Olarreaga (2006).

Figure 7.9   Contribution of Textiles to Change in Employment Coefficient:
Formal Manufacturing Sector
Source: Authors' calculation from ASI data sets and Nicita and Olarreaga (2006).

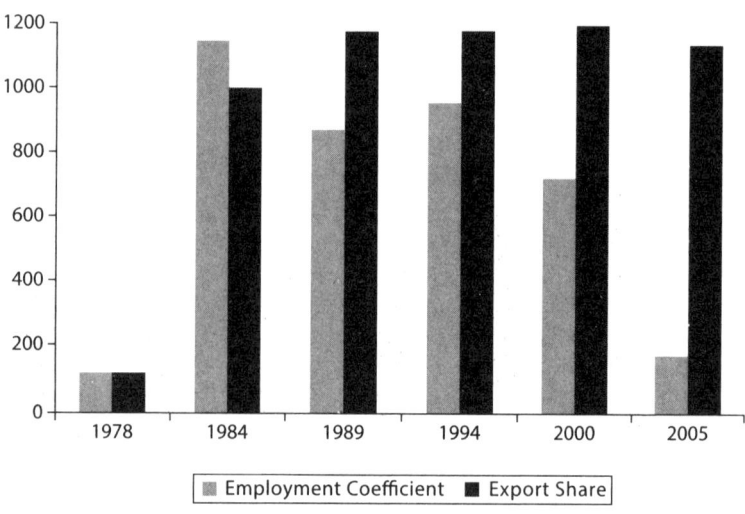

Figure 7.10   Contribution of Textiles to Change in Employment Coefficient:
Informal Manufacturing Sector
Source: Authors' calculation from NSSO data sets and Nicita and Olarreaga (2006).

Figure 7.11   Contribution of Basic Chemicals to the Change in Employment
Coefficient: Formal Manufacturing Sector
Source: Authors' calculation from ASI data sets and Nicita and Olarreaga (2006).

Figure 7.12   Contribution of Basic Chemicals to the Change in Employment
Coefficient: Informal Manufacturing Sector
Source: Authors' calculation from NSSO data sets and Nicita and Olarreaga (2006).

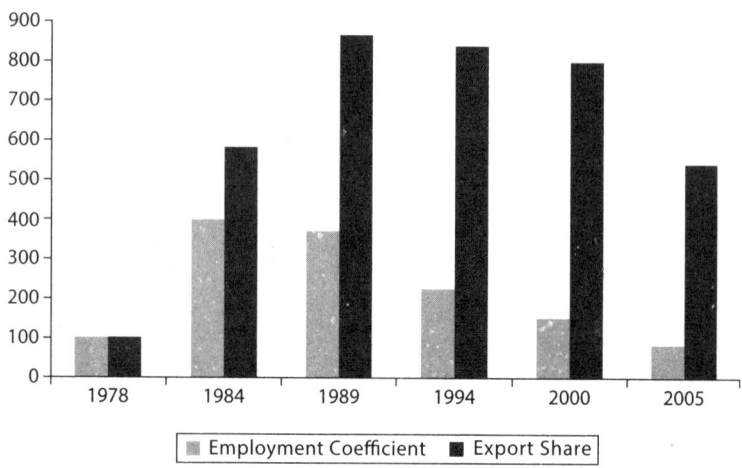

Figure 7.13   Contribution of Other Manufacturing Goods (including jewellery, sporting goods, and toys) to the Change in Employment Coefficient: Formal Manufacturing Sector
Source: Authors' calculation from ASI data sets and Nicita and Olarreaga (2006).

Figure 7.14   Contribution of Other Manufacturing Goods (including jewellery, sporting goods and toys) to the Change in Employment Coefficient: Informal Manufacturing Sector
Source: Authors' calculation from NSSO data sets and Nicita and Olarreaga (2006).

employment coefficient reported a decline in all the industries except chemicals for the same period. The employment coefficient in the informal segment of the chemicals industry, on the other hand, increased steadily during the period 1978–94 and then declined. Export shares increased from the late 1970s to the mid-1980s and then remained more or less stable for the remaining period in industries producing textiles and chemicals. In the cotton products industry, the export share declined between 1978 and 1989, remained stagnant till late 1990s, and declined thereafter. In the case of other manufacturing products, the share in manufacturing exports increased till the mid-1980s, remained stagnant between 1989 and 2000, and declined thereafter. In essence, these findings suggest that the principal reason for the decrease in the overall employment coefficient for India's exports over the period 1978–2005 was the fall in employment intensity of production, and not in the lack of specialization in labour-intensive products.[6] Furthermore, the fact that employment intensity of production had been falling both in the informal and formal sectors suggests that the decline may not be due to India's stringent laws relating to the firing of workers, which pertains only to the formal manufacturing sector.

Decomposition of Employment Changes

As was seen in the previous section, there have been substantial changes for India in terms of openness in recent years, with both exports and imports growing rapidly. A first stab at estimating the effects of increased openness on manufacturing employment can be made using a growth accounting methodology which divides employment changes over a period of time into that attributable to changes in domestic demand, exports, import penetration, and productivity.

The employment decomposition has been carried out for the entire manufacturing sector, including both formal and informal sectors, in India for the period 1978–2005. The two-digit ISIC data for imports and exports has been taken from the trade database developed by Nicita and Olarreaga (2006). Data on manufacturing output and employment at the two-digit level are drawn from the National Sample

---

[6] A decline in the employment intensity of production has also been observed by Das et al. (2009).

Survey Office (NSSO) (for the informal sector) and the Annual Survey of Industries (ASI) (for the formal sector) data sets.[7]

Much of the employment increase has been driven by increases in domestic demand (Table 7.3). Increases in labour productivity have led to labour shedding in the late 1980s, 1990s, and the early 2000s. Exports also contributed to the increase in employment all through the 1980s, 1990s, and the early 2000s. The contribution of exports to employment growth has been greater in the late 1990s and early 2000s, than in the preceding periods. Import penetration has led to few jobs being lost for much of the period under consideration, especially in the late 1990s.[8] However, this trend reversed in the early

Table 7.3   Decomposition of Manufacturing Employment Changes in India

Year	Total Employ- ment Effect	Domestic Demand	Productivity Growth	Export Growth	Import Penetration	Net Employment Growth from Trade
Absolute Numbers (in '000s)						
1978–84	18,388	9,509	5,938	3,038	–97	2,941
1984–89	–1,528	8,650	–13,174	3,324	–328	2,997
1989–94	–2,375	–3,975	–6,821	3,976	4,445	8,421
1994–2000	6,975	10,730	–8,211	5,669	–1,213	4,456
2000–5	641	16,387	–24,448	4,007	4,694	8,702
Percentage Contribution						
1978–84		51.7	32.3	16.5	–0.5	16.0
1984–89		–566.2	862.3	–217.6	21.4	–196.1
1989–94		167.4	287.2	–167.4	–187.2	–354.6
1994–2000		153.8	–117.7	81.3	–17.4	63.9
2000–5		2,555.1	–3,811.8	624.8	732.0	1,356.8

Source: Estimated using industry and trade data.

[7] To arrive at the data for the total manufacturing sector, the figures on the informal sector obtained from the NSSO data sets were added with the figures on the formal sector obtained from the ASI data sets for the corresponding year for the respective variables.

[8] Our finding for India contrasts with the findings of Kucera and Milberg (2002) for OECD countries where it is found that trade expansion with non-OECD countries led to a decline in employment.

2000s, when import penetration led to creation of jobs in the manu-facturing sector.

Labour Demand Estimation

The previous section examined the direct effects of international trade on manufacturing employment via trade-induced adjustments in output. This section studies the indirect impact of international trade on employment via changes in the efficiency of labour use. To capture the indirect effects of trade, we estimate constant-output labour demand equations at the industry level, augmented by variables that capture trade orientation.

In labour demand modelling, it is usually assumed that due to large adjustment costs related to hiring and firing of workers, employment adjusts to output and wage changes slowly over time. This implies that there are lagged employment terms in Equation 7.5 and the possible correlation between these terms and industry-specific time-invariant effects (fixed effects). Generalized Method of Moments (GMM) estimator proposed by Arellano and Bond (1991) is the ideal estimator in this situation as it helps the data to get rid of any time invariant industry-specific variable (such as labour-saving technological progress that may differ across industries). This also eliminates any endogeneity that may be due to the correlation of the industry-specific effects and the independent variables. The estimator also allows for possible endogeneity of the independent variables, by using lags of the right hand side variables as instruments for the possible endogenous variables. Thus, the GMM estimator allows for the possibility of some of the independent variables in Equation 7.5—output, wages, import penetration, and export orientation—to be correlated with the error term. For example, positive productivity shocks may lead industries to withstand import competition better. To test whether the Arellano–Bond GMM estimator is correctly specified, two diagnostic statistics are normally reported—tests for first and second order serial correlation. The GMM estimator is appropriately specified if the test for first order serial correlation does not reject the null of no correlation and test for second order serial correlation rejects the null of no correlation by any standard levels of significance.

A double logarithmic function is specified and estimated using GMM. The function is expressed as:

$$\log L_{it} = \beta_0 + \beta_1 \log Q_{it} + \beta_2 \log W_{it}$$
$$+ \beta_3 \, IM_{it} + \beta_4 EO_{it} + u, \qquad (7.6)$$

where L, Q, W, IM, and EO represent employment, output, wage rate, import penetration, and export orientation, respectively. The equation is estimated for the period 1978–9 to 2000–1 for 15 industries.[9] The analysis is based on pooled cross-section (industry level) and time series (five rounds) data. Data for the formal (obtained from ASI) and informal (obtained from NSSO surveys) manufacturing sectors are combined together to arrive at the figures for the total manufacturing sector.

The results of the regression analysis are reported in Table 7.4. The diagnostic statistics reported in the table are satisfactory in all cases. In the estimation, the Sargan test[10] does not reject the null hypothesis that the over-identifying restrictions are valid. The null hypothesis of no first order autocorrelation is rejected, but the null hypothesis of no second-order autocorrelation is not rejected. Thus, specification tests support the overall validity of the model. The lagged employment term is not significant, implying that there are no adjustment costs to changing employment levels—a finding that is expected as the analysis focuses on the total manufacturing sector which also includes units from the informal sector.[11] The coefficients on real output and real wage have the expected signs and are statistically significant at the 1 per cent level. A 1 per cent increase in output leads to a 0.4 per cent increase in employment, and a 1 per cent increase in the real wage rate leads to a fall in employment by around 0.62 per cent. It is found that the

[9] We omit 2005–6 from this estimation as the data for this year is not strictly comparable with earlier years.

[10] The Sargan test is a statistical test used for testing over-identifying restrictions in a statistical model. The test is used to test the validity of the instruments used in the estimations.

[11] However, as Sen (2009) has shown, there are significant adjustment costs to changing employment when the analysis is confined to the formal manufacturing sector.

Table 7.4   Regression Results: Labour Demand Estimation

Variable	Combined Sector
Constant	0.061
	(1.42)
Log L (−1)	−0.115
	(1.36)
Log Q	0.399*
	(4.05)
Log W	−0.619*
	(5.37)
IM	0.763*
	(3.20)
EO	−1.371*
	(3.22)
Estimation Method	Arellano-Bond Estimator
First Order Serial Correlation (p value in parenthesis)	1.91
	(0.056)
Second Order Serial Correlation (p value in parenthesis)	1.20
	(0.23)
Sargan Test (prob > chi^2)	7.29
	(0.20)
Number of Industries	15
Number of Observations	45

Source: Estimated using industry and trade data.

Notes: (a) Log L is the dependent variable.

(b) * denotes statistical significance at the 5 per cent level.

(c) t ratios in brackets, except where mentioned otherwise.

coefficients of import penetration and export orientation are statistically significant at 1 per cent level. Results show that export orientation has led to a reduction in employment for a given level of output, suggesting that increasing outward orientation has led to labour productivity gains in export-oriented industries. However, import penetration seems to have led to an increase in employment. This puzzling finding may be explained by increasing outsourcing of production from the more capital-intensive formal sector to the more labour-intensive informal sector in the face of increasing import competition (Ramaswamy 1999).

☆   ☆   ☆

This chapter examines the effect of international trade on manufacturing employment in India, combining both the formal and informal segments of the manufacturing sector. Using the factor content approach, it is found that the share of unskilled-labour-intensive goods in India's export basket has increased over time, but that the employment coefficients of exports and imports in India have consistently fallen over the period, along with the fact that the difference between the employment coefficient of exports and that of imports has narrowed over time. What is remarkable is that employment intensity of production for all major exports of the Indian economy has been steadily declining, and this phenomenon has not been confined to the formal manufacturing sector where there may be policy impediments that may restrict the use of labour in this sector. The analysis suggests that the employment impacts of trade for a given change in output may be actually less in the post-reform period than it was in the pre-reform period.

The growth accounting approach suggests that some of the employment growth in the 1990s can be linked to the growth of exports. However, most of the employment increase that has occurred over the period 1978–2005 can be attributed to increases in domestic demand and less to international trade. Finally, by estimating a labour demand equation that allows for trade to affect employment via changes in labour productivity, we find that trade (or more specifically, export orientation) can explain part of the labour productivity increases that was seen in the Indian manufacturing sector in 1978–2000, and may have contributed to labour shedding in the manufacturing sector. Thus, we find that international trade has not had a significant positive effect on manufacturing employment via scale and composition effects, and that it may have had a negative effect via the process effect. The weak effect of international trade on employment in the informal manufacturing sector is particularly striking, given the large number of the poor who are located in this sector. While the reasons for this is outside the scope of this chapter, the lack of a beneficial effect of India's increasing integration with the world economy on urban labour markets should be a matter of concern for Indian policymakers.

Appendix 7A: Construction of Variables

The basic variables used in the study are gross output, employment, wages, export, and imports.

Gross Output

Gross output is used as the measure of output in the analysis carried out in this chapter. The implicit deflators of gross domestic product of the respective registered and unregistered manufacturing available at the two-digit industry level are used to deflate gross output in the two sectors.

Employment

Labour input is measured by total number of persons employed, which includes both production and non-production workers.

Real Wages

To estimate real wages, the nominal wages have been deflated by Consumer Price Index (CPI).

Export and Imports

The exports and imports data matched to the ISIC three-digit level is obtained from the World Bank trade data set (Nicita and Olarreaga 2006).[12] The export and import figures are then deflated using the GDP deflators at the two-digit industry level for the total manufacturing sector. All values are in 1993–4 prices.

[12] The concordance between ISIC three-digit level and NIC two-digit level is presented in Appendix A1 (see Table A1.4).

8

OUT OF THE SHADOWS?
Lessons and Policy Implications

Most firms in Indian manufacturing are located in the informal sector. These firms tend to be much less productive than firms in the formal sector and the individuals that own, manage, and work in these enterprises comprise a large proportion of the urban working poor. The majority of these firms are not able to grow in size and make the transition to the formal sector. In spite of over two decades of economic reforms, there is no evidence of the decline of the informal manufacturing sector in India.

In this book, we examined the evolution of the informal manufacturing sector in the post-reform period. We took a specific 'production lens' to the informal manufacturing sector, focusing on the characteristics and performance of informal firms, and analysed how these have changed over time, and the determinants of informal sector growth in India. We began with a discussion of the alternate theoretical perspectives that are there on the informal economy. We described the economic policies enacted in India that have directly or indirectly impacted on the informal sector. We then described the growth experience of the informal manufacturing sector, in the aggregate and also by industry, sector, and region. We also looked at the characteristics of informal firms and how these have changed over time. Next, we examined the effects of economic reforms on the performance of informal firms relative to formal firms. We then studied the constraints to firm growth in the informal sector. Finally, we looked at the effects of globalization on job creation in the informal sector. In this chapter, we summarize the key findings of the book and draw some overall lessons to inform policy in the future.

Key Findings

Growth and Structural Change

In setting out the 'stylized facts' of the Indian informal manufacturing sector in the post-reform period, we found that there have been quite remarkable changes in the informal manufacturing sector in this period, which has witnessed strong growth in most industries in the post-reform period. We also found that the urban informal manufacturing sector has grown at a faster rate than the rural informal manufacturing sector with a steady decline of rural informal enterprises in total informal enterprises across most Indian states, suggesting a clear urban bias in the growth of informal manufacturing firms in India. No significant change is found in the distribution of output, employment, and the share of enterprises across Indian states in the informal sector, which is contrary to what one may expect in a period of significant change in the Indian economy.

Disaggregating informal enterprises by types of enterprise—Own Account Manufacturing Enterprises (OAMEs), Non-directory Manufacturing Enterprises (NDMEs), and Directory Manufacturing Enterprises (DMEs)—we saw a clear fall in the relative share of OAMEs in total enterprises, and a relative increase in the share of DMEs over time. This is evident for both rural and urban areas. While OAMEs are very different in their characteristics than NDMEs and DMEs, little evidence is found of segmentation in industrial location across these three types of enterprises, with all three categories present in industries such as food and beverages, cotton goods and textiles. However, there is a larger presence of NDMEs and DMEs in the more capital-intensive sectors such as chemicals and basic metals. The decline in OAME's share in total enterprises is also evident from most states, though there are important exceptions such as Gujarat.

Digging deeper into the Indian informal manufacturing sector through the analysis of detailed firm-level data, we found that there has been a downward shift in the size of the average informal firm in the Indian manufacturing sector over time. We found the average firm size to be declining in both OAMEs and NDMEs, while firm's size increased among the large firms—the DMEs. There were also differences in firm size across other firm characteristics; for example, firm's size was considerably higher in firms that operated on a partnership basis as compared to firms that operated at the household level. In terms of labour productivity, we noticed an inverted-U relationship between firm size and firm performance: productivity increases to a large size till a certain point and then stagnates and declines. Not surprisingly, across the types of enterprises, OAMEs turned out to be the least productive, followed by NDMEs and DMEs. We also found that productivity is the highest among firms that operate from fixed premises and have permanent structures.

Further, we found that there are social and economic barriers to informal enterprises in increasing their productivity. Controlling for other factors, enterprises owned by members of disadvantaged social groups such as the Scheduled Castes (SCs) and Scheduled Tribes (STs), and female-owned enterprises are less productive than those headed by Other Backward Classes (OBCs) and the general category social groups and by males. Finally, while exploring the nature of interlinkages between informal and formal firms, we found that both home-based enterprises and larger firms in the informal sector are likely to subcontract more, and that firms that enter into a subcontracting relationship are actually less productive than firms which do not enter into such a relationship.

The Effects of Economic Reforms on Performance

Examining the labour productivity of informal firms relative to formal firms, we found that labour productivity witnessed a consistent increase in both the formal and informal manufacturing segments in the post-reform period. At the regional level, overall evidence points to reforms generating significant gains in labour productivity in the informal sector in majority of the states. We also observed a considerable inter-industry variation in labour productivity levels, though all industries except rubber products recorded considerable gains in labour productivity in the period following reforms.

We found that economic reforms have had an unambiguous positive effect on the absolute levels of technical efficiency in the entire manufacturing sector. However, while average efficiency levels in both the informal and the formal manufacturing sectors have increased, the increase has been more for the formal firms. Therefore, economic reforms have increased the efficiency differentials between the more efficient formal firms and the less efficient informal firms in Indian manufacturing. We also found that all the three types of reforms we studied—tariff cuts, delicensing, and dereservation—contributed to greater dualism in the manufacturing sector in the post-reform period.

Understanding Firm Transition

Investigating the determinants of firm transition within the informal manufacturing sector, we found that the firm capabilities seem to matter significantly for the firm transition in the informal sector. Among the variables capturing firm capabilities, registration status of the firm and whether or not the owner–manager maintains accounts play a crucial role in the transition of firms to larger sizes. We also found that relative to firms in rural areas, urban firms have a greater chance of being in the larger size type in the informal sector, and that improvement in infrastructure such as the construction of paved roads in villages and access to electricity can significantly accelerate firm transition within the informal sector. We also found that the presence of human capital in the region (proportion of those individuals in the district where the firm is located who are educated at secondary level and above) increases the likelihood that the firm will make a transition from a household level to non-household level in the informal sector. Surprisingly, we found that financial constraints do not contribute significantly to a firm's expansion in the informal sector, as compared to the firm capabilities, locational and infrastructural variables, and human capital. This finding is consistent with a growing body of work that small-scale interventions designed solely to alleviate credit market frictions have little effect on firm growth (see de Mel et al. 2010).

The Effects of International Trade

We examined the effect of international trade on manufacturing employment in India, combining both the formal and informal segments of the manufacturing sector, using three different approaches— the factor content approach, the growth accounting approach, and the labour demand approach. Using the factor content approach, we found that the share of unskilled-labour-intensive goods in India's export basket has increased over time, but that the employment coefficients of exports and imports in India have consistently fallen over the period, along with the fact that the difference between the employment coefficient of exports and that of imports has narrowed over time. We found that the employment intensity of production for all major exports of the Indian economy has been steadily declining, both in the informal and formal manufacturing sectors, and that the employment impacts of trade for a given change in output may have actually become less in the post-reform period than it was in the pre-reform period.

The growth accounting approach suggests that most of the increase in employment that occurred over the period 1978–2005 in the manufacturing sector can be attributed more to the increase in domestic demand and less to international trade. Finally, by estimating a labour demand equation that allows for trade to affect employment via changes in labour productivity, we found that trade (or more specifically, export orientation) can explain part of the increase in labour productivity that was seen in the Indian manufacturing sector in 1978–2000, and may have contributed to labour shedding in the informal manufacturing sector. Thus, international trade has not had a significant, positive direct effect on manufacturing employment in the informal sector through an increase in exports from this sector, and may actually have had a negative indirect effect via the shedding of labour in the informal sector due to cost-cutting measures that were linked to attempts to increase the competitiveness of exports.

The overall finding in the book is that while there has been impressive growth of the informal sector in terms of output and productivity in the post-reform period, the effects of reforms on the informal sector has been quite mixed. The reforms have exacerbated the 'manufacturing dualism' by increasing the efficiency of formal firms relative to informal firms. Globalization in terms of greater integration with world markets has not had the desired positive effects, in that, job creation in the informal manufacturing sector due to international trade has been weak. The informal manufacturing sector seems to be still in the shadows of the formal manufacturing sector, despite two decades of economic reforms. Even within the informal sector, the likelihood that household enterprises will move out of 'the bottom of the economy' by making the transition to non-household enterprises remains a distant possibility for many household enterprises, especially those without access to electricity, those situated in remote rural regions of the country without access to a literate workforce or village-level infrastructure, and those where owners and managers lack basic capabilities such as knowledge of book-keeping.

Chapter 1 of the book posed the question, which theoretical perspective among the ones that were discussed—the dualist approach, the neo-Marxian approach, the legalist approach, and the institutionalist approach—is most consistent with the empirical reality of the informal manufacturing sector in India. The answer to this question depends partly in understanding which component of the informal sector we look at. Many household enterprises (OAMEs) operate in exploitative conditions and with a great deal of surplus unproductive labour. For this part of the informal sector, the dualist and the neo-Marxian theoretical perspectives are possibly the approaches that have the closest approximation to the empirical reality. However, many of the non-household enterprises that we studied (NDMEs and DMEs) exhibit a great deal of economic dynamism that is most consistent with the legalist approach. The positive news is that the proportion of these enterprises is gradually increasing amongst the informal firms in the Indian manufacturing sector. In addition, many of these firms are gradually becoming larger in size and becoming more productive, though there is not enough evidence to suggest that they are moving to the formal sector. Further, relational contracts/interlinkages also characterize many of the firms in the Indian informal sector, and so the institutionalist approach has some analytical purchase in understanding the behaviour of informal firms in the Indian context.[1]

Policy Implications

Our study has three main policy implications. First, it is important to recognize that there is a large continuum of firms in the informal sector—from very small household enterprises, which are quite unproductive and use mostly traditional technologies, to slightly larger non-household enterprises, some of which use modern technologies.

---

[1] However, the data was not reasonably fine enough to discern the nature of inter-firm relationships, and whether they were formal or informal, in the Indian informal sector.

Therefore, policies need to be tailored to the type of firm one is concerned with—for OAMEs, ensuring access to electricity, training programmes for entrepreneurs (such as targeted support for training in account maintenance), and the development of the skills of the workers in these enterprises should be the priority of policymakers. On the other hand, for larger NDMEs and DMEs, a stronger emphasis on credit availability should be the focus of policy. In addition, policymakers need to simplify the registration process for the DMEs as well as to provide greater incentives for registering with the relevant authorities.[2]

Second, our study clearly shows that neither the view that the informal sector is a means of accumulation nor the view that the informal sector is a means of exploitation is unequivocally supported by the empirical evidence. While some informal firms are engaged in subcontracting relationships with other firms that allow them to grow, others are engaged in more exploitative relationships built around asymmetric bargaining power with formal firms. Firms exhibit very diverse behaviour in terms of their growth trajectories, depending on the industry they belong to, whether they are rural or urban, the gender and caste background of their owners, whether they have access to permanent structures for their operations, and so on. In the same informal sector in India, we see De Soto's entrepreneurial firm (1989) that is dynamic and able to grow as well as Sanyal's stagnant firm

---

[2] As Kanbur (2014) notes, there are broadly three categories of firms in the informal sector. The first are those that evade government regulations—such as the Factories Act—even though they are all under the ambit of such government regulations. (These may be firms with more than 10 workers.) The second are those that avoid regulations by adjusting their operations (for example, those who remain at nine workers to avoid being within the ambit of the Factories Act). The third are those whose 'natural size' keeps them outside the ambit of government regulation. In our terminology, DMEs are in the first and second category, NDMEs in the second category, and OAMEs (and some NDMEs) are in the third category. Clearly, deregulation or the easing of registration procedures has little relevance to firms in the third category, which are mostly OAMEs and many NDMEs. On the other hand, many DMEs in the second category would quite clearly benefit from the easing of registration procedures.

(2007) that is locked in a subordinated relationship with the capitalist sector and is simply the repository of surplus or expendable labour. Policy prescriptions that are 'one size fits all' and that do not take into account the heterogeneity of firms in the informal sector are of limited relevance in the Indian context. The key policy lesson here is to understand the context in which the informal firm is operating, its characteristics, and its potential growth trajectory better. This may mean that (a) there is less of a role for central bodies or agencies and (b) as far as possible, policies for small industry need to be devolved down from the central government to municipal authorities and district industrial centres. This will allow for the possibility of policies being formulated that are more in accord with the needs of the firms in their geographical area.

The final policy implication is that the economic reforms that have been enacted in India since 1991 have been a mixed blessing for the informal manufacturing sector, while their effects on the formal manufacturing sector has been largely positive. Although the performance of informal firms has improved due to the reforms and the fact that there has been a remarkable growth of informal firms in many industries in the post-reform period, it also has been the case that the economic reforms have increased the gap in the performance between informal and formal firms, with the informal firms falling behind the formal firms. In addition, trade reforms have not had the expected benefits in terms of job creation in the informal manufacturing sector. While this does not imply that certain reforms targeted at small firms, such as dereservation, need to be reversed (as we have documented, reservation policy had significant economic costs on small firms in India), it does mean that greater care must be taken by policymakers to provide complementary reforms that can allow informal firms to catch up with formal firms (such as rationalizing the system of inspection of small firms to minimize the level of corruption and red tape that these firms face), and also to provide critical public goods such as uninterrupted electricity supply, roads, secondary schools in rural areas, and skill training through vocational institutions, which are important enablers for the growth of informal firms in India.

An unfortunate aspect of Indian economic policy, whether in the pre-reform or post-reform period, has been that it has mostly focused on the agricultural sector (for example, with the Green Revolution) and to the larger entities in the manufacturing sector (with industrial policy, both old and new). The informal manufacturing sector has been mostly ignored in economic policymaking, largely due to the fact that it remains hidden from the view of the formal policy apparatus. While the informal manufacturing sector in India is not yet 'out of the shadows', concerted government action and strong public interest is needed to bring it into the limelight it deserves, so that millions of individuals who populate the informal sector as owners, managers, and workers of informal firms are able to enjoy sustained increases in their standard of living, and to participate more fully in India's economic growth and development.

APPENDIX A I

Unorganized Manufacturing Sector Surveys in India: An Overview

There is no periodical collection and publication of statistics of the unorganized manufacturing sector as a whole or on an all-India basis. Recognizing the significance of the unorganized manufacturing sector in terms of its share in Gross Domestic Product (GDP) as well as in total employment, the National Sample Survey Office (NSSO) had taken up this subject of surveying the manufacturing enterprises belonging to the unorganized sector in many of its rounds. That way, the collection of data on unorganized manufacture has a long history in the NSSO (NSSO 2008). The first such survey was conducted from October 1953 to March 1954 (7th Round) covering only the household enterprises. The same exercise was repeated in the 10th (1955–6) and 14th (1958–9) Rounds of the NSSO. During the 23rd (1968–9) and 29th (1974–5) Rounds, the data were collected on a sample basis from household and non-household enterprises.[1] The main objective was to cover the entire unorganized sector which could be combined with data for the organized

[1] These surveys had used the list of villages from population census and the list of census enumeration blocks, or the lists of urban frame survey (UFS) blocks of NSSO (subject to their availability) as the sampling frame for selection of villages/urban blocks (NSSO 2008).

sector, so that an overall picture of the manufacturing sector in India can be obtained. However, due to incomplete coverage, the results for the non-household sector were not encouraging and an overall picture of the unorganized sector remained incomplete during these periods.

A review of the NSSO rounds of surveys recognized the need for a better sampling frame to generate more accurate statistics of unorganized sector. This finally culminated in the conduct of periodic economic censuses (EC), which form the basis for preparing a sample frame for conducting follow-up sample surveys to collect detailed information on establishments. The Central Statistical Organization (CSO) launched a central plan scheme on economic censuses and surveys in 1976 and conducted the first EC in 1977. Five ECs followed, one each in 1980, 1990, 1998, 2005, and 2012–13, covering unregistered enterprises in manufacturing, trade, transport, and services sectors. While the first census covered units with at least one hired worker, all subsequent censuses also covered units employing family labour. The follow-up surveys covered non-factory manufacturing, trade, hotels and restaurants, transport, storage and warehousing, mining and quarrying, and services sectors. These surveys were designed to collect detailed industry-wise information on the nature of activity, employment, emoluments, inputs, output, inventory of fixed assets, working capital, outstanding loans, etc., and form a rich source of data for the unorganized manufacturing sector.

The surveys on the unorganized manufacturing sector have been conducted for the years 1978–9, 1984–5, 1989–90, 1994–5, 2000–1, 2005–6, and 2010–11. In the beginning, the surveys on directory manufacturing establishments (DMEs), employing six or more persons with at least one hired worker were conducted by the CSO, while non-directory manufacturing establishments (NDMEs), employing less than six persons with at least one hired worker and own account manufacturing enterprises (OAMEs), employing only family labour were surveyed by the NSSO. Since 1994–5, the responsibility for collecting and analysing data and publishing the results for the entire unorganized sector has been vested with the NSSO.

In all the surveys, the enterprise formed the basic unit of inquiry. These survey reports give information on certain indicators at the industry level and state level, specifically for the OAMEs, NDMEs, and DMEs, and also for rural and urban areas. These large-scale surveys covered all the states and union territories (UTs). For instance, the surveys conducted in 2000–1 and 2005–6 covered the whole of the Indian union except (a) Leh and Kargil districts of Jammu and Kashmir, (b) villages situated beyond 5 kilometres of bus route in the state of Nagaland, and (c) inaccessible villages of Andaman and Nicobar Islands. In the survey conducted in 2010–11, Leh and Kargil districts of Jammu and Kashmir were also covered.[2]

In all these rounds, a stratified sampling design was adopted for the selection of the first stage units (FSUs) sample. The FSUs were villages (panchayat wards in the case of Kerala) in rural areas and urban frame survey (UFS) blocks in urban areas. List of villages/urban blocks, along with enterprise-level information available from economic censuses, was used as the sampling frame with some exceptions. Table A1.1 presents the list of FSUs surveyed for the latest four rounds (51st, 56th, 62nd, and 67th Rounds) of surveys on the unorganized manufacturing sector carried out by the NSSO. The ultimate stage units (USUs) for the survey were enterprises. The method of circular sampling was employed for selecting the USUs from the corresponding frame in the FSUs. If there were large FSUs, there were subdivided into smaller parts called hamlet groups (rural)/sub-blocks (urban). In the end, three of these smaller parts were selected; one having maximum enterprises with certainty and two others with circular, systematic sampling. The former was called segment 1 and the latter two were called as segment 2. The USUs were selected independently from each of these segments. The number of enterprises (USUs) surveyed in different rounds of NSSO is given in Table A1.2.

Table A1.1 Number of FSUs Surveyed

Round	Year	First Stage Units (FSUs)		
		Villages	Urban Blocks	Total FSUs
51st	1994–5	8,214	5,258	13,472
56th	2000–1	5,586	8,942	14,528
62nd	2005–6	4,798	5,125	9,923
67th	2010–11	8,296	7,602	15,898

Source: NSSO, various rounds.

[2] For these two districts, sample FSUs that were drawn as 'state sample' have been treated as 'central sample'.

Table A1.2   Number of USUs Surveyed

Round	Year	Number of Enterprises (USUs)					
		Rural	Urban	OAME	NDME	DME	Total
51st	1994–5	120,609	71,420	146,337	30,445	15,247	192,029
56th	2000–1	60,770	91,724	101,830	32,994	17,670	152,494
62nd	2005–6	42,050	40,847	55,045	18,060	9,792	82,897
67th	2010–11	51,608	47,674	63,305	27,757	8,220	99,282

Source: NSSO, various rounds.

Differences in sampling approach and conceptual modifications introduced to accommodate the need for improvement have, to an extent,
affected the comparability of data over time. There are also differences
across rounds in terms of coverage of the survey. The 33rd Round of the
NSSO replaced the household approach (used by the previous three
rounds) with the establishment approach. Some researchers were suspi-
cious on the effectiveness of the establishment approach to accurately
predict the size of the sector as they believed that this approach is likely
to underestimate the number of OAMEs in the sector. Others argued
for following a dual approach—establishment approach for DMEs and
the household approach for relatively small units (Saluja 1988).

The criteria used to categorize enterprises in the sector also witnessed significant changes over time. In the 33rd Round (1978–9), the
units were classified on the basis of annual turnover criterion in which
NDMEs having an annual turnover of more than one lakh rupees were
treated as DMEs irrespective of their employment size. Beginning with
the 40th Round for 1984–5, employment-based criterion was adopted
for selecting enterprises. There have been also considerable differences
in the presentation of information pertaining to many variables. For
instance, data on emoluments were presented 'per enterprise' in the
40th Round and 'per employee' in the subsequent surveys. Again, the
direct presentation of data on emoluments has been omitted in the 56th
Round, and is reported as a percentage component of total inputs under
the income method of data presented on estimates of gross value added
(GVA). Additionally, to minimize errors in the data furnished, the reference period for collecting the data on GVA has been changed to '30 days
preceding the date of survey' in 2000–1, while in the earlier rounds it
was collected with reference to a period of '365 days preceding the date

of survey'. Further, in the 56th Round, the data on gross output was not directly presented and the data on 'total receipts' was used for the computation of GVA (that is, value of total receipts less value of total inputs) while in the earlier NSSO rounds value of gross output was exclusively mentioned and used for the calculation of GVA. This pattern has been followed in the subsequent rounds too. The value of total receipts presented for 2000–1, therefore, needs to be used as indicating the value of gross output while relating it to the data on gross output for earlier rounds. Unlike the previous survey rounds, the 67th Round of NSSO principally covered all unincorporated enterprises in the non-agricultural sector of the economy, excluding those engaged in construction and electricity, gas, and water supply. The enterprises covered in this round are selected from three broad industry groups: (a) manufacturing, (b) trade, and (c) other service sector enterprises. The unincorporated enterprises are those enterprises which are not incorporated/registered under Companies Act, 1956. Thus, the data set for this round (on the manufacturing sector) is largely comparable with that of the earlier rounds.

An important problem encountered while comparing the NSSO rounds is the differences in the National Industrial Classification (NIC) followed by the NSSO in its various survey reports. The reports used in the study relate to the 40th, 45th, 51st, 56th, 62nd, and 67th Rounds of NSSO. Among them, the report for the 40th Round followed NIC 1970, those for the 45th and 51st Rounds followed NIC 1987, and the 56th Round report followed NIC 1998. For the last two rounds, 62nd and 67th, NIC 2004 and NIC 2008 were followed, respectively. While concordance of NIC 1987 with 1970 required only interchanging of industry divisions 30 and 31, matching of NIC 1987 with NIC 1998 required a greater degree of approximation by relevant grouping. The exact concordance of the two-digit industry groups of NIC 1987 with that of NIC 1998 and NIC 2004 required data on some three-digit and four-digit industrial divisions, which are not readily available in the report published for 56th Round (NSSO 2002a, 2002b). Hence, for the purpose of comparison across rounds, unit-level data for 56th and 62nd Rounds available from the NSSO have been used. In the end, the industries have been reclassified using the concordance table published by the CSO. Details of 15 industry groupings clubbed for the purpose of this study (which may differ with the groupings made in other studies) are given below.

Table A1.3   Concordance between NIC 1987 and NIC 1998

Name of the Industry	Terminology Used in the Book	NIC 1987 (Two digit)	NIC 1998
Manufacture of food products	Food Products	20–21	151 + 152 + 153 + 154 + 15544
Manufacture of beverages, tobacco, and related products	Beverages	22	(155 – 15544) + 16
Manufacture of cotton textiles, wool, silk and man-made fibre textiles and jute, and other vegetable-fibre textiles	Cotton Products	23 + 24 + 25	171 + 01405
Manufacture of textile products (including wearing apparel)	Textiles	26	172 + 173 + (181 – 18104)
Manufacture of wood and wood products; furniture and fixtures	Wood Products	27	20 + 361
Manufacture of paper and paper products and printing, publishing, and allied industries	Paper Products	28	21 + 22
Manufacture of leather and products of leather, fur, and substitutes of leather	Leather Products	29	18104 + 182 + 19
Manufacture of basic chemicals and chemical products (except products of petroleum and coal)	Chemicals	30	24
Manufacture of rubber, plastic, petroleum, and coal products; processing of nuclear fuels	Rubber Products	31	23 + 25
Manufacture of non-metallic mineral products	Non-metallic Minerals	32	26
Basic metal and alloys industries	Basic Metals	33	27 + 371
Manufacture of metal products and parts except machinery and equipment	Metal Products	34	2811 + 2812 + 289
Manufacture of machinery and equipment other than transport equipment	Machinery	35–36	2813 + 29 + 30 + 31 + 32 + 3311

		37	34 + 35
Manufacture of transport equipment and parts	Transport Equipment and Parts	37	34 + 35
Other manufacturing industries	Other Manufacturing Products	38	(33 – 33111) + 369

Source: Authors' construction based on NIC 1987 and NIC 1998.

Table A1.4 Concordance between ISIC Three-digit Level and NIC Two-digit Level

ISIC Code (Revision 2)	Industry	NIC Code 1987	Industry
311	Food Products	20–21	Manufacture of food products
313 + 314	Beverages + Tobacco	22	Manufacture of beverages, tobacco, and tobacco products
321	Cotton Products	23 + 24 + 25	Manufacture of cotton textiles + Manufacture of wool, silk, and synthetic fibre textiles + Manufacture of jute, hemp, and mesta textiles
322	Textiles that include all kinds of wearing apparel, except footwear	26	Manufacture of textile products (including wearing apparel other than footwear)
331 + 332	Wood products, except furniture + Furniture, except metal	27	Manufacture of wood and wood products, furniture and fixtures
341 + 342	Paper and products + Printing and publishing	28	Manufacture of paper and paper products and printing, publishing, and allied industries
323 + 324	Leather products + Footwear, except rubber or plastic	29	Manufacture of leather and leather and fur products
351 + 352	Industrial chemicals + Other chemicals	30	Manufacture of chemical and chemical products

(Contd.)

Table A1.4 (*Contd.*)

ISIC Code (Revision 2)	Industry	NIC Code 1987	Industry
353 + 354 +355 + 356	Petroleum refineries + Miscellaneous petroleum and coal products + Rubber products + Plastic products	31	Manufacture of rubber, plastic, petroleum, and coal products
361 + 362 + 369	Pottery, china, earth-enware + Glass and products + Other non-metallic mineral products	32	Manufacture of non-metallic mineral products
371	Iron and steel	33	Basic metal and alloy industries
372 + 381	Non-ferrous metals + Fabricated metal products	34	Manufacture of metal products and parts, except machinery and transport equipment
382 + 383	Machinery, except electrical + Machinery, electrical	35 + 36	Manufacture of machin-ery, machine tools and parts except electrical machinery + Manufacture of electrical machinery, apparatus, appliance, and supplies and parts
384	Transport equipment	37	Manufacture of transport equipment and parts
385 + 390	Professional and scientific equipment + Other manufactured products	38	Other manufacturing industries

Source: Authors' construction based on ISIC 1968 and NIC 1987.
Note: ISIC refers to International Standard Industrial Classification.

Table A1.5   National Industrial Classification (NIC): 1998 (at two-digit level)

NIC Two-digit Classification	ISIC Code	Description
15	311, 313	Manufacture of food products and beverages
16	314	Manufacture of tobacco products
17	321	Manufacture of textiles

18	322	Manufacture of wearing apparel; dressing and dyeing of fur
19	323, 324	Tanning and dressing of leather; manufacture of luggage, handbags, saddle, harness, and footwear
20	331	Manufacture of wood and of products of wood and cork, except furniture; manufacture of articles of straw and plaiting materials
21	341	Manufacture of paper and paper products
22	342	Publishing, printing, and reproduction of recorded media
23	353, 354	Manufacture of coke, refined petroleum products, and nuclear fuel
24	351, 352	Manufacture of chemicals and chemical products
25	355, 356	Manufacture of rubber and plastics products
26	361, 362, 369	Manufacture of other non-metallic mineral products
27	371, 372	Manufacture of basic metals
28	381	Manufacture of fabricated metal products, except machinery and equipment
29	382	Manufacture of machinery and equipment, not classified elsewhere
30	382	Manufacture of office, accounting, and computing machinery
31	383	Manufacture of electrical machinery and apparatus, not classified elsewhere
32	385	Manufacture of radio, television, and communication equipment and apparatus
33	385	Manufacture of medical, precision and optical instruments, watches and clocks
34	384	Manufacture of motor vehicles, trailers, and semi-trailers
35	384	Manufacture of other transport equipment
36	332	Manufacture of furniture; manufacturing not classified elsewhere

Source: Authors' construction based on NIC 1998 and ISIC 1968.

APPENDIX A2

A Note on the Use of NSSO Multipliers

There has been considerable discussion in the literature on whether to weigh observations during the estimation of parameters. This is an important issue that needs to be discussed here as the present study too relies heavily on the unit-level data published by the NSSO. As mentioned in Appendix A1, the NSSO collects data by employing a proper sampling procedure and it depends on the census data to calculate appropriate multipliers to inflate its samples so as to be representative of the overall central and state populations. These multipliers are supplied along with the unit-level data and presented against each unit surveyed in these rounds.

Many researchers have highlighted the role of weights in estimations and the various pros and cons associated with them (Bhattacharya 2005; Deaton 1997; DuMouchel and Duncan 1983; Solon et al. 2013). In most large-scale surveys, as is the case with the NSSO surveys too, the survey samples are generally selected by using a stratified, clustered design, and hence, all elements in the populations will not enjoy the equal probability of getting selected in the sample (Bhattacharya 2005). This necessitates the need to assign weights to these sample observations, with the weight for an observation denoting the number of duplicated observations in the population it represents. It is thus suggested to use weighted-estimation technique whenever the purpose of estimation is to derive the population parameters from such data sets (Bhattacharya 2005).

Solon et al. (2013) maintain that weighting is a serious issue when the purpose of estimation is to arrive at population-descriptive statistics (populations means and proportions) using sample data. In other words, computing weighted averages using survey weights is clearly justified when it is needed to make the sample representative of the target population (Zanutto and Gelman 2001). On the other hand, the weighting issue is more nuanced for cases where the objective is to capture causal effects between variables (Solon et al. 2013). Method of incorporating survey weights when fitting more complex statistical models such as linear regression models and log-linear models is less obvious (Zanutto and Gelman 2001). One reason that is often highlighted for using weights while estimating causal effects is to realize the accurate estimates by correcting heteroskedasticity. (See Solon et al. 2013 for a discussion on this.) In contrast, Dickens (1990) argues that the use of weighting could, in fact, harm the precision of estimation. With the help of a simple example, he shows how the robust standard errors are smaller for ordinary least squares (OLS) than for weighted least squares (WLS) and resulting in less precise estimates for the latter. Deaton (1997) suggests a number of strategies for dealing with heterogeneity. One strategy is to assume that the behaviour is homogeneous across (statistical or substantive) subunits, the data is pooled, and that the weights are ignored. On the other hand, if the distinctions between groups are of fundamental interest, one may go for testing the differences between them using covariance analysis (Johnston 1972).

Two other reasons often highlighted for the motive behind weighting in research on causal effects are: (a) to achieve consistent estimation in the presence of endogenous sampling, and (b) to identify average partial effects in the presence of unmodelled heterogeneity of effects (Solon et al. 2013). In a detailed discussion on each of these two cases, Solon et al. (2013) have referred to instances where the use of weights to understand causal effects may not be as good an idea as empirical researchers sometimes think. The authors note that using weighting procedure to reflect population shares may not identify average marginal effects in the presence of unmodelled heterogeneous effects.

In essence, there is now a consensus on the use of weights for computing population-descriptive statistics. The discussion is largely confined to the question of whether and how this procedure extends from the estimation of means to the estimation of regressions (Deaton

1997). Some suggest that estimates will be biased in the case of those estimations where weights are not used. Others contend that sample weights are unnecessary because multivariate analyses typically include the same set of variables that go into the sample design and calculation of sample weights. That is, one can fit the model without survey weights if all variables that are used in the design or the weighting of the survey are included as explanatory variables in the model (DuMouchel and Duncan 1983; Korn and Graubard 1999). Solon et al. (2013) suggest using robust standard errors as a solution for overcoming many of these issues associated with using weights in regression estimations.

In the context of this unresolved puzzle, the present volume employs the weighting procedure only to derive population-descriptive statistics. To estimate causal effects, we follow Solon et al. (2013) in not using weighted regressions. The discussion above suggests that this would not affect our estimates for two reasons: (a) we use most of the behavioural variables as explanatory variables in regression estimations; and (b) in all estimations (except where specified), we use robust standard errors.

BIBLIOGRAPHY

Acar, A. 1993. 'The Impact of Key Internal Factors on Firm Performance: An Empirical Study of Small Turkish Firms', *Journal of Small Business Management*, 31(4): 86–92.

Adams, C. and B. Harriss-White. 2007. 'From Monet to Mondrian: Characterizing Informal Economic Activity in Field Research and Simulation Models', in B. Harriss-White and A. Sinha (eds), *Trade Liberalization and India's Informal Economy*, pp. 15–41. New Delhi: Oxford University Press.

Agarwala, Rina. 2013. *Informal Labor, Formal Politics, and Dignified Discontent in India*. Cambridge: Cambridge University Press.

Ahluwalia, I.J. 1999. 'India's Economic Reforms: An Appraisal', in J.D. Sachs, A. Varshney, and N. Bajpai (eds), *India in the Era of Economic Reforms*, pp. 26–80. New Delhi: Oxford University Press.

Ahsan, R.N. and D. Mitra. 2014. 'Trade Liberalization and Labor's Slice of the Pie: Evidence from Indian Firms', *Journal of Development Economics*, 108: 1–16.

Aigner, D.J., C.A.K. Lovell, and P. Schmidt. 1977. 'Formulation and Estimation of Stochastic Frontier Production Function Models', *Journal of Econometrics*, 6(1): 21–37.

Alessandrini, M., B. Fattouh, B. Ferrarini, and P. Scaramozzino. 2011. 'Tariff Liberalization and Trade Specialization: Lessons from India', *Journal of Comparative Economics*, 39(4): 499–513.

Almeida, R. and P. Carneiro. 2005. 'Enforcement of Regulation, Informal Labour and Firm Performance', Discussion Paper No. 1759. Bonn: Institute for the Study of Labour.

Arellano, M. and S. Bond. 1991. 'Some Tests of Specification for Panel Data: Monte Carlo Evidence and an Application to Employment Equations', *Review of Economic Studies*, 58(2): 277–97.

Arend, R.J. 2014. 'Entrepreneurship and Dynamic Capabilities: How Firm Age and Size Affect the "Capability Enhancement–SME Performance" Relationship', *Small Business Economics*, 42(1): 33–57.

Aterido, R. and M. Hallward-Driemeier. 2008. 'Putting African Employment Growth in a Global Context: Impact of Access to Finance, Infrastructure and Regulations Across Firms', Conference Paper. Oxford: St Catherine's College.

Aterido, R., M. Hallward-Driemeier, and C. Pages. 2011. 'Big Constraints to Small Firms' Growth? Business Environment and Employment Growth across Firms', *Economic Development and Cultural Change*, 59(3): 609–47.

Balakrishnan, P. and K. Pushpangadan. 1994. 'Total Factor Productivity Growth in Manufacturing Industry: A Fresh Look', *Economic and Political Weekly*, 29(31): 2028–35.

———. 1998. 'What Do We Know About Productivity Growth in Indian Industry?', *Economic and Political Weekly*, 33(33/34): 2241–6.

Balasubramanyam, V.N. 2003. 'India: Trade Policy Review', *The World Economy*, 26(9): 1357–68.

Banerjee, N. 1984. *Women Workers in the Unorganized Sector: The Calcutta Experience*. Calcutta: Orient Longman.

Basile, E. 2013. *Capitalist Development in India's Informal Economy*. Oxon: Routledge.

Beck, T. 2007. 'Financing Constraints of SMEs in Developing Countries: Evidence, Determinants and Solutions', mimeo, Tilburg: Tilburg University.

Beck, T. and A. Demirgüç-Kunt. 2006. 'Small and Medium-Size Enterprises: Access to Finance as Growth Constraint', *Journal of Banking and Finance*, 30(11): 2931–43.

Beck, T., A. Demirgüç-Kunt, L. Laeven, and R. Levine. 2008. 'Finance, Firm Size, and Growth', *Journal of Money, Credit and Banking*, 40(7): 1379–405.

Beck, T., A. Demirgüç-Kunt, and V. Maksimovic. 2005. 'Financial and Legal Constraints to Firm Growth: Does Firm Size Matter?', *Journal of Finance*, 60(1): 137–77.

Becker, K. 2004. *The Informal Economy*. Stockholm: Swedish International Development Agency.

Berry, A., E. Rodrigues, and H. Sandee. 2002. 'Firm and Group Dynamics in the Small and Medium Enterprise Sector in Indonesia', *Small Business Economics*, 18(1–3): 141–61.

Besley, T. and R. Burgess. 2004. 'Can Labour Regulation Hinder Economic Performance? Evidence from India', *The Quarterly Journal of Economics*, 119(1): 91–134.

Bhagwati, J. 1993. *India in Transition: Freeing the Economy*. Oxford: Clarendon Press.

Bhagwati, J. and P. Desai. 1970. *India: Planning for Industrialization*. London: Oxford University Press.

Bhagwati, J. and T.N. Srinivasan. 1975. *Foreign Trade Regimes and Economic Development: India.* New York: Columbia University Press.

Bhattacharya, D. 2005. 'Asymptotic Inference from Multi-stage Samples', *Journal of Econometrics*, 126(1): 145–71.

Bigsten, A. and M. Gebreeyesus. 2007. 'The Small, the Young, and the Productive: Determinants of Manufacturing Firm Growth in Ethiopia', *Economic Development and Cultural Change*, 55(4): 813–40.

Binks, M.R. and C.T. Ennew. 1996. 'Growing Firms and the Credit Constraint', *Small Business Economics*, 8(1): 17–25

Bond, S.R. and A. Malik. 2007. 'Explaining Cross-country Variation in Investment: The Role of Endowments, Institutions and Finance', mimeo, Oxford: Oxford University.

Bourguignon, F. and C. Morrison. 1998. 'Inequality and Development: The Role of Dualism', *Journal of Development Economics*, 57(2): 233–57.

Breman, Jan. 1985. *Of Peasants, Migrants and Paupers: Rural Labour Circulation and Capitalist Production in West India.* New Delhi: Oxford University Press.

———. 1996. *Footloose Labour: Working in India's Informal Economy.* Cambridge: Cambridge University Press.

———. 2010. *Outcast Labour in India: Circulation and Informalization of the Workforce at the Bottom of the Economy.* New Delhi: Oxford University Press.

———. 2013. *At Work in the Informal Economy of India: A Perspective from the Bottom Up.* New Delhi: Oxford University Press.

Brown, J.D., J.S. Earle, and D. Lup. 2005. 'What Makes Small Firms Grow? Finance, Human Capital, Technical Assistance, and the Business Environment in Romania', *Economic Development and Cultural Change*, 54(1): 33–70.

Burgess, R. and R. Pande. 2005. 'Do Rural Banks Matter? Evidence from the Indian Social Banking Experiment', *American Economic Review*, 95(3): 780–95.

Burki, A.A. and D. Terrell. 1998. 'Measuring Production Efficiency of Small Firms in Pakistan', *World Development*, 26(1): 155–69.

Carlton, D.W. and J. M. Perloff. 2004. *Modern Industrial Organization.* New York: Prentice-Hall.

Carr, M. and M.A. Chen. 2002. 'Globalization and Informal Economy: How Global Trade and Investment Impact on the Working Poor', Working Paper on the Informal Economy. Geneva: International Labour Office.

Carswell, G. and G. De Neve. 2013. 'From Field to Factory: Tracing Transformations in Bonded Labour in the Tiruppur Region, South India', *Economy and Society*, 42(3): 430–54.

Castells, M. and A. Portes. 1989. 'World Underneath: The Origins, Dynamics, and Effects of the Informal Economy', in A. Portes, M. Castells, and L.A. Benton (eds), *The Informal Economy: Studies in Advanced and Less Advanced*

Developed Countries, pp. 11–40. Baltimore: The Johns Hopkins University Press.

Catao, L.A.V., C. Pages, and M.F. Rosales. 2009. 'Financial Dependence, Formal Credit and Informal Jobs', Working Paper 118, Washington, DC: Inter-American Development Bank.

Central Statistical Organization. 2008. 'National Industrial Classification' (All Economic Activities), Ministry of Statistics and Programme Implementation, Government of India, New Delhi.

Chadha, R., D.K. Brown, A.V. Deardorff, and R.M. Stern. 2003. 'Computational Analysis of the Impact on India of the Uruguay Round and the Doha Development Agenda Negotiations', in A. Mattoo and R. Stern (eds), *India and the WTO*, pp. 13–46. Washington, DC: Oxford University Press and World Bank.

Chari, S. 2004. 'Provincializing Capital: The Work of an Agrarian Past in South Indian Industry', *Comparative Studies in Society and History*, 46(4): 760–85.

Chatterjee, U. and R. Kanbur. 2013. 'Regulation and Non-Compliance: Magnitudes and Patterns for India's Factories Act', mimeo, Ithaca: Cornell University.

Coelho, K. and A. Maringanti. 2012. 'Understanding Urban Poverty in India: Tools, Treatment and Politics at the Neo-Liberal Turn', *Economic and Political Weekly*, 47(47/48): 39–41.

Coelho, K., T. Venkat, and R. Chandrika. 2012. 'The Spatial Reproduction of Urban Poverty: Labour and Livelihood in a Slum Resettlement Colony', *Economic and Political Weekly*, 47(47/48): 53–63.

Dabla-Norris, E., M. Gradstein, and G. Inchauste. 2005. 'What Causes Firms to Hide Output? The Determinants of Informality', IMF Working Paper No. 05/160, Washington, DC: International Monetary Fund.

Daniels, L. and D.C. Mead. 1998. 'The Contribution of Small Enterprises to Household and National Income in Kenya', *Economic Development and Cultural Change*, 47(1): 45–71.

Das, D. K., D. Wadhwa, and G. Kalita. 2009. 'The Employment Potential of Labour Intensive Industries: An Appraisal of India's Organised Manufacturing', Working Paper, New Delhi: Indian Council for Research on International Economic Relations.

Davidsson, P., L. Achtenhagen, and L. Naldi. 2005. 'Research on Small Firm Growth: A Review', Conference Paper, Barcelona: Spain.

de Mel, S., D. McKenzie, and C. Woodruff. 2010. 'Wage Subsidies for Microenterprises', *American Economic Review*, 100(2): 614–18.

De Neve, G. 2005. *The Everyday Politics of Labour: Working Lives in India's Informal Economy*. New Delhi: Social Science Press.

De Soto, H. 1989. *The Other Path*. New York: Harper and Row.

———. 2000. *The Mystery of Capital*. New York: Basic Books.

Deaton, A. 1997. *The Analysis of Household Surveys: A Microeconometric Approach to Development Policy*. Baltimore: The Johns Hopkins University Press.

Demirgüç-Kunt, A. and V. Maksimovic. 1998. 'Law, Finance and Firm Growth', *Journal of Finance*, 53(6): 2107–37.

Desai, A.V. and N. Taneja. 1993. 'Small Firms in Indian Industry: Economic Characteristics and Functioning', *Journal of Indian School of Political Economy*, 5(2): 203–14.

Deshpande, A. and S. Sharma. 2013. 'Entrepreneurship or Survival? Caste and Gender of Small Business in India', *Economic and Political Weekly*, 28(28): 38–49.

Dessy, S. and S. Pallage. 2003. 'Taxes, Inequality and the Size of the Informal Sector', *Journal of Development Economics*, 70(1): 225–33.

Dickens, W.T. 1990. 'Error Components in Grouped Data: Is It Ever Worth Weighting?', *The Review of Economics and Statistics*, 72(2): 328–33.

Dollar, D., M. Hallward-Driemeier, and T. Mengistae. 2005. 'Investment Climate and Firm Performance in Developing Economies', *Economic Development and Cultural Change*, 54(1): 1–31.

Dougherty, S.M. 2009. 'Labour Regulation and Employment Dynamics at the State Level in India', *Review of Market Integration*, 1(3): 295–337.

DuMouchel, W.H., and G.J. Duncan. 1983. 'Using Sample Survey Weights in Multiple Regression Analyses of Stratified Samples', *Journal of the American Statistical Association*, 78(383): 535–43.

Fafchamps, M. 2004. *Market Institutions in Sub-Saharan Africa*. Cambridge: MIT Press.

Feenstra, R.C. and G.H. Hanson. 2005. 'Ownership and Control in Outsourcing to China: Estimating the Property Rights Theory of the Firm', *Quarterly Journal of Economics*, 120(2): 729–62.

Gang, I. 1992. 'Small Firm "Presence" in Indian Manufacturing', *World Development*, 20(9): 1377–89.

Gang, I., K. Sen, and M.S. Yun. 2012. 'Is Caste Destiny? Occupational Diversification among Dalits in Rural India', BWPI Working Paper No. 162, Manchester: Brooks World Poverty Institute.

Garcia-Santana, M. and J. Pijoan-Mas. 2014. 'The Reservation Laws in India and the Misallocation of Production Factors', *Journal of Monetary Economics*, 66: 193–209.

Ghani, E., W. Kerr, and S. O'Connell. 2013. 'Input Usage and Productivity in Indian Manufacturing Plants', Policy Research Working Paper No. 6656, Washington, DC: World Bank.

Ghosh, Arun. 1988. 'Government Policies Concerning Small Scale Industries: An Appraisal', in Suri, K.B. (ed.), *Small Scale Enterprises in Industrial Development: The Indian Experience*, pp. 299–325. London: Sage Publications.

Giunta, A., N. Annamaria, and S. Domenico. 2012. 'Subcontracting in Italian Industry: Labour Division, Firm Growth and the North–South Divide', *Regional Studies*, 46(8): 1067–83.

Glinskaya, E. and M. Lokshin. 2005. 'Wage Differentials between the Public and Private Sectors in India', *Journal of International Development*, 19(3): 333–55.

Godfrey, P.C. 2011. 'Toward a Theory of the Informal Economy', *The Academy of Management Annals*, 5(1): 231–77.

Gokarn, S., A. Sen, and R. Vaidya (eds). 2004. *The Structure of Indian Industry*. Delhi: Oxford University Press.

Goldar, B. 1986. *Productivity Growth in Indian Industry*. New Delhi: Allied Publishers.

Gollin, D. 2008. 'Nobody's Business but My Own: Self-Employment and Small Enterprise in Economic Development', *Journal of Monetary Economics*, 55(2): 219–33.

———. 2014. 'The Lewis Model: A 60-Year Retrospective', *Journal of Economic Perspectives*, 28(3): 71–88.

Government of India. 1997. *Report of the Expert Committee on Small Enterprises*, Ministry of Commerce and Industry. New Delhi: Government of India.

———. 2001. *Report of the Study Group on Development Small-Scale Enterprises*, Planning Commission. New Delhi: Government of India.

Greenaway, D., R. Hine, and P. Wright. 1999. 'An Empirical Assessment of Impact of Trade on Employment in the United Kingdom', *European Journal of Political Economy*, 15(3): 485–500.

Greene, W. 2006. 'A General Approach to Incorporating "Selectivity" in a Model', Working Paper EC-06-10, Stern School of Business, New York: New York University.

———. 2007. 'NLOGIT Version 4.0: Student Reference Guide', Econometric Software, Inc., New York.

———. 2010. 'A Stochastic Frontier Model with Correction for Sample Selection', *Journal of Productivity Analysis*, 34(1): 15–24.

Guhathakurta, S. 1993. 'Economic Independence through Protection? Emerging Contradictions in India's Small-Scale Sector Policies', *World Development*, 21(12): 2039–54.

Gulyani, S. and D. Talukdar. 2010. 'Inside Informality: The Links between Poverty, Microenterprises, and Living Conditions in Nairobi's Slums', *World Development*, 38(12): 1710–26.

Harris, J.R. and M.P. Todaro. 1970. 'Migration, Unemployment, and Development: A Two Sector Analysis', *American Economic Review*, 60(1): 126–42.

Harriss-White, B. 2002. *Globalization and Insecurity: Political, Economic and Physical Challenges*. London: Palgrave.

———. 2003. *India Working: Essays on Society and Economy*. Cambridge: Cambridge University Press.

———. 2010. 'Work and Wellbeing in Informal Economies: The Regulative Roles of Institutions of Identity and the State', *World Development*, 38(2):170–83.

Hart, K. 1973. 'Informal Income Opportunities and Urban Employment in Ghana', *Journal of Modern African Studies*, 11(1): 61–89.

Heckman, J.J. 1976. 'The Common Structure of Statistical Models of Truncation, Sample Selection and Limited Dependent Variables and a Simple Estimator for Such Models', *Annals of Economic and Social Measurement*, 5(4): 475–92.

Hill, H. 1985. 'Subcontracting, Technological Diffusion and the Development of Small Enterprise in Philippine Manufacturing', *The Journal of Developing Areas*, 19(2): 245–62.

Himanshu and K. Sen. 2014. 'Poverty in India: Measurement, Patterns, and Determinants', in Nandini Gooptu and Jonathan Parry (eds.), *The Persistence of Poverty in India*, pp. 67–88. New Delhi: Social Science Press.

Hine, R. and P. Wright. 1998. 'Trade with Low Wage Economies, Employment and Productivity in UK Manufacturing', *Economic Journal*, 108(450): 1500–10.

Hnatkovska, V., A. Lahiri, and S. Paul. 2012. 'Castes and Labor Mobility', *American Economic Journal: Applied Economics*, 4(2): 274–307.

Holl, A. 2012. 'Market Potential and Firm-Level Productivity in Spain', *Journal of Economic Geography*, 12(6): 1191–215.

Holmström, M. 1993. 'Flexible Specialisation in India?', *Economic and Political Weekly*, 28(35): M82–M86.

Hoogstra, G.J. and J.V. Dijk. 2004. 'Explaining Firm Employment Growth: Does Location Matter?', *Small Business Economics*, 22(3/4): 179–92.

Hossain, M.A. and N.D. Karunaratne. 2004. 'Trade Liberalization and Technical Efficiency: Evidence from Bangladesh Manufacturing Industries', *The Journal of Development Studies*, 40(3): 87–114.

Hsieh, C. and P.J. Klenow. 2009. 'Misallocation and Manufacturing TFP in China and India', *The Quarterly Journal of Economics*, 124(4): 1403–48.

———. 2014. 'The Life Cycle of Plants in India and Mexico', *Quarterly Journal of Economics*, 129(3): 1035–084.

Hussain, Abid. 1997. 'Report of the Expert Committee on Small Enterprises', Ministry of Commerce and Industry, New Delhi: Government of India.

International Labour Office (ILO). 2002. *Decent Work and the Informal Economy*. Geneva: ILO.

———. 2009. 'Globalization and Informal Jobs in Developing Countries', mimeo, Geneva: ILO.

Iversen, V., A. Verschoor, K. Sen, and A. Dubey. 2009. 'Job Recruitment Networks and Migration to Cities in India', *Journal of Development Studies*, 45(4): 522–43.

Iyer, L., T. Khanna, and A. Varshney. 2013. 'Caste and Entrepreneurship in India', *Economic and Political Weekly*, 48(6): 52–60.

Johnson, S., J. McMillan, and C. Woodruff. 2002. 'Property Rights and Finance', *American Economic Review*, 92(5):1335–56.

Johnston, J. 1972. *Econometric Methods*. Tokyo: McGraw-Hill.

Joshi, V. and I.M.D. Little. 1997. 'India: Reform on Hold', *Asian Development Review*, 15(2): 1–42.

Kanbur, R. 2011. 'Avoiding Informality Traps', in E. Ghani (ed.), *Reshaping Tomorrow: Is South Asia Ready for the Big Leap?*, pp. 260–78. New Delhi: Oxford University Press.

———. 2014. 'Informality: Causes, Consequences and Policy Responses', Working Paper, Ithaca: Cornell University.

Kapur, D., C.B. Prasad, L. Pritchett, and D. Shyam Babu. 2010. 'Rethinking Inequality in Uttar Pradesh in the Market Reform Era', *Economic and Political Weekly*, 46(35): 39–49.

Kathuria, V., S.N. Rajesh Raj, and K. Sen. 2013. 'The Effects of Economic Reforms on Manufacturing Dualism: Evidence from India', *Journal of Comparative Economics*, 41(4): 1240–62.

Katrak, H. 1999. 'Small-Scale Enterprise Policy in Developing Countries: An Analysis of India's Reservation Policy', *Journal of International Development*, 11(5): 701–15.

Keeble, D. and P. Tyler. 1995. 'Enterprising Behaviour and the Urban–Rural Shift', *Urban Studies*, 32(6): 975–97.

Keeble, D., P. Tyler, G. Broom, and J. Lewis. 1992. 'Business Success in the Countryside: The Performance of Rural Enterprise', mimeo, London: HMSO.

Kimura, F. 2002. 'Subcontracting and the Performance of Small and Medium Firms in Japan', *Small Business Economics*, 18(1–3): 163–75.

Korn, E.L. and B.I. Graubard. 1999. *Analysis of Health Surveys*. New York: Wiley.

Krause, L.B. 1982. 'U.S Economic Policy towards the Association of Southeast Asian Nations: Meeting the Japanese Challenge', Washington, DC: The Brookings Institution.

Krueger, A.O. 2013. 'The Missing Middle', in N.C. Hope, A. Kochar, R. Noll, and T. N. Srinivasan (eds), *Economic Reform in India: Challenges, Prospects, and Lessons*, pp. 299–318. Cambridge: Cambridge University Press.

Krueger, A.O. and S. Chinoy. 2002. 'The Indian Economy in a Global Context', in A.O. Krueger (ed.), *Economic Policy Reforms and the Indian Economy*, pp. 9–46. Chicago: University of Chicago Press.

Kucera, D. and W. Milberg. 2002. 'Trade and the Loss of Manufacturing Jobs in the OECD: New Factor Calculations for 1978–1995', Discussion Paper, Geneva: International Institute for Labour Studies.

Kulshreshtha, A.C. 2011. 'Measuring the Unorganised Sector in India', *Review of Income and Wealth*, 57(s1): S123–S134.

Kumar, R. and A.S. Gupta. 2008. 'Towards a Competitive Manufacturing Sector', in R. Kumar and A.S. Gupta (eds), *India and the Global Economy*, pp.187–239. New Delhi: Academic Foundation.

Kumar, S. 2006. 'A Decomposition of Total Productivity Growth: A Regional Analysis of Indian Industrial Manufacturing Growth', *International Journal of Productivity and Performance Management*, 55(3/4): 311–31.

Kumbhakar, S. and C.A.K. Lovell. 2000. *Stochastic Frontier Analysis*. Cambridge: Cambridge University Press.

Kuntchev, V., R. Ramalho, J. Rodriguez-Meza, and J.S. Yang. 2012. 'What Have We Learned from the Enterprise Surveys Regarding Access to Finance by SMEs?', mimeo, Washington, DC: World Bank.

La Porta, R. and A. Shleifer. 2008. 'The Unofficial Economy and Economic Development', Brookings Papers on Economic Activity, 39(2): 275–363.

———. 2014. 'Informality and Development', *Journal of Economic Perspectives*, 28(3): 109–26.

Lall, S. 1980. 'Vertical Inter-Firm Linkages in LDCs: An Empirical Study', *Oxford Bulletin of Economics and Statistics*, 42(3): 203–26.

Lall, S. V., Z. Shalizi, and U. Deichmann. 2004. 'Agglomeration Economies and Productivity in Indian Industry', *Journal of Development Economics*, 73(2): 643–73.

Lewis, W.A. 1954. 'Economic Development with Unlimited Supplies of Labour', *The Manchester School*, 22(2): 139–91.

Liedholm, C. and D. Mead. 1987. 'Small Scale Industries in Developing Countries: Empirical Evidence and Policy Implications', Development Paper, Michigan: Michigan State University.

———. 1999. *Small Enterprises and Economic Development: The Dynamic Role of Micro and Small Enterprises*. London: Routledge.

Little, I.M.D. 1987. 'Small Manufacturing Enterprises in Developing Countries', *The World Bank Economic Review*, 1(2): 203–35.

Little, I.M.D., D. Mazumdar, and J.M. Page. 1987. *Small Manufacturing Enterprises: A Comparative Analysis of India and Other Economies*. New York: Oxford University Press.

Mahadevan, R. 2004. *The Economics of Productivity in Asia and Australia.* Cheltenham: Edward Elgar.

Maiti, D. and K. Sen. 2010a. 'The Informal Sector in South Asia: An Introduction', *Indian Journal of Labour Economics*, 53(2): 195–98.

———. 2010b. 'The Informal Sector in India: A Means of Accumulation or Exploitation?', *Journal of South Asian Development*, 5(1): 1–13.

Marjit, S. and S. Kar. 2007. 'The Urban Informal Sector and Poverty: Effect of Trade Reform and Capital Mobility in India', Working Paper, Canada: Poverty and Economic Policy Network.

Martin, L., S. Nataraj, and A. Harrison. 2014. 'In with the Big, Out with the Small: Removing Small-Scale Reservations in India', Working Paper, Cambridge: National Bureau of Economic Research.

Mazumdar, D. 2010. 'Decreasing Poverty and Increasing Inequality in India', in OECD (ed.), *Tackling Inequalities in Brazil, China, India and South Africa: The Role of Labour Market and Social Policies*, pp. 157–207. Paris: OECD.

Mazumdar, D. and S. Sarkar. 2008. *Globalization, Labour Markets and Inequality in India.* Oxford: Routledge.

———. 2009. 'The Employment Problem in India and the Phenomenon of the "Missing Middle"', *The Indian Journal of Labour Economics*, 52(1): 43–56.

———. 2013. *Manufacturing Enterprises in Asia: Size Structure and Economic Growth.* London and New York: Routledge.

McPherson, M.A. and J.J. Rous. 2010. 'Access to Finance and Small Enterprise Growth: Evidence from East Java', *Journal of Developing Areas*, 43(2): 159–72.

Mead, D.M. and C. Liedholm. 1998. 'The Dynamics of Micro and Small Enterprises in Developing Countries', *World Development*, 26(1):61–74.

Mean, D. 1984. 'Of Contracts and Subcontracts: Small Firms in Vertically Disintegrated Production/Distribution Systems in LDCs', *World Development*, 12(11–12): 1095–106.

Memili, E., J.J. Chrisman, and J.H. Chua. 2011. 'Transaction Costs and Outsourcing Decisions in Small- and Medium-Sized Family Firms', *Family Business Review*, 24(1): 47–61.

Ministry of Commerce and Industry. 1989. *Annual Report 1988-1989*, Development Commissioner (Small-Scale Industries). New Delhi: Small Industries Development Organization (SIDO), Ministry of Commerce and Industry, Government of India.

Mohan, R. 2002. 'Small-Scale Industry Policy in India: A Critical Evaluation', in Anne O. Krueger (ed.), *Economic Policy Reforms and the Indian Economy*, pp. 213–302. Chicago: University of Chicago Press.

Mookherjee, D. 1995. 'Introduction', in Mookherjee, D. (ed.), *Indian Industry: Policies and Performance*, pp. 1–43, Oxford: Oxford University Press.

Moreno-Monroy, A.I., J. Pieters, and A.A. Erumban. 2012. 'Subcontracting and the Size and Composition of the Informal Sector: Evidence from Indian Manufacturing', IZA Discussion Paper. Bonn: Institute for the Study of Labor.

Morris, S., R. Basant, K. Das, and K. Ramachandran. 2001. *The Growth and Transformation of Small Firms in India*. New Delhi: Oxford University Press.

Planning Commission. 1989. *Report of the Advisory Group on Consumer Industry - Part-I*. New Delhi: Government of India.

———. 2006. *Report of the Working Group on Labour Laws and Other Labour Regulations*. New Delhi: Government of India.

Nafziger, E.W. and D. Terrell. 1996. 'Entrepreneurial Human Capital and the Long-Run Survival of Firms in India', *World Development*, 24(4): 689–96.

Narayana, M.R. 2003. 'Implications of Recent Changes in Economy-wide Industrial and Trade Policies on Small-Scale Industries in India', *Journal of Indian School of Political Economy*, 15(4): 717–43.

Nataraj, S. 2011. 'The Impact of Trade Liberalization on Productivity: Evidence from India's Formal and Informal Manufacturing Sectors', *Journal of International Economics*, 85(2): 292–301.

National Commission for Enterprises in the Unorganized Sector (NCEUS). 2007. 'Conditions of Work and Promotion of Livelihood in the Unorganised Sector', Report, New Delhi: Government of India.

———. 2009. 'The Challenge of Employment in India: An Informal Economy Perspective', Report, New Delhi: Government of India.

National Sample Survey Organization (NSSO). 2002a. *Unorganized Manufacturing Sector in India, 2000–2001: Characteristics of Enterprises*, Report No: 478. New Delhi: NSSO, Ministry of Statistics and Programme Implementation, Government of India.

———. 2002b. *Unorganized Manufacturing Sector in India, 2000–2001: Employment, Asset and Borrowings*, Report No: 479. New Delhi: NSSO, Ministry of Statistics and Programme Implementation, Government of India.

———. 2008. *Unorganized Manufacturing Sector in India: Employment, Assets and Borrowings*, Report No. 525. New Delhi: NSSO, Ministry of Statistics and Programme Implementation, Government of India.

Nichter, S. and L. Goldmark. 2009. 'Small Firm Growth in Developing Countries', *World Development*, 37(9): 1453–64.

Nicita, A. and M. Olarreaga. 2006. 'Trade, Production and Protection 1976–2004', *World Bank Economic Review*, 21(1): 165–71.

North, D. 1990. *Institutions, Institutional Change and Economic Performance*. Cambridge: Cambridge University Press.

North, D. and S. Smallbone. 2000. 'The Innovativeness and Growth of Rural SMEs during the 1990s', *Regional Studies*, 34(2): 145–57.

Ojah, K., T. Gwatidzo, and S. Kaniki. 2010. 'Legal Environment, Finance Channels and Investment: The East African Example', *Journal of Development Studies*, 46(4): 724–44.

Oliveira, B. and A. Fortunato. 2006. 'Firm Growth and Liquidity Constraints', *Small Business Economics*, 27(2): 139–56.

Ostrom, E. 1990. *Governing of the Commons: The Evolution of Institutions for Collective Actions*. Cambridge: Cambridge University Press.

Pais, Jesim. 2008. *Effectiveness of Labour Regulations in Indian Industry*. New Delhi: Bookwell Publishers.

Palmer-Jones, R. and K. Sen. 2003. 'What has Luck Got to Do with It? A Regional Analysis of Poverty and Agricultural Growth in India', *Journal of Development Studies*, 40(1):1–33.

Panagariya, Arvind. 2008. *India: The Emerging Giant*. New Delhi: Oxford University Press.

Parker, J. 1994. 'Patterns of Business Growth: Micro and Small Enterprises in Kenya', PhD Dissertation, East Lansing: Michigan State University.

Penrose, E.G. 1959. *The Theory of the Growth of the Firm*. New York: Wiley.

Rajan, G.R. and L. Zingales. 1998. 'Financial Dependence and Growth', *American Economic Review*, 88(3): 559–86.

Rajiv Gandhi Institute for Contemporary Studies. 2006. *Small Sector in India: Status, Growth and De-reservation*. New Delhi: Rajiv Gandhi Institute for Contemporary Studies.

Ramaswamy, K.V. 1999. 'The Search for Flexibility in Indian Manufacturing: New Evidence on Outsourcing Activities', *Economic and Political Weekly*, 34(6): 363–68.

———. 2013. 'Understanding the "Missing Middle" in Indian Manufacturing: The Role of Size-Dependent Labour Regulations and Fiscal Incentives', Working Paper, Chiba: Institute of Developing Economies.

Rani, Uma and Jeemol Unni. 2004. 'Unorganized and Organized Manufacturing in India: Potential for Employment Generating Growth', *Economic and Political Weekly*, 39(41): 4568–80.

Ranis, G. and Stewart, F. 1999. 'V-Goods and the Role of the Urban Informal Sector in Development', *Economic Development and Cultural Change*, 47(2): 259–88.

Rao, R.R. 2014. 'Priority Sector Lending (PSL) and Inclusive Growth', *Industry Insights*, New Delhi: Federation of Indian Chambers of Commerce and Industry.

Ray, S.C. 2002. 'Did India's Economic Reforms Improve Efficiency and Productivity? A Nonparametric Analysis of the Initial Evidence from Manufacturing', *Indian Economic Review*, 37(1): 23–57.

Rice, P., A.J. Venables, and E. Patacchini. 2006. 'Spatial Determinants of Productivity: Analysis for the Regions of Great Britain', *Regional Science and Urban Economics*, 36(6): 727–52.

Rijkers, B., M. Söderbom, and J.L. Loening. 2010. 'A Rural–Urban Comparison of Manufacturing Enterprise Performance in Ethiopia', *World Development*, 38(9): 1278–96.

Romjin, H. 2001. 'Technology Support for Small-Scale Industry in Developing Countries: A Review of Concepts and Project Practices', *Oxford Development Studies*, 29(1): 57–76.

Sahu, P.P. 2010. 'Subcontracting in India's Unorganised Manufacturing Sector: A Mode of Adoption Or Exploitation?', *Journal of South Asian Development*, 5(1): 53–83.

Salim, R.A. and K.P. Kalirajan. 1999. 'Sources of Output Growth in Bangladesh Food Processing Industries: A Decomposition Analysis', *The Developing Economies*, 37(3): 247–69.

Saluja, M.R. 1988. 'Data Base of the Unorganized Manufacturing Industry: An Appraisal', in K.B. Suri (ed.) *Small-Scale Enterprises in Industrial Development: The Indian Experience*, pp. 54–71. New Delhi: Sage Publications.

Sandesara, J.C. 1993. 'Modern Small Industry, 1972 and 1987–88: Aspects of Growth and Structural Change', *Economic and Political Weekly*, 28(6): 223–9.

Sanyal, K. 2007. *Rethinking Capitalist Development: Primitive Accumulation, Governmentality and Post-colonial Capitalism*. Routledge: New Delhi.

Sanyal, K. and R. Bhattacharya. 2009. 'Beyond the Factory: Globalisation, Informalisation of Production and the New Locations of Labour', *Economic and Political Weekly*, 34(2): 35–9.

Scherer, F.M. and D. Ross. 1990. *Industrial Market Structure and Economic Performance*. Boston: Houghton Mifflin Company.

Schmitz, H. 1982. 'Growth Constraints on Small-Scale Manufacturing in Developing Countries: A Critical Review', *World Development*, 10(6): 429–50.

Schmitz, H. and K. Nadvi. 1999. 'Clustering and Industrialisation: Introduction', *World Development*, 27(9): 1503–14.

Sen, K. 2008. *Trade Policy, Inequality, and Performance in Indian Manufacturing*. London: Routledge.

———. 2009. 'International Trade and Manufacturing Employment: Is India following the Footsteps of Asia or Africa?', *Review of Development Economics*, 13(4): 765–77.

———. 2014. 'Inclusive Growth, Social Exclusion and the Urban Poor: Taking a "Production Lens" to Informality in India', in O.P. Mathur (ed.), *State of the Urban Poor Report 2013*, pp. 97–115. New Delhi: Oxford University Press.

Sen, K. and R.R. Vaidya. 1997. *The Process of Financial Liberalization in India*. Delhi: Oxford University Press.

Sen, S. and S.K. Ghosh. 2005. 'Basel Norms, Indian Banking Sector and Impact on Credit to SMEs and the Poor', *Economic and Political Weekly*, 40(12): 1167–80.

Shanmugam, K.R. and S.N. Bhaduri. 2002. 'Size, Age and Firm Growth in the Indian Manufacturing Sector', *Applied Economics Letters*, 9(9): 607–13.

Sharma, S. 2014. 'Benefits of a Registration Policy for Microenterprise Performance in India', *Small Business Economics*, 42(1): 153–64.

Shaw, A. and Pandit, K. 2001. The Geography of Segmentation of Informal Labor Markets: The Case of Motor Vehicle Repair in Calcutta, *Economic Geography*, 77(2): 180–96.

Sher, P.J. and P.Y. Yang. 2005. 'The Effects of Innovative Capabilities and R&D Clustering on Firm Performance: The Evidence of Taiwan's Semiconductor Industry', *Technovation*, 25(1): 1–82.

Shiferaw, A., M. Söderbom, E. Siba, and G. Alemu. 2013. 'Road Infrastructure and Enterprise Dynamics in Ethiopia', Working Paper No. 128, Virginia: College of William and Mary.

Shridharan, L. 2002. 'Impact of Dereservation on SSI Sector: Case Studies of Four Industries around Hyderabad', *The Asian Economic Review*, 44(3): 492–502.

Sinha, A. 2011. 'Trade and the Informal Economy', in M. Jansen, R. Peters, and J.M. Salazar-Xirinachs (eds), *Trade and Employment: From Myths to Facts*, pp. 125–70. Geneva: International Labour Office.

Sinha, A., K.A. Siddiqui, and P. Munjal. 2007. 'A SAM Framework of the Indian Informal Economy', in B. Harriss-White and A. Sinha (eds), *Trade Liberalization and India's Informal Economy*, pp. 233–306. New Delhi: Oxford University Press.

Sleuwaegen, L. and M. Goedhuys. 2002. 'Growth of Firms in Developing Countries, Evidence from Côte d'Ivoire', *Journal of Development Economics*, 68(1): 117–35.

Solon, G., S.J. Haider, and J.M. Wooldridge. 2013. "What Are We Weighting for?", *The Journal of Human Resources*, 50(2): 301–16.

Sonobe, T., A.J. Akoten, and K. Otsuka. 2011. 'Growth Process of Informal Enterprises in Sub-Saharan Africa: A Case Study of a Jua Kali Cluster in Nairobi', *Small Business Economics*, 36(3): 323–35.

Stallings, B. and W. Peres. 2000. *Growth, Employment and Equity: The Impact of the Economic Reforms in Latin America and the Caribbean*. Washington, DC: Brookings Institution Press.

Stephen, A. 1997. 'The Impact of Road Infrastructure on Productivity and Growth: Some Preliminary Results for the German Manufacturing Sector', Discussion Paper, Berlin: Social Science Research Center.

Subrahmanya, M.H.B. 1995. 'Reservation Policy for Small-Scale Industry: Has It Delivered the Goods?', *Economic and Political Weekly*, 30(21): M51–M54.

Taymaz, E. 2005. 'Are Small Firms Really Less Productive?', *Small Business Economics*, 25(5): 429–45.

Taymaz, E. and G. Saatci. 1997. 'Technical Change and Efficiency in Turkish Manufacturing Industries', *Journal of Productivity Analysis*, 8(4): 461–75.

Temple, J.R.W. 2005. 'Dual Economy Models: A Primer for Growth Economists', *The Manchester School*, 73(4): 435–78.

Thorat, S. and K.S. Newman. 2012. *Blocked by Caste: Economic Discrimination in Modern India*. New Delhi: Oxford University Press.

Trivedi, P. 2004. 'An Inter-state Perspective on Manufacturing Productivity in India: 1980–81 to 2000–01', *Indian Economic Review*, 39(1): 203–37.

Trivedi, P., A. Prakash, and D. Sinate. 2000. 'Productivity in Major Manufacturing Industries in India: 1973–74 to 1997–98', DRG Study No. 20, Reserve Bank of India, August.

Tsai, K.S. 2004. 'Imperfect Substitutes: The Local Political Economy of Informal Finance and Microfinance in Rural China and India', *World Development*, 32(9): 1487–1507.

Tybout, J. 2000. 'Manufacturing Firms in Developing Countries: How Well Do They Do, and Why?', *Journal of Economic Literature*, 38(1): 11–44.

Uchikawa, S. 2011. 'Linkage between Organised and Unorganised Sectors in Indian Machinery Industry', *Economic and Political Weekly*, 46(1): 45–54.

UNCTAD. 2004. *The Least Developed Countries Report: 2004: Linking International Trade with Poverty Reduction*. New York and Geneva: United Nations.

Unni, J., N. Lalitha, and U. Rani. 2001. 'Economic Reforms and Productivity Trends in Indian Manufacturing', *Economic and Political Weekly*, 36(41): 3915–22.

van der Sluis, J., M. van Praag, and W. Vijverberg. 2005. 'Entrepreneurship Selection and Performance: A Meta-Analysis of the Impact of Education in Developing Economies', *World Bank Economic Review*, 19(2): 225–61.

Variyam, J.N. and D.S. Kraybill. 1992. 'Empirical Evidence on Determinants of Firm Growth', *Economics Letters*, 38(1): 31–6.

Voulgaris, F., T. Papadogonas, and G. Agiomirgianakis. 2003. 'Job Creation and Job Destruction in Greek Manufacturing', Conference Paper, Bologna: Italy.

Williams, R. 2006. 'Generalized Ordered Logit/Partial Proportional Odds Models for Ordinal Dependent Variables', *The Stata Journal*, 6(1): 58–82.

Williamson, O. 1985. *The Economic Institutions of Capitalism*. New York: Free Press.

Winker, P. 1999. 'Causes and Effects of Financing Constraints at the Firm Level', *Small Business Economics*, 12(2): 169–81.

Wood, A. 1994. *North–South Trade, Employment and Inequality: Changing Fortunes in a Skill-Driven World*. Oxford: Clarendon Press.

Woodruff, C. 2012. 'What Do(n't) We Know about Self-Employment in LICs?', Workshop Paper. Available at http://glm-lic.iza.org/files/Paper_Woodruff_GLM_LIC.pdf, last accessed on 14 September 2014..

Woodruff, C. and R. Zenteno. 2007. 'Migration Networks and Microenterprises in Mexico', *Journal of Development Economics*, 82(2): 509–28.

World Bank. 2004. *India Investment Climate Assessment, 2004: Improving Manufacturing Competitiveness*. Washington, DC: The World Bank.

———. 2005. *World Development Report, 2005: A Better Investment Climate for Everyone*. Washington, DC: The World Bank.

———. 2010. *World Development Indicators, 2010*. Washington, DC: World Bank Publications.

———. 2013. *World Development Report, 2013: Jobs*. Washington, DC: The World Bank.

World Trade Organization (WTO) 2009. *Globalization and Informal Jobs in Developing Countries*. Geneva: World Trade Organization and International Labour Office.

Yang, C.H. and J.H. Chen. 2009. 'Are Small Firms Less Efficient?', *Small Business Economics*, 32(4): 375–95.

Yang, C.H. and C.H. Huang. 2005. 'R&D, Size and Firm Growth in Taiwan's Electronics Industry', *Small Business Economics*, 25(5): 477–87.

Yasuda, T. 2005. 'Firm Growth, Size, Age and Behaviour in Japanese Manufacturing', *Small Business Economics*, 24(1): 1–15.

Zagha, R. 1998. 'Labor and India's Economic Reforms', *The Journal of Policy Reform*, 2(4): 403–26.

Zanutto, E.L. and A. Gelman. 2001. 'Analysis of Large-Scale Social Surveys', in N.J. Smelser and P.B. Baltes (eds), *International Encyclopaedia of the Social and Behavioural Sciences*, pp. 8376–82. Oxford: Elsevier Science Ltd.

INDEX

ABOUT THE AUTHORS

Rajesh Raj S.N. is an Associate Professor at the Department of Economics, Sikkim University, Gangtok, India. He is also an Honorary Research Fellow at the School of Environment, Education and Development (SEED), the University of Manchester, UK. Previously, he has been associated with the Centre for Multi-Disciplinary Development Research (CMDR), Karnataka, India. He has a PhD in economics from the Indian Institute of Technology Madras, Chennai, India. He has published articles in various international peer-reviewed journals, including *Journal of Comparative Economics*, *The Manchester School*, and *Oxford Development Studies*.

Kunal Sen is Professor of Development Economics at the Institute for Development Policy and Management (IDPM), the University of Manchester, UK. He is also the Joint Research Director of the Effective States and Inclusive Development (ESID) Research Centre, UK. Previously, he has taught at the University of East Anglia, UK; the Australian National University, Canberra, Australia; and the Indira Gandhi Institute of Development Research (IGIDR), Mumbai, India. He has been awarded the Dudley Seers and Sanjaya Lall prizes for his publications. Among his recent publications is the edited book *The Politics of Inclusive Development: Interrogating the Evidence* (Oxford University Press, 2014).